Debt in Times of Crisis

Thomas Poufinas
Editor

Debt in Times of Crisis

Does Economic Crisis Really Impact Debt?

palgrave
macmillan

Editor
Thomas Poufinas
Department of Economics
Democritus University of Thrace
Komotini, Greece

ISBN 978-3-030-74161-7 ISBN 978-3-030-74162-4 (eBook)
https://doi.org/10.1007/978-3-030-74162-4

This Palgrave Macmillan imprint is published by the registered company Springer Nature Switzerland AG
The registered company address is: Gewerbestrasse 11, 6330 Cham, Switzerland

To Angelina and Katherine

Preface

Debt, private and public, and in particular excessive debt, has been debated to be one of the root causes of the economic crises we have experienced—financial and sovereign. At the same time, economic crises are believed to lead to an increase of debt—also private and public. Since 2007 and for about a decade, the exit from the consequences of the crises that started in that year was still questionable for the economies of some of the countries. However, in most cases, debt has increased and continued to increase until the end of this decade (2020). The central banks have launched a series of quantitative easing programs that have resulted in more affordable debt to such an extent that some countries are being paid to borrow, as interest rates have turned negative. As a matter of fact, at the present time (November 2020), all of the Eurozone countries enjoy negative yields for at least one of their government bond issues and some of them post negative yields for all their government bond issues, such as Germany and the Netherlands, whose 30-year bond yields are below zero. In Switzerland even the 50-year bond yield is negative. In the United States, the yields, positive though they may be, they are the lowest for the last 40 years.

In the midst of a pandemic, countries around the world are looking still for ways to support the economies and weather a new crisis that this time has a totally different cause. With a forecasted drop of -4.9% for the world output, -8.0% for the United States and -10.2% for the Eurozone,[1] the central banks along with the governments are injecting funds in the economies and the markets in order to successfully get through it. Most likely this will increase both public and private debt as governments and individuals will have to somehow repay the funds that flew in their economies, households or enterprises. This makes the quest of the link between debt and crisis more relevant than ever.

In this book, we look at certain constituents of an economy and attempt to identify their contribution to debt, especially in times of crisis, as well as in periods of tranquility; these are government debt (bonds), tariffs, social security, non-performing loans as well as demography. In addition, we calculate the reserve that a state may want to provision for, in order to secure its economy from defaulting within a certain time horizon. This calculation offers an alternative valuation/pricing of debt. Last but not least, we offer a comparative study of countries with a history of (excessive versus non-excessive) debt and try to realize whether an economic crisis can genuinely deteriorate debt or the "debt illness" is preexisting to the crisis. Furthermore, the role of the central banks and the impact of the quantitative easing programs are investigated, especially for the countries that have more fragile economies, such as the southern or periphery members of the Eurozone.

Through the chapters of this book, the contributors attempt to capture the entire grid of debt—private and/or public—as created by its determinants. A wide range of countries were considered; from the OECD to G20 to the European Union to Eurozone to the periphery of the Eurozone. The studies undertaken confirm that debt is definitely influenced by certain macroeconomic variables that capture the fiscal position, the economic activity, the external competitiveness, the international risk factor and the size of the financial sector. The debt is also affected by social security and tariffs, which are in their turn determined among others by demographic parameters. Sovereign debt is linked with non-performing loans and the central bank purchase programs have a beneficial effect on both of them, as well as the government bond yields. Finally, evidence is found that both the financial and sovereign debt crises had an impact on the bond yields which is stronger to the countries of the south.

[1] IMF, (2020), World Economic Outlook, A Crisis Like No Other, An Uncertain Recovery. https://www.imf.org/en/Publications/WEO/Issues/2020/06/24/WEOUpdateJune2020.

All findings have added value for a series of stakeholders, authorities, policymakers, central banks, regulators, social security organizations, pension schemes, bankers, insurers, investors, entrepreneurs both at institutional and individual levels. As such, they may be used proactively to steer the appropriate drivers so as to prevent each of the unpleasant situations that have been studied from arising or to succeed in securing the desired conditions. At the same time, they may be employed reactively every time one of the investigated cases arises in order to contain its consequences. As such, this book on one hand introduces novelties in the field and on the other hand provides directions that can be readily applied when the relation of debt with a crisis is considered.

Komotini, Greece

Thomas Poufinas

Acknowledgments

My gratitude is in order to my co-authors, colleagues and friends that contributed to the completion of this book. We made an effort to cover all aspects of debt in relation to crises. The trigger point for writing this book was the previous financial and sovereign crisis and its impact on debt, and vice versa. Until the completion of the book a different cause that made the connection of debt with crisis emerged; this of the pandemic. This makes the analysis provided more relevant than ever, as several stakeholders attempt to find ways to weather the consequences of the new challenge.

The chapters of this book constitute original research on the relevant topics and attempt to address anew the long-standing link between debt and crisis and in particular whether economic crisis really impacts debt. The trust of the co-authors in this effort is very much appreciated.

Many thanks are due to the members of Palgrave Macmillan who believed in the proposal, accepted its publication and guided me until the submission of the chapters. With the order met—in most cases remotely, my gratitude is expressed to Mmes and Messrs Rachel Sangster, Wyndham Hacket Pain, Lavanya Devgun, Naveen Dass, Anette Weiss and Preetha Kuttiappan.

Contents

Notes on Contributors

Charalampos Agiropoulos is a Visiting Lecturer in the Department of Economics and a Postgraduate fellow in the Department of International and European Studies at the University of Piraeus. He holds a Ph.D. in Economics and a Master's degree in Applied Statistics from the University of Piraeus. His research interests focus on Applied Econometrics, Financial Analysis, Labor Economics, Tourism and Machine Learning.

Nicholas Apergis is Professor of Economics at the University of Derby. Previously he was with the University of Piraeus. His research is within Macrofinance and Energy Economics. He has over 250 papers in peer-reviewed journals and a Scopus h-index=42. He is the Editor-in-Chief of the Energy Research Letters.

James Ming Chen is Professor of Law at Michigan State University. He also holds visiting or honorary appointments at universities in Croatia, France and Finland. Jim is executive vice-president of Silver Leaf Capital LLC. He edits a series on behavioral economics and finance for Palgrave Macmillan. He received his law degree from Harvard and a degree in data science from Northwestern.

Giuseppina Chesini is Associate Professor of Banking and Finance at the University of Verona (Italy), where she currently teaches undergraduate and graduate courses in financial markets and financial intermediaries. Her research interests include banking, international financial systems and corporate finance. She has participated in many international congresses on these topics with a large number of published papers.

Dionysios Chionis is currently Professor of Economics in Democritus University of Thrace (DUTH) and Research Fellow in Economic Chamber of Greece. He holds a Ph.D. in Economics from the University of Strathclyde and an M.Sc. from the University of Glasgow. His research interests focus on Macroeconomics, International Economics, Financial Markets and Monetary Policy.

Evaggelos Drimpetas is a Professor in the Department of Economics at the Democritus University of Thrace. He is currently the Dean of the School of Social, Political and Economic Sciences. His work has appeared in various scientific journals and international conferences. His research interests are on financial economics, mergers and acquisitions, strategic management, corporate governance and international financial markets.

George Galanos is an Assistant Professor in the field of Economic Policy and Competitiveness at the University of Piraeus, Department of International and European Studies. He holds a Ph.D. in International Economics and Tourism Competitiveness from the University of Piraeus, an M.B.A. focused in Tourism Management and a B.Sc. in Economics.

Fotios Mitropoulos is a Postdoc Researcher in Economics at Democritus University of Thrace, after completing his Ph.D. in Economics and a Research Fellow at the Economic Chamber of Greece. He was a visitor researcher at Brunel University. His research interests focus on the field of Macroeconomics, Labor Economics and Political Economics.

Thomas Poufinas is an Assistant Professor in the Department of Economics of the Democritus University of Thrace. He holds a Ph.D. in Financial Mathematics from the Ohio State University and a Bachelor's Degree in Mathematics from the University of Athens. His research interests focus on finance, investments, risk management, actuarial science and their applications.

Antonios Sarantidis holds a Ph.D. in Economics with a specialization in Econometrics from the School of Social Sciences of the Hellenic Open University. His research interests focus on the fields of Applied Financial Econometrics, Applied Macroeconomics, Economic growth and Political and Economic instability.

List of Figures

List of Tables

CHAPTER 1

Debt Valuation: An Alternative Method to Avoid Future Default

Thomas Poufinas and Evaggelos Drimpetas

1.1 Introduction

1.1.1 Trigger

Public debt evaluation has been debated for years—if not for ever—among the competent authorities of the interested countries, as well as the affected institutions, such as the International Monetary Fund (IMF), the European Commission (EC), etc. It was escalated several times as an important issue, especially during the latest financial crisis that commenced in 2008 and until recently it tantalized several countries, especially in the South of Europe. Public debt projections became of utmost importance, as they were indicative of the sustainability of the sovereign debt of the countries, especially the ones with troubled economies. The country officials and the organization experts produced and continue to produce numerous studies and reports, which are not always fully aligned. The discrepancies are most likely due to the different

T. Poufinas (✉) · E. Drimpetas
Department of Economics, Democritus University of Thrace, Komotini, Greece
e-mail: tpoufina@econ.duth.gr

T. Poufinas (ed.), *Debt in Times of Crisis*,
https://doi.org/10.1007/978-3-030-74162-4_1

assumptions used for the estimation of the debt projection, which result in higher or lower levels of public debt as a percent of GDP (Gross Domestic Product).

To illustrate that, consider for example the case of Greece, a country that has been in the spotlight for years due to the prolonged adverse environment it had to weather. According to the IMF (2018), the debt to GDP ratio is projected to drop from 188.1% in 2018 to 151.3% in 2023 to 142.3% by 2027 to approximately 138% by 2038 and rise gradually to almost 180% by 2060. The EC (European Commission, 2020) forecasts are more optimistic as they drop from 181.2% in 2018 to 140.1% in 2023 to 122.7% in 2027 and to 111.9% in 2030. The difference between the two projections is of the magnitude of 20 percentage points in 2027. Most likely, both can be justified when the assumptions on which they rely are explained.

As a matter of fact, the Debt Sustainability Monitor (European Commission, 2020) notes that the European as well as the world economies were weaker in 2019 with several characteristics of the global slowdown expected to be persistent. Growth is not expected to come back within the next two years, as a consequence of which central banks are most likely to prolong their quantitative easing policies (even if mentioned with different names). Interest rates, as well as the yields of a big part of sovereign bonds, are anticipated to move in negative territories. As far as Greece is concerned, there appear to be a series of debt sustainability challenges (European Commission, 2020) that make the viability of the Greek debt questionable post 2038 (IMF, 2018).

The blend becomes even more explosive as the IMF in its World Economic Outlook (IMF, 2020) projects for 2020 a contraction of −3% for the world economy, which breaks down to −5.9% for the USA and −7.5% for the Euro Area. The trigger this time is the pandemic that has paused a big portion of the global activity. This is expected to be followed by a growth of 5.8% for the world economy, translated to 4.7% growth both for the USA and The Euro Area in 2021. These are conditional on returning gradually to the normal pace at the second half of 2020 as the outbreak fades and that there is a generous policy support.

Consequently, in the midst of these new and unprecedented conditions, the question of whether countries have the capability to repay their debt becomes more relevant than ever. Countries that have had manageable debts may find themselves with debt levels in excess of their

GDPs. Countries whose debt sustainability was already questionable may experience even higher debt to GDP ratios.

1.1.2 *Reserve Funds*

Debt estimates and projections constitute one side of the coin; the other side pertains to the capacity of a country to repay its debt and avoid failing to pay its obligations. Apparently, a forward-looking approach that covers a mid- to long-term horizon is more appropriate. A country may need to consider setting aside funds to meet future commitments. The concept is not new; several countries have put in place sovereign wealth funds (SWFs), which have a range of targets and among which are stabilization funds, savings or future generation funds, pension reserve funds and others. Consequently, it would make sense to think about establishing a default protection scheme.

There are several well-known sovereign wealth funds whose total assets under management were in the area of 8 trillion US dollars in 2019 (SWFI, 2020). The most popular and biggest fund in terms of assets under management is the Norwegian Government Pension Fund Global with almost 1.2 trillion US dollars in assets under management as of 2019 (Norges Bank Investment Management, 2020; SWFI, 2020). The fund was established after the country discovered oil in the North Sea. Its purpose is to shield the economy from ups and downs in oil revenue and serves as financial reserve and long-term savings plan that gives the opportunity to current and future generations to benefit from the wealth created from oil revenues. The top five list is completed with the China Investment Corporation, the Abu Dhabi Investment Authority, the Kuwait Investment Authority and the Hong Kong Monetary Authority Investment Portfolio, all of which had assets under management between 0.5 and 1 trillion US dollars in 2019 (SWFI, 2020).

1.1.3 *Proposed Approach: An Insurance Pricing Technique*

In the midst (or at the rise) of a potentially new crisis, this time with a different cause—a pandemic, it is more than relevant to assess whether a country can be prepared against a potential default through an appropriate default-protection reserve. Insurance and pensions are the best-placed disciplines to provide with means to describe the mechanics of this idea, combined with the principle of a sovereign wealth fund.

The protection mechanism uses the approach employed by standard insurance—actuarial techniques to calculate the burning cost of a life protection scheme. The model deployed in this study can be applied to any type of debt projection; it does not question the assumptions of the available forecasts. As a matter of fact, all different debt projections can be inserted as inputs; the model outputs can serve as a range of the amount that needs to be set aside to avoid a future default. It offers more of a pricing of the country debt, i.e. it indicates what amount the country has to pay as a premium to buy protection against a future default.

1.1.4 Resemblance and Differences with CDS

The route followed and the semantics referred to—even in the previous paragraph—remind also the setup and evaluation of the spread of a Credit Default Swap (CDS). The origins of our research though reflect more the need to create an appropriate reserve to avoid default and not to compensate bond bearers for the risk they undertook—as is the purpose of a CDS. Consequently, the rationale, the notation and the algebra of insurance have been preferred.

1.1.5 Benefits: Support to and from the Development of a European Safe Asset

This approach can facilitate but can also be supported by the development of one safe asset at a Pan-European level. The trigger for a euro-area safe asset is primarily the need to achieve financial integration and capital markets union within the EU (Constâncio, 2018). However, it can support (among other things) the functioning of the EU economies during financial crises (Monti, 2010), which is in line with our rationale. As the intention is to create an insurance-type of reserve that will serve as a cushion to prevent future default, the cause is almost sacred. What would be a better instrument than a single asset (or pool of assets) that will be designated to avoid future defaults from the member-states of the Eurozone or the entire European Union?

Opponents of the one safe asset are probably afraid that it will be used to replace existing debt. Attention is needed here so as not to misinterpret the proposal; the prescribed safe asset will be earmarked as the underlying asset of the reserve that will be created to prevent countries from not meeting their future debt obligations (in excess let's say of their GDP).

In addition, such a special-purpose asset could serve as a pilot for a global Pan-European asset to be introduced at a later stage—when convergence of opinions is achieved. Consequently, finding the amount necessary to fund an insurance-type reserve can definitely facilitate the introduction of one safe asset.

The opposite direction holds true as well; if a safe asset is launched, then it can serve as the underlying asset to support the reserve that will be funded by the contributions of the countries that have been estimated with actuarial techniques, in order to avoid future default. Such an asset will be free from the risk of default of each country and will be of premium quality, thus securing that the necessary funds will be there if there is a need for them to be drawn.

Of course, there may be concerns as to the return of such a good quality asset; they may be nil or negative. This is true; but the primary purpose is to globally preserve the accumulated reserve for potential future use. The long-term horizon allows for potential low returns for certain periods of time when safekeeping is a priority. As a result, the existence of one safe asset (or a series of Pan-European safe assets) would support the placement of the burning-cost-type contributions of the member countries.

1.1.6 *The Role of the European Commission*

Can the European Commission play a role? The success of the undertaking starts from the will of the European Commission to address such an important issue as the viability of the debt of its member states ad infinitum or for a specific time horizon; the recommended path resembles to a whole of life insurance or a term life insurance, respectively. Insurance serves a good cause; the concept of solidarity is well embedded in it and the participants of an insurance scheme contribute to receive benefits when in need. The contributions are held aside in a reserve to be drawn when necessary. We employ the same functioning; the disbursement of the benefit though is to avoid a default and not a physical condition of an individual. Even if not all of the properties of insurance are in place so that an individual insurer can offer coverage, at an EU level, the mechanism could work.

1.1.7 The European Stability Mechanism (ESM)

There are definitely similarities with the European Stability Mechanism (ESM) as far as the concept is concerned. The ESM provides financial assistance to the countries of the eurozone that face severe financial problems. This assistance is provided only if it is deemed necessary so as to secure the financial stability of the euro area as a whole and of its members. The ESM provides financing through loans. Even the credit lines offered by the ESM so that the member countries can maintain access to the markets are essentially loans (ESM, 2020).

The recommended insurance-based approach aims primarily at preventing countries from reaching such a state at which they will not be able to draw money from the markets or they will have a hard time repaying their debts. The ESM funding is primarily for curing the problem; even when it is for preventing it, the same medicine is used—a loan. In contrast, the creation of a pool that will work as a safety net by the participating countries does not necessarily involve lending, as the countries have prepaid some sort of premium protection.

One could say that the latter resembles to the contributions that the countries of the eurozone have made in order to accumulate the capital of ESM. However, this capital (approximately 80 Billion Euro) is not used to make loans; it serves as a guarantee. Having the experience of the ESM, the European Commission could create a protection branch of ESM or an independent body.

Furthermore, even if the ESM is in charge of the eurozone countries and this mechanism is considered sufficient for the time being, the recommended insurance protection reserve could be established for countries that are not members of the eurozone. It can be used by countries that are not even states of the European Union with the aim of avoiding future defaults.

1.1.8 Debt Sustainability

The concept is immediately linked to the mid- to long-term debt sustainability of the countries under examination. If the member states manage to have access to funds that they can draw upon so as to avoid defaults, then their debt would be viable longer. Our study is not linked and does not deploy any debt sustainability analysis (DSA) framework. The European institutions are better placed to develop multi-block, DSA frameworks consisting of deterministic, stochastic and indicator-linked approaches for the assessment of the risks related to the sustainability of sovereign debt (see for example Bouabdallah et al., 2017).

1.1.9 Originality and Novelty of the Approach

Such an approach has not been presented so far to the best of the knowledge of the authors and introduces a fresh and novel approach to the public debt valuation of a country, through an actuarial pricing perspective. It does not limit the flexibility of the responsible parties in predicting the evolution of debt in the future. It equips the policymakers though with a tool that can help the country avoid a potential default and have an estimate of how much it would cost to acquire such a protection.

1.2 Background Discussion

There is ample literature in the pricing or rather estimation of debt. It can be categorized in terms of (i) the type of debt, i.e. corporate, sovereign, private or structured; (ii) the method employed, such as option pricing techniques or econometric—macroeconomic modeling; (iii) the events that occurred, such as market events or a crisis; and (iv) the default, which pertains to the probability of default, the sovereign default, its avoidance or prevention, as well as the issuing law that facilitates the latter. We follow the literature by the type of debt (as in (i)) and in a chronological order grouped were possible so as to match (ii), (iii) and (iv). Interestingly enough it seems that in most of the cases, the chronological order determines the methods employed.

Starting with corporate debt, Merton (1974) prices corporate debt with the use of the newly introduced (at the time) Black-Scholes option pricing formula. His approach is applicable to almost any type of (fixed income) financial instrument from risky discount bonds to callable coupon bonds as exhibited in his manuscript. Claessens and van Wijnbergen (1990) use option pricing to assess the impacts of different debt reduction strategies and forms of enhancement on secondary market prices of debt. They find that debt reduction influences significantly the value of the remaining claims. At the same time, they offer a valuation of fixed and rolling guarantees, realizing that rolling guarantees dominate the fixed ones as a credit enhancement technique; this value is also affected by debt reliefs. Bicksler and Chen (1992) price corporate risky debt with event-risk provisions using contingent claims analysis. They show that this type of debt can be replicated by a portfolio that consists of an outright position on risky debt, a protective put option and a conversion call option that can be exercised before the maturity date if designated corporate-control-related events occur. Risky debt issuance with event-risk provisions results in lower explicit cost than that of straight risky debt. In the same wavelength, Reneby (1998) applies contingent claims analysis to price corporate debt instruments, such as non-investment grade bonds, with closed-form solutions. In particular, he employs combinations of barrier contracts and extends his framework to compound claims such as embedded options on corporate bonds.

On a different route, Datta et al. (1999) investigate whether the cost of public debt is influenced by the existence of a relation of the firm with a bank, as well as by the reputation of the firm. They find that the existence of bank debt and the reputation of the firm are negatively related to the at-issue yield spread for initial public offerings. As a matter of fact, the impact of the former was estimated to be 68 basis points on average.

Ortiz-Molina (2006) investigates the link between managerial ownership structure and at-issue yield spreads on corporate bonds to find that there is a positive relation between the two, which becomes weaker at higher levels of ownership. The same holds true for managerial stock options, which seem to have a stronger influence impact on yield spreads versus stock ownership. Bruche and Naqvi (2010) build a continuous-time asset pricing model of debt and equity in an environment where equity holders decide when to default and creditors decide when to liquidate, which leads to an early default of the equity holders and early liquidation of creditors. They assess in a quantitative manner how the timing of default and liquidation is affected, the optimal capital structure and the spreads.

Colla et al. (2012) examine the pricing of debt in LBOs to realize that there is a positive relationship between the profitability of the firm prior to the LBO and the deal leverage and thus the pricing. They recommend grouping the debt tranches used in LBOs into two main categories, senior and junior, whose pricing depends on their relative use and on bankruptcy risk.

Going to sovereign debt, which is closer to our universe of interest, Babbel, in Babbel and Bertozzi (1996), discusses the insurability of sovereign debt against default by replacing the traditional approach of risk-pooling with a modern (at the time) approach of risk hedging. He argues that sovereign debt does not necessarily meet the insurability criteria required in the risk pooling approach (in particular high frequency and small severity) but realizes that they are not necessary, as what matters is that the insurer has the necessary assets to cover the claims. He thus proposes a risk-hedging technique as an alternative, with the use of put options—a long put and a short put (i.e. a bear spread), that is not capital intensive and draws from the approach of Merton (1974) as presented above. It pretty much builds on the idea of portfolio insurance with the use of options. Kletzer (2005) suggests that derivative contracts may be used for risk sharing and allow debtors on one hand to insure themselves as parties to the contracts and bondholders to reduce the default and restructuring risk. If markets in these securities are feasible, then they may assist in reducing macroeconomic volatility in indebted countries and in increasing capital flows to emerging market economies.

Blundell-Wignall and Slovik (2011) focus on the four countries that were hit the most by the latest sovereign debt crisis, namely Greece, Ireland, Portugal and Spain. They examine the probabilities of default that are implied by observable market spreads to find that they differ between countries according to certain criteria that affect the probability of debt restructuring. Bi and Traum (2012) use Bayesian methods to estimate the probability of default of Italy and Greece in the post EMU period through a real business cycle model that embeds fiscal policy instruments, sovereign default risk and the level of debt that the government is willing to finance. They find that (i) Greece historically had a lower probability of default than Italy for a given level of debt; but (ii) the Italian government seemed to be more willing to service debt compared to the Greek one.

O'Kane (2012) analyzes the relationship between the price of Eurozone sovereign-linked CDSs and the same sovereign bond markets during the Eurozone debt crisis of 2009–2011 to find that there is (i) a relationship with a one day lag from CDS to bonds for Greece and Spain; (ii) the reverse relationship for France and Italy; and (iii) a feedback relationship for Ireland and Portugal. Aizenman et al. (2013) show that there is complex and time-varying association between credit ratings and the pricing of sovereign debt during the Euro crisis, which changes between the pre and at the crisis periods. As a matter of fact, European countries had similar moves in CDS spreads as a result of credit rating changes before the crisis; however, they exhibited large differences during the crisis, with GIIPS being more sensitive than the other European countries.

Cruces and Trebesch (2013) create a database of haircuts in debt restructurings to show that debt restructurings that entail higher haircuts lead to significantly higher subsequent bond yield spreads and longer periods of capital market exclusion.

Camba-Méndez et al. (2016) use the quotes of sovereign CDS contracts to find the probability of default and the loss given default in an emerging market (Poland). They employ fixed and time-varying LGD to realize that there is a low loss given default and a high probability of default for Poland during the crisis. The latter received its highest values in the months that followed the default of Lehman Brothers. The correlations between the probabilities of default and the CDS spreads depend heavily on the maturity of the sovereign CDS. Soytas and Volkan (2016) recommend the application of the Hotz-Miller estimation technique to dynamic general equilibrium models of sovereign default as an alternative to improve their ability to estimate the ex-ante probability of default of economies. They do that with the use of the structural parameter values that the country-specific business cycle statistics and the relevant literature provide.

Beirne and Fratzscher (2013) investigate the drivers of sovereign risk for 31 advanced and emerging economies during the European sovereign debt crisis to find that (i) a deterioration in the fundamentals of the countries and a fundamentals contagion explain the rise in the sovereign yield spreads and CDS spreads during the crisis globally and not only for the eurozone; (ii) regional spillovers and contagion have been of lower importance; (iii) herd contagion has been less concentrated in time and among a few markets; and (iv) empirical models using economic fundamentals did generally a poor job in explaining sovereign risk in the pre-crisis period for European economies, implying that the market priced the sovereign risk without completely embedding the fundamentals prior to the crisis.

The role of monetary policy fluctuations for the macroeconomy and the bond markets is researched by Yamarthy (2017). He finds that the former significantly impact bond risk exposures and contribute about 20% to the variation of bond risk premia. To achieve that, he employs an asset pricing framework incorporating a time-varying Taylor rule for monetary policy, macroeconomic factors and risk pricing restrictions as stemming from the preferences of the investors with the use of the US term structure. Gumus and Koeda (2018) employ a sovereign default model for

Argentina with the use of a maximum simulated likelihood estimation to predict default events. Their model closely matches the default data and performs better than a logit model in predicting the onset of default events. Bradley et al. (2018) examine three parameters that influence the pricing of sovereign bonds, namely governing law, currency and stock exchange listing. They find that investors perceive sovereign debt issued under foreign parameters as less risky than the debt issued under local parameters, both for investment and non-investment grade bonds.

McGregor (2019) proposes a stochastic general equilibrium model in order to link the sovereign default risk with moving oil price and output process of resource-rich (oil-rich) economies. To that end, he realizes that the joint movement of risk premium with oil price is affected by higher risk aversion, government impatience, larger oil shares and strong correlation between domestic output and oil price shocks, thus offering an explanation of the counter-cyclicality of interest rate spreads and oil prices of oil-exporting emerging market economies.

As far as private debt is concerned, Blanc-Brude and Yim (2019) examine the evolution and the drivers of credit spreads in private infrastructure debt, with the use of a factor model. They realize that common risk factors (market trend, credit risk, liquidity and cost of funds) partly explain infrastructure and corporate debt spreads and that the private infrastructure debt pricing is considered fair even after the 2008 credit crisis.

The study that could be considered conceptually the closest to ours, from the papers presented in this section, is the one of Babbel, in Babbel and Bertozzi (1996), in the sense that it refers to the insurability of sovereign debt. The author however questions whether sovereign debt meets the conditions set by a private insurer to offer traditional insurance coverage against default and thus proposes the use of options to implement risk-hedging strategies in a way similar to portfolio insurance. We also do not examine the insurability of sovereign debt but rather employ actuarial techniques in order to price the creation of a reserve, trusting that if it runs under the auspices of the EU, several of the limitations are lifted.

The role of the EU is key in such an undertaking for reputational reasons as well. Following the work of English (1996) on the defaults of US States in the 1840s, it appears that as the defaulting states were part of a large and economically integrated nation, creditors could not enforce payment by imposing military or trade sanctions. However, most states eventually repaid in full in order to maintain access to capital markets and preserve their reputation. As a parallelism, if we replace the US States with EU (member) States, then we have a similar framework, with the EU fostering the debt repayment of its member countries.

Our study focuses on the pricing of the total debt of a country in excess of its GDP and not only related to the bonds issued, in a way that a reserve is created so as to prevent future defaults. The actual contributions required by each of the EU countries, based on the projections performed by the IMF (2018) and the European Commission (2020), are estimated. As such, it covers almost all of the aforementioned categories (with the exception of an event such as a crisis) offering an innovative pricing/reserve accumulation approach; therefore there lies its contribution in the field.

1.3 Problem Description

The problem that this study addresses is the valuation of the public debt of a country via an insurance—actuarial approach. From this perspective, it can be considered more of a pricing of the debt. It also resembles to a reserve accumulation technique. The methodology employed mimics the pricing of a term life insurance product. Term life insurance provides an amount in case of death of the insured; likewise, the default of an entity can be considered as the financial death of this entity, equivalent to the physical death of an individual. Consequently, putting a lump sum amount or a periodic amount aside that could help prevent such a default—by making the required payment when the risk appears—is a legitimate action on behalf of the interested country. This amount is similar to the lump sum or period premium of a term life policy.

The default rate is taken as a proxy of the probability of default, which in turn is considered as a replica of the probability of death in the relevant actuarial model that is used to price term life insurance. It is assumed that a country can avoid default if it can repay at any time the debt that is in excess of its GDP. The excess debt is regarded as comparable to the sum assured that is paid in case of default—instead of death. The former is not flat, as is normally the latter assumed to be. It is worth noticing that this choice is not restrictive. Depending on the target set by the country, other options may include a fixed percentage of the GDP (e.g. 20%) or the debt in excess of a certain percent of the GDP (e.g. 150% of the GDP) or any other set of cash flows.

No matter what the choice of the flows to be protected is, the output of the model is analogous to the burning cost (premium net of loadings) of the corresponding insurance product and it indicates the cost of obtaining protection against default—similar to death. It is calculated as the present value of the payments made in case of default, adjusted by the probability of default.

As most studies, this one has certain limitations that stem primarily from its focus on a specific aspect of debt financing; this of an alternative valuation of public debt. First of all, it does not question either the debt projections or the credit ratings assigned, along with the resulting default rates; it takes them for granted—debt projections are extracted from official reports and default rates are assumed to be the corporate (not sovereign) default rates that correspond to the associated credit rating. Furthermore, credit ratings remain unchanged over time. Second, the interest rate term structures used—a flat interest rate corresponding to the credit rating of the country and the EIOPA risk-free curve—also do not move during the period under consideration. Third, it does not inquire from what sources the required amount will be paid. Although it makes some recommendations and drafts certain directions, it assumes that the interested countries will reallocate their finances to make room for such payments if they find it useful. Fourth, it does not tackle how to create a pool of interested countries or who is better placed to launch it; normally an insurance product is sold to the insured population and the reserve that is built—from the premia paid by the insured individuals—is used to cover for the sum assured in case of death of one or more of them. It highlights potential institutions that could pick up this role; nevertheless, it centers primarily on the calculation of the protection cost per country. Fifth, it assumes no recoveries and no correlations among the countries, as the interest is to secure each and every country at all times, thus pursuing a more prudent assessment.

1.4 Model Analysis

Following the path that was sketched in the aforementioned paragraph, the relative actuarial notation is introduced, enhanced with the necessary symbols to reflect debt (Table 1.1).

If a state wishes to estimate the amount needed to secure that it will not default, within a specific time horizon of n years, then it needs to add the present value of the excess debt for each year within its time horizon,

Table 1.1 Variable notation and interpretation

Variable	*Explanation*
(x)	The entity of interest. In the standard actuarial notation, it usually denotes an individual of age x. However, it is assumed that all countries have age 0 as the history of debt is embedded in the debt projections
$_{m/}q_x$	The probability that (x) does not default for m years but defaults between years m and $m + 1$. It is derived from the cumulative default rates as posted by the rating agencies
i	The interest rate used for discounting
u	$(1+i)^{-1}$
$_n p_x$	The probability that (x) does not default for n years
$_n q_x$	The probability that (x) defaults within n years. It is equal to $1 - {_n p_x}$
$A^{1}_{x:\overline{n}\vert}$	The lump sum cost that (x) undertakes for setting up a default protection scheme for n years
$P^{1}_{x:\overline{n}\vert}$	The periodic (annual) cost that (x) undertakes for setting up a default protection scheme for n years
$_{m/}A^{1}_{x:\overline{n}\vert}$	The lump sum cost that (x) undertakes for setting up a default protection scheme for n years, with a delay of m years
$P^{1}_{x:\overline{n}\vert}$	The periodic (annual) cost that (x) undertakes for setting up a default protection scheme for n years, with a delay of m years
$\ddot{a}_{x:\overline{n}\vert}$	The present value of a term life annuity—in advance for n years
ed_n	Excess debt amount over GDP at year n

multiplied by the probability of defaulting in that year, given that it has not defaulted the previous years. This mirrors the lump sum burning cost (premium) of a term life insurance policy. Without loss of generality, we assume that default takes place only on integer time instants, although the model can be easily adjusted for fractional time instants. This amount is derived by the following equation:

$$A^{1}_{x:\overline{n}\vert} = u \cdot q_x \cdot ed_1 + u^2 \cdot {_{1/}q_x} \cdot ed_2 + \cdots + u^n \cdot {_{n-1/}q_x} \cdot ed_n$$
$$= \sum_{t=1}^{n} u^t \cdot {_{t-1/}q_x} \cdot ed_t. \qquad (1.1)$$

This is a variation of the corresponding actuarial equation that has 1 monetary unit instead of the excess debt amount at each year.

If the state wishes to have this expense made annually, then the annual figure is deduced from the following formula:

$$P^1_{x:\bar{n}|} = \frac{A^1_{x:\overline{n}|}}{\ddot{a}_{x:\overline{n}|}}. \tag{1.2}$$

This echoes the annual (periodic) burning cost (premium) of a term life insurance policy. The denominator is equal to:

$$\begin{aligned}\ddot{a}_{x:\overline{n}|} &= 1 + u \cdot {}_1p_x + u^2 \cdot {}_2p_x + \cdots u^{n-1} \cdot {}_{n-1}p_x \\ &= 1 + \sum\nolimits_{t=1}^{n-1} u^t \cdot {}_{t-1}p_x.\end{aligned} \tag{1.3}$$

If the state wishes to delay the payment and start the accumulation earlier, i.e. wait for a certain number of years, let us say m, before activating such a default protection, then the lump sum amount is given by the relation:

$$\begin{aligned}{}_{m/}A^1_{x:\overline{n}|} &= u^{m+1} \cdot {}_{m/}q_x \cdot ed_{m+1} + \cdots + u^n \cdot {}_{n-1/}q_x \cdot ed_n \\ &= \sum\nolimits_{t=m+1}^{n} u^t \cdot {}_{t-1/}q_x \cdot ed_t.\end{aligned} \tag{1.4}$$

The matching annual disbursement, provided that it starts form year 1, is obtained by:

$${}_{m/}P^1_{x:\overline{n}|} = \frac{A^1_{x:\overline{n}|}}{\ddot{a}_{x:\overline{n}|}}. \tag{1.5}$$

Additional versions can be quoted; for example, the annual payments can last for less than n years. We do not list them, as the applicable formulas can be readily inferred from these, by keeping only the years of interest.

1.5 Numerical Application

To elaborate the implementation of the recommended technique, we reflect on the debt of the European Union countries. The projections of the public debt and the GDP come from the IMF or the European Commission reports (European Commission, 2018, 2020; IMF, 2018) for Greece. We use two sources for this country as it seemed to have the most turbulent times, and the viability of its debt has been debated, with different sources posting differing points of view. For the other countries, the projections of the public debt and the GDP come from the European Commission (2018, 2020). The default rates are taken from S&P (2019). The interest rates are either based on the authors' assumptions—reflecting the current (rounded) interest rates or acquired from EIOPA (European Insurance and Occupational Pensions Authority, 2018).

As the assumption we made earlier is that countries will avoid default if they keep their debt always below their GDP, we apply our model to the countries that have had in the recent years a public debt that was higher than or close to their GDP and/or are anticipated to have debt to GDP ratio higher than or close to 100% for at least one year in the period under examination (2019–2030). These countries are Greece, Italy, Cyprus, Portugal, Spain and Ireland as per the baseline scenario and France and Belgium based on adverse scenarios. The remaining countries have a debt to GDP ratio lower than 100% according to all scenarios.

1.5.1 Greece

Starting with Greece, a first set of default protection cost calculations is based on the debt and GDP projections of the Debt Sustainability Monitor prepared by the European Commission (2020). With regard to GDP, the 2019 GDP of 187,457 Million Euro was entered as seed and the GDP real growth rate as projected by the European Commission (2020) was applied for the years 2020–2030. As the GDP real growth rate was given for the years 2020 and 2030, the interim GDP growth rate was estimated with linear interpolation. Subsequently, the debt to GDP ratio was applied to the GDP amount in order to produce the debt amount for the same years. The amount to be protected in case of default is the debt in excess of GDP.

The annual default rates were calculated as the differences of the cumulative default rates of two consecutive years as computed by S&P Global (2019) per credit score (rating). The latter are available for a period of 15 years. As mentioned earlier, the annual default rates are proxies of the probability of default within a specific year. The credit rating of Greece was assumed to remain at BB—for the entire period 2019–2030 (Table 1.2).

Two interest rate variances were utilized; a flat 1.5% and the risk-free term structure of EIOPA as of December 2018. The rationale behind

Table 1.2 Default protection cost—European Commission debt projections until 2030—Greece

Greece/Year	*2018*	*2019*	*2020*	*2021*	*2022*	*2023*	*2024*	*2025*	*2026*	*2027*	*2028*	*2029*	*2030*
Cumulative probability of default BB-		0.95	2.98	5.11	7.33	9.27	11.15	12.71	14.21	15.42	16.46	17.28	17.99
Annual probability of default BB-		0.95	2.03	2.13	2.22	1.94	1.88	1.56	1.5	1.21	1.04	0.82	0.71
GDP (Eurostat Million Euro)	184,714	187,457	191,768	195,929	199,926	203,745	207,372	210,793	213,997	216,972	219,706	222,188	224,410
GDP growth (%) real—European Commission		1.80	2.3	2.17	2.04	1.91	1.78	1.65	1.52	1.39	1.26	1.13	1
Debt (Million Euro)	334,701	322,425	313,924	304,866	291,892	285,447	280,574	275,718	270,921	266,224	261,230	256,183	251,115
Debt to GDP (%) European Commission	181.2	172	163.7	155.6	146	140.1	135.3	130.8	126.6	122.7	118.9	115.3	111.9
Amount to protect in case of default													
Debt-GDP	149,987	134,969	122,156	108,937	91,966	81,702	73,202	64,924	56,923	49,253	41,524	33,995	26,705
Interest rate flat 1.5%		1.50%	1.50%	1.50%	1.50%	1.50%	1.50%	1.50%	1.50%	1.50%	1.50%	1.50%	1.50%
u		0.99	0.97	0.96	0.94	0.93	0.91	0.90	0.89	0.87	0.86	0.85	0.84
Single premium protection amount	13,502	1263	2407	2219	1924	1471	1259	913	758	521	372	237	159

(continued)

Table 1.2 (continued)

Greece/Year	*2018*	*2019*	*2020*	*2021*	*2022*	*2023*	*2024*	*2025*	*2026*	*2027*	*2028*	*2029*	*2030*
Regular premium protection amount	1342												
Annuity in advance PV $\ddot{a}_{x:\overline{n}\rvert}$	10.06	1	0.98	0.94	0.91	0.87	0.84	0.81	0.79	0.76	0.74	0.72	0.70
Interest rate EIOPA 12.2018		−0.33%	−0.28%	−0.18%	−0.05%	0.10%	0.24%	0.37%	0.50%	0.62%	0.73%	0.82%	0.91%
u		1.00	1.01	1.01	1.00	1.00	0.99	0.97	0.96	0.95	0.93	0.91	0.90
Single premium protection amount	14,290	1286	2493	2333	2045	1577	1357	987	821	564	402	255	170
Regular premium protection amount	1343												
Annuity in advance PV $\ddot{a}_{x:\overline{n}\rvert}$	10.64	1	0.99	0.98	0.95	0.93	0.90	0.88	0.85	0.82	0.80	0.78	0.76

Source Author calculations based on debt and GDP projections by the European Commission (2020) and cumulative default rates by S&P Global (2019)

these choices is that the first corresponds to the ten-year Greek Government Bond yield to maturity, whereas the second is the yield curve suggested by EIOPA to insurance companies and occupational pension funds. Formulas (1.1) and (1.2) were used to derive the lump sum and the periodic cost for setting up a default protection scheme for 12 years, i.e. the interval 2019–2030 (Table 1.2). The lump sum that had to be in place on January 1, 2019 was estimated to be 13,502 Million Euro when a flat interest rate of 1.5% was used. It increased to 14,290 Million Euro when the EIOPA risk-free term structure was inserted. The periodic amounts were found to be 1342 Million Euro and 1343 Million Euro respectively (Table 1.2).

A second round of default protection cost estimates originates from the GDP and debt projections made by the IMF (2018) in the Consultation and Proposal for Post-Program Monitoring for Greece. This time the GDP and debt amount projections are explicit until 2023. For the years 2024–2027, the IMF forecasted GDP real growth rate and debt to GDP ratios were engaged to find the GDP and debt figures. The amount to be protected in case of default is again the debt in excess of GDP.

The annual default rates and the interest rate variants were the same as before. Equations (1.1) and (1.2) were employed once and again to find that the lump sum that was required on January 1, 2019 was 16.54 Billion Euro when a flat interest rate of 1.5% was assumed and 17.54 Billion Euro, when the EIOPA risk-free term structure was applied. The periodic amounts were calculated to be 1.64 Billion Euro and 1.65 Billion Euro, respectively (Table 1.3).

Finally, the IMF projections were extended to 2060, as IMF (2060) has made debt to GDP forecasts until that year in the Consultation and Proposal for Post-Program Monitoring for Greece. Linear interpolation was used between the years 2027 and 2038, as well as the years 2038 and 2060 due to the fact that these forecasts are presented in a chart only. The GDP real growth rate was assumed to remain unchanged for the years following 2027. The GDP projections were multiplied by the debt to GDP ratio projections to estimate the debt projections. The amount to be protected again in case of default is once more the debt in excess of GDP.

The annual default rates and the interest rate versions remain the same. However, as the default rates are given only for a period of 15 years, the moving average annual default rate of the last four years

Table 1.3 Default protection cost—IMF debt projections until 2027—Greece

Greece/Year	*2018*	*2019*	*2020*	*2021*	*2022*	*2023*	*2024*	*2025*	*2026*	*2027*
Cumulative probability of default BB-		0.95	2.98	5.11	7.33	9.27	11.15	12.71	14.21	15.42
Annual probability of default BB-		0.95	2.03	2.13	2.22	1.94	1.88	1.56	1.5	1.21
GDP (IMF Billion Euro)	183.1	189.2	196.0	202.6	208.6	214.6	217.18	219.78	222.42	224.64
GDP growth (%) real—IMF	2	2.4	2.2	1.6	1.2	1.2	1.2	1.2	1.2	1
Debt (Billion Euro)	344.4	335	332.5	330	324	324.7	321.64	319.78	319.39	319.67
Debt to GDP (%) IMF	188.1%	177.1%	169.6%	162.9%	155.3%	151.3%	148.1%	145.5%	143.6%	142.3%
Amount to protect in case of default										
Debt-GDP	161	146	137	127	115	110	104	100	97	95
Interest rate flat 1.5%		1.50%	1.50%	1.50%	1.50%	1.50%	1.50%	1.50%	1.50%	1.50%
u		0.99	0.97	0.96	0.94	0.93	0.91	0.90	0.89	0.87
Single premium protection amount	16.54	1.36	2.69	2.60	2.41	1.98	1.80	1.41	1.29	1.01
Regular premium protection amount	1.64									
Annuity in advance PV $\ddot{a}_{x:\overline{n}\rvert}$	10.063	1	0.98	0.94	0.91	0.87	0.84	0.81	0.79	0.76
Interest rate EIOPA 12. 2018		−0.33%	−0.28%	−0.18%	−0.05%	0.10%	0.24%	0.37%	0.50%	0.62%
u		1.00	1.01	1.01	1.00	1.00	0.99	0.97	0.96	0.95
Single premium protection amount	17.54	1.39	2.79	2.73	2.57	2.13	1.94	1.52	1.40	1.09
Regular premium protection amount	1.65									
Annuity in advance PV $\ddot{a}_{x:\overline{n}\rvert}$	10.64	1	0.99	0.98	0.95	0.93	0.90	0.88	0.85	0.82

Source Author calculations based on debt and GDP projections by the IMF (2018) and cumulative default rates by S&P Global (2019)

was used to produce the step for the cumulative default rates until 2060. Consequently, the annual default rates remain almost unchanged.

Formulas (1.1) and (1.2) were put to use to yield that the lump sum cost as of January 1, 2019 came up to 18.62 Billion Euro when the flat interest rate of 1.5% was used and increased to 19.78 Billion Euro when the EIOPA risk-free term structure was introduced. The corresponding periodic costs were computed to be 1.85 Billion Euro and 1.86 Billion Euro (Table 1.4).

Our findings indicate that in the case of Greece, the lump sum amount that needs to be set aside so that default protection is acquired varies between 13.5 and almost 20 Billion Euro, depending on the source of the projections and the time horizon. The corresponding periodic disbursements range between 1.3 and almost 1.9 Billion Euro, again depending on the origin of the forecasts and the time span.

A natural question is what body is in a position to offer such a protection scheme in case of default, even if a country could afford the lump sum or the periodic expense. The European Union could create such a default protection pool, which would resemble to the reserve that insurance companies build for life protection products. The outlay is still high; the lump sum varies between 7.20 and 10.45% of GDP, whereas the periodic amount ranges between 0.72 and 0.98% of GDP for Greece, depending on the projections employed (European Commission until 2030, IMF until 2027 and IMF until 2060) and the yield curve. Imposing additional taxes or launching special-purpose bonds are two potential routes; the former would imply a lump sum tax between approximately 2700 Euro and 3955 Euro and an annual tax between approximately 268 Euro and 372 Euro (again depending on the source of the forecasts, the time horizon and the yield curve employed) per taxpayer if 5 million taxpayers are assumed in Greece (roughly 50% of the population) (Tables 1.12a and 1.12b).

1.5.2 *Italy*

Going to Italy, we repeat the same calculations with debt and GDP projections (baseline no-policy change scenario) brought from the European Commission Debt Sustainability Monitor (2020). The 2019 GDP of 1,787,664 Million Euro is as per the Eurostat database (Eurostat, 2020), whereas the following year amounts were estimated with the GDP real growth rate as forecasted by the European Commission (2020) for the

Table 1.4 Default protection cost—IMF debt projections until 2060—Greece

Greece/Year	*2018*	*2019*	*2020*	*2021*	*2022*	*2023*	*2024*	*2025*	*2026*	*2027*	*2038*	*2060*
Cumulative probability of default BB-		0.95	2.98	5.11	7.33	9.27	11.15	12.71	14.21	15.42	23.72	39.36
Annual probability of default BB-		0.95	2.03	2.13	2.22	1.94	1.88	1.56	1.5	1.21	0.71	0.71
GDP (IMF Billion Euro)	183.1	189.2	196.0	202.6	208.6	214.6	217.18	219.78	222.42	224.64	250.63	311.96
GDP growth (%) real—IMF	2	2.4	2.2	1.6	1.2	1.2	1.2	1.2	1.2	1	1	1
Debt (Billion Euro)	344.4	335	332.5	330	324	324.7	321.64	319.78	319.39	319.67	345.87	561.53
Debt to GDP (%) IMF	188.1%	177.1%	169.6%	162.9%	155.3%	151.3%	148.1%	145.5%	143.6%	142.3%	138.0%	180.0%
Amount to protect in case of default												
Debt-GDP	161	146	137	127	115	110	104	100	97	95	95	250
Interest rate flat 1.5%		1.50%	1.50%	1.50%	1.50%	1.50%	1.50%	1.50%	1.50%	1.50%	1.50%	1.50%
u		0.99	0.97	0.96	0.94	0.93	0.91	0.90	0.89	0.87	0.74	0.54
Single premium protection amount	18.62	1.36	2.69	2.60	2.41	1.98	1.80	1.41	1.29	1.01	0.50	0.95
Regular premium protection amount	1.85											
Annuity in advance PV $\ddot{a}_{x:\overline{n}\vert}$	10.06	1	0.98	0.94	0.91	0.87	0.84	0.81	0.79	0.76	0.58	0.33
Interest rate EIOPA 12.2018		−0.33%	−0.28%	−0.18%	−0.05%	0.10%	0.24%	0.37%	0.50%	0.62%	1.28%	2.41%

Greece/Year	*2018*	*2019*	*2020*	*2021*	*2022*	*2023*	*2024*	*2025*	*2026*	*2027*	*2038*	*2060*
u		1.00	1.01	1.01	1.00	1.00	0.99	0.97	0.96	0.95	0.78	0.37
Single premium protection amount	19.78	1.39	2.79	2.73	2.57	2.13	1.94	1.52	1.40	1.09	0.53	0.65
Regular premium protection amount	1.86											
Annuity in advance PV $\ddot{a}_{x:\overline{n}\rvert}$	10.64	1	0.99	0.98	0.95	0.93	0.90	0.88	0.85	0.82	0.61	0.23

Source Author calculations based on debt and GDP projections by the IMF (2018) and cumulative default rates by S&P Global (2019)

years 2020–2030. The growth rate for the years 2021, 2026, 2028 and 2030 is as per the EC report (2020) and the missing years were filled in with linear interpolation. The amount of debt was calculated by applying the debt to GDP ratio to the GDP amount. The difference of the GDP from the debt amount is the amount to be protected. The annual default rates were found again as the differences of the cumulative default rates of two consecutive years as per the S&P Global (2019) study under the assumption that the credit rating of Italy will remain at BBB through the 2019–2030 time interval. Again two interest rate scenarios were tested; a level of 1.4% corresponding to the ten-year Italian Government Bond yield to maturity and the EIOPA risk-free rate curve.

The output of formulas (1.1) and (1.2) this time is that the lump sum amount that had to be in place as of January 1, 2019 comes up to 24,071 Million Euro and 25,568 Million Euro with the flat and the EIOPA interest rate curves, respectively. The corresponding periodic amounts were computed to be 2196 Million Euro and 2215 Million Euro, respectively (Table 1.5). These correspond to 1.35% to 1.43% of the 2019 GDP for the lump sum and 0.12% for the periodic amount depending on the yield curve employed. The bill would be between 802 Euro and 852 Euro for the lump sum and between 73 Euro and 74 Euro per taxpayer for the level and the EIOPA interest rate curve, respectively, under the assumption that there are 30 million taxpayers in Italy (roughly 50% of the population) (Table 1.12a). The financing means could be similar to the ones mentioned in the case of Greece.

1.5.3 Cyprus

Turning to Cyprus, we observe that although in the recent years it exhibits debt to GDP ratio higher than 100%, it drops below 100% after 2019 as per the European Commission Debt Sustainability Monitor (2020). Moreover, this is true not only for the baseline scenario, but even for the most adverse scenario. Consequently, applying Eqs. (1.1) and (1.2) yields a zero lump sum and periodic amount (Table 1.6).

1.5.4 Portugal

Portugal is one of the countries that have been severely hit by the latest crisis; however, the projections (European Commission Debt Sustainability Monitor, 2020) indicate that it will revert to a debt to GDP

Table 1.5 Default protection cost—European Commission debt projections until 2030—Italy

Italy/Year	*2018*	*2019*	*2020*	*2021*	*2022*	*2023*	*2024*	*2025*	*2026*	*2027*	*2028*	*2029*	*2030*
Cumulative probability of default BBB		0.16	0.41	0.64	1.01	1.36	1.72	2.04	2.36	2.72	3.08	3.46	3.77
Annual probability of default BBB		0.16	0.25	0.23	0.37	0.35	0.36	0.32	0.32	0.36	0.36	0.38	0.31
GDP (Eurostat Million Euro)	1,766,168	1,787,664	1,794,815	1,807,378	1,819,307	1,830,587	1,841,204	1,851,147	1,860,403	1,866,914	1,870,648	1,874,389	1,878,138
GDP growth (%) real–European Commission		0.10	0.40	0.70	0.66	0.62	0.58	0.54	0.50	0.35	0.20	0.20	0.20
Debt (Million Euro)	2,380,795	2,434,799	2,455,307	2,483,338	2,512,463	2,531,702	2,542,703	2,550,880	2,561,774	2,574,474	2,588,976	2,609,150	2,633,149
Debt to GDP (%) European Commission	134.8	136.2	136.8	137.4	138.1	138.3	138.1	137.8	137.7	137.9	138.4	139.2	140.2
Amount to protect in case of default													
Debt-GDP	614,627	647,134	660,492	675,960	693,156	701,115	701,499	699,733	701,372	707,560	718,329	734,761	755,011
Interest rate flat 1.2%		1.20%	1.20%	1.20%	1.20%	1.20%	1.20%	1.20%	1.20%	1.20%	1.20%	1.20%	1.20%

(continued)

Table 1.5 (continued)

Italy/Year	*2018*	*2019*	*2020*	*2021*	*2022*	*2023*	*2024*	*2025*	*2026*	*2027*	*2028*	*2029*	*2030*
u		0.99	0.98	0.96	0.95	0.94	0.93	0.92	0.91	0.90	0.89	0.88	0.87
Single premium protection amount	24,404	1023	1612	1500	2445	2312	2351	2060	2040	2288	2295	2449	2028
Regular premium protection amount	2203												
Annuity in advance PV $\ddot{a}_{x:\overline{n}\rvert}$	11.07	1	0.99	0.97	0.96	0.94	0.93	0.91	0.90	0.89	0.87	0.86	0.85
Interest rate EIOPA 12.2018		−0.33%	−0.28%	−0.18%	−0.05%	0.10%	0.24%	0.37%	0.50%	0.62%	0.73%	0.82%	0.91%
u		100.33%	100.55%	100.53%	100.18%	99.51%	98.58%	97.43%	96.10%	94.61%	93.02%	91.39%	89.71%
Single premium protection amount	25,568	1039	1660	1563	2569	2442	2490	2182	2157	2410	2406	2552	2100
Regular premium protection amount	2215												
Annuity in advance PV $\ddot{a}_{x:\overline{n}\rvert}$	11.54	1	1.00	1.00	1.00	0.99	0.98	0.97	0.95	0.94	0.92	0.90	0.88

Source Author calculations based on debt and GDP projections by the European Commission (2020) and cumulative default rates by S&P Global 2019)

Table 1.6 Default protection cost—European Commission debt projections until 2030—Cyprus

Cyprus/Year	*2018*	*2019*	*2020*	*2021*	*2022*	*2023*	*2024*	*2025*	*2026*	*2027*	*2028*	*2029*	*2030*
Cumulative probability of default BBB-		0.24	0.73	1.35	2.04	2.77	3.42	4.00	4.55	5.00	5.39	5.83	6.19
Annual probability of default BBB-		0.24	0.49	0.62	0.69	0.73	0.65	0.58	0.55	0.45	0.39	0.44	0.36
GDP (Eurostat Million Euro)	21,138	21,944	22,514	23,032	23,543	24,047	24,542	25,028	25,504	25,989	26,482	26,946	27,377
GDP growth (%) real—European Commission		2.90	2.60	2.30	2.22	2.14	2.06	1.98	1.90	1.90	1.90	1.75	1.60
Debt (Million Euro)	21,265	20,583	19,767	18,840	18,222	17,747	17,376	16,744	16,042	15,359	14,592	13,850	13,168
Debt to GDP (%) European Commission	100.6	93.8	87.8	81.8	77.4	73.8	70.8	66.9	62.9	59.1	55.1	51.4	48.1
Amount to protect in case of default													
Debt-GDP	127	–	–	–	–	–	–	–	–	–	–	–	–
Interest rate flat 0.5%		0.50%	0.50%	0.50%	0.50%	0.50%	0.50%	0.50%	0.50%	0.50%	0.50%	0.50%	0.50%
u		1.00	0.99	0.99	0.98	0.98	0.97	0.97	0.96	0.96	0.95	0.95	0.94

(continued)

Table 1.6 (continued)

Cyprus/Year	*2018*	*2019*	*2020*	*2021*	*2022*	*2023*	*2024*	*2025*	*2026*	*2027*	*2028*	*2029*	*2030*
Single premium protection amount	–	–	–	–	–	–	–	–	–	–	–	–	–
Regular premium protection amount	–												
Annuity in advance PV $\ddot{a}_{x:\overline{n}\vert}$	11.34	1	0.99	0.98	0.97	0.96	0.95	0.94	0.93	0.92	0.91	0.90	0.89
Interest rate EIOPA 12.2018		−0.33%	−0.28%	−0.18%	−0.05%	0.10%	0.24%	0.37%	0.50%	0.62%	0.73%	0.82%	0.91%
u		100.33%	100.55%	100.53%	100.18%	99.51%	98.58%	97.43%	96.10%	94.61%	93.02%	91.39%	89.71%
Single premium protection amount	–	–	–	–	–	–	–	–	–	–	–	–	–
Regular premium protection amount	–												
Annuity in advance PV $\ddot{a}_{x:\overline{n}\vert}$	11.38	1	1.00	1.00	0.99	0.98	0.97	0.95	0.94	0.92	0.90	0.88	0.86

Source Author calculations based on debt and GDP projections by the European Commission (2020) and cumulative default rates by S&P Global (2019)

ratio of less than 100% after 2026 (included). The 2019 GDP amounts to 253,702 Million Euro according to the Eurostat database (Eurostat, 2020). As for Italy, the GDP for the following years is computed with the GDP real growth rate as mapped by the European Commission (2020) for the years 2020–2030, with the growth rate being actual for 2021, 2026, 2028 and 2030 and linearly interpolated for the interim years. The annual default rates are calculated by taking the differences of the cumulative default rates of any two adjacent years according to the S&P Global (2019) study; as with Italy, we assume that the credit rating will remain at BBB. We employ two interest rate scenarios, a flat 0.4% corresponding to the ten-year Portuguese Government Bond yield to maturity and the EIOPA risk-free interest rate term structure.

Formulas (1.1) and (1.2) give that the lump sum required on January 1, 2019 amounts to 427 Million Euro with the horizontal and 433 Million Euro with the EIOPA term structures, respectively. The periodic amounts are found to be 37 Million Euro in both cases (rounded to the million) (Table 1.7). These correspond to 0.2% of the 2019 GDP for the lump sum and 0.02% of the 2019 GDP for the periodic amount for both yield curves (rounded to the second decimal). The cost per taxpayer would be 85 Euro and 87 Euro for the lump sum for the flat and the EIOPA interest rates, respectively, and 7 Euro for the periodic amount for both curves, assuming 5 million taxpayers (approximately 50% of the population) (Table 1.12a). This could be financed with the ways described above for Greece.

1.5.5 Spain

Coming to Spain, we recall that it was one of the first countries to be affected by the crisis, with the unemployment rate jumping to higher than 20% and public debt flirting with 100% of GDP; however, for the period under examination, it remains below 100% according to the baseline scenario. Therefore, applying Eqs. (1.1) and (1.2) produces a zero lump sum and periodic amount (Table 1.8a). It could exceed 100% if an adverse scenario comes true (European Commission Debt Sustainability Monitor, 2020).

We proceed as we did for Italy and Portugal with one additional intervention; as under the adverse scenario, the debt to GDP forecasts are given only for the years 2019, 2020, 2021, 2026, 2028 and 2030; we linearly interpolate the debt to GDP ratios for the years in between. We

Table 1.7 Default protection cost—European Commission debt projections until 2030—Portugal

Portugal/Year	*2018*	*2019*	*2020*	*2021*	*2022*	*2023*	*2024*	*2025*	*2026*	*2027*	*2028*	*2029*	*2030*
Cumulative probability of default BBB		0.16	0.41	0.64	1.01	1.36	1.72	2.04	2.36	2.72	3.08	3.46	3.77
Annual probability of default BBB		0.16	0.25	0.23	0.37	0.35	0.36	0.32	0.32	0.36	0.36	0.38	0.31
GDP (Eurostat Million Euro)	204,305	212,303	215,912	219,582	222,964	226,041	228,799	231,224	233,305	235,288	237,170	239,068	240,980
GDP growth (%) real—European Commission		2.00	1.70	1.70	1.54	1.38	1.22	1.06	0.90	0.85	0.80	0.80	0.80
Debt (Million Euro)	249,660	253,702	252,833	249,665	246,375	243,446	240,467	236,080	231,672	227,053	222,703	218,747	214,954
Debt to GDP (%) European Commission	122.2	119.5	117.1	113.7	110.5	107.7	105.1	102.1	99.3	96.5	93.9	91.5	89.2
Amount to protect in case of default													
Debt-GDP	45,356	41,399	36,921	30,083	23,411	17,405	11,669	4856	–	–	–	–	–
Interest rate flat 0.4%		0.40%	0.40%	0.40%	0.40%	0.40%	0.40%	0.40%	0.40%	0.40%	0.40%	0.40%	0.40%
u		1.00	0.99	0.99	0.98	0.98	0.98	0.97	0.97	0.96	0.96	0.96	0.95
Single premium protection amount	427	66	92	68	85	60	41	15	–	–	–	–	–

Portugal/Year	*2018*	*2019*	*2020*	*2021*	*2022*	*2023*	*2024*	*2025*	*2026*	*2027*	*2028*	*2029*	*2030*
Regular premium protection amount	37												
Annuity in advance PV $\ddot{a}_{x:\overline{n}\rceil}$	11.56	1	0.99	0.99	0.98	0.97	0.97	0.96	0.95	0.95	0.94	0.93	0.92
Interest rate EIOPA 12.2018		−0.33%	−0.28%	−0.18%	−0.05%	0.10%	0.24%	0.37%	0.50%	0.62%	0.73%	0.82%	0.91%
u		100.33%	100.55%	100.53%	100.18%	99.51%	98.58%	97.43%	96.10%	94.61%	93.02%	91.39%	89.71%
Single premium protection amount	433	66	93	70	87	61	41	15	–	–	–	–	–
Regular premium protection amount	37												
Annuity in advance PV $\ddot{a}_{x:\overline{n}\rceil}$	11.54	1	1.00	1.00	1.00	0.99	0.98	0.97	0.95	0.94	0.92	0.90	0.88

Source Author calculations based on debt and GDP projections by the European Commission (2020) and cumulative default rates by S&P Global (2019)

Table 1.8a Default protection cost—European Commission debt projections until 2030 Spain (base)

Spain/Year	*2018*	*2019*	*2020*	*2021*	*2022*	*2023*	*2024*	*2025*	*2026*	*2027*	*2028*	*2029*	*2030*
Cumulative probability of default A		0.06	0.14	0.23	0.35	0.48	0.65	0.83	1.00	1.19	1.41	1.59	1.73
Annual probability of default A		0.06	0.08	0.09	0.12	0.13	0.17	0.18	0.17	0.19	0.22	0.18	0.14
GDP (Eurostat Million Euro)	1,202,193	1,245,331	1,264,011	1,281,707	1,298,882	1,315,508	1,331,557	1,347,003	1,361,820	1,376,800	1,391,945	1,407,256	1,422,736
GDP growth (%) real—European Commission		1.90	1.50	1.40	1.34	1.28	1.22	1.16	1.10	1.10	1.10	1.10	1.10
Debt (Million Euro)	1,173,340	1,204,235	1,221,035	1,230,439	1,248,226	1,269,465	1,290,279	1,302,552	1,314,156	1,325,858	1,336,267	1,348,151	1,361,558
Debt to GDP (%) European Commission	97.6	96.7	96.6	96	96.1	96.5	96.9	96.7	96.5	96.3	96	95.8	95.7
Amount to protect in case of default													
Debt-GDP	–	–	–	–	–	–	–	–	–	–	–	–	–
Interest rate flat 0.4%		0.40%	0.40%	0.40%	0.40%	0.40%	0.40%	0.40%	0.40%	0.40%	0.40%	0.40%	0.40%
u		1.00	0.99	0.99	0.98	0.98	0.98	0.97	0.97	0.96	0.96	0.96	0.95
Single premium protection amount	–	–	–	–	–	–	–	–	–	–	–	–	–

Spain/Year	*2018*	*2019*	*2020*	*2021*	*2022*	*2023*	*2024*	*2025*	*2026*	*2027*	*2028*	*2029*	*2030*
Regular premium protection amount	–												
Annuity in advance PV $\ddot{a}_{x:\overline{n}\rceil}$	11.66	1	1.00	0.99	0.99	0.98	0.98	0.97	0.96	0.96	0.95	0.95	0.94
Interest rate EIOPA 12.2018		−0.33%	−0.28%	−0.18%	−0.05%	0.10%	0.24%	0.37%	0.50%	0.62%	0.73%	0.82%	0.91%
u		100.33%	100.55%	100.53%	100.18%	99.51%	98.58%	97.43%	96.10%	94.61%	93.02%	91.39%	89.71%
Single premium protection amount	–	–	–	–	–	–	–	–	–	–	–	–	–
Regular premium protection amount	–												
Annuity in advance PV $\ddot{a}_{x:\overline{n}\rceil}$	11.65	1	1.00	1.00	1.00	1.00	0.99	0.98	0.97	0.95	0.93	0.92	0.90

Source Author calculations based on debt and GDP projections by the European Commission (2020) and cumulative default rates by S&P Global (2019)

find (with the use of formulas [1.1] and [1.2]) that starting with a GDP of 1,245,331 Million Euro in 2019 (Eurostat database [Eurostat, 2020]), assuming a credit rating of A and utilizing two interest rate variants—a flat 0.40% and the EIOPA risk-free curve—the lump sum is 550 Million Euro and 532 Million Euro, respectively; the respective periodic amount is 47 and 46 million, respectively (Table 1.8b). These come up to 0.04% and 0.00% of GDP for the lump sum and the periodic amount for both interest rate term structures. Assuming 23.5 million taxpayers (about 50% of the population), we realize that the share per taxpayer would be 23 Euro and 2 Euro per taxpayer for the lump sum and the periodic amount for both yield variants. This could be financed with the ways that have been proposed earlier for Greece.

1.5.6 Ireland

Looking at Ireland, we observe that although it was one of the countries that was initially hit by the most recent financial crisis, it has fully recovered and the anticipated debt to GDP ratio is far below 100% under all scenarios according to the European Commission Debt Sustainability Monitor (2020). As a matter of fact, the same held true for 2018 and 2019. Therefore, applying Eqs. (1.1) and (1.2) produces a zero lump sum and periodic amount (Table 1.9).

1.5.7 France

France is a country similar to Spain, in the sense that in the baseline scenario the debt to GDP ratio remains under 100% (for some years just a little under it), but in the adverse scenario, it may exceed 100%. We proceed exactly as we did in the adverse scenario of Spain (we do not post the baseline scenario as it results in zero protection cost) to find the respective amounts. More precisely, commencing with a GDP of 2,418,997 Million Euro in 2019 (Eurostat database [Eurostat, 2020]), maintaining an unchanged credit rating of AA throughout the years under examination and using two interest rate curves, a flat of 0.07% and the EIOPA risk-free interest rate term structure, we find that the lump sum amount is 975 Million Euro and 931 Million Euro, whereas the period amount is 82 Million Euro and 80 Million Euro, respectively (Table 1.10). These figures represent 0.04% of GDP for the lump sum and 0.00% of GDP for the periodic amount, under both term structures

Table 1.8b Default protection cost—European Commission debt projections until 2030—Spain (adverse)

Spain/Year—adverse	*2018*	*2019*	*2020*	*2021*	*2022*	*2023*	*2024*	*2025*	*2026*	*2027*	*2028*	*2029*	*2030*
Cumulative probability of default A		0.06	0.14	0.23	0.35	0.48	0.65	0.83	1.00	1.19	1.41	1.59	1.73
Annual probability of default A		0.06	0.08	0.09	0.12	0.13	0.17	0.18	0.17	0.19	0.22	0.18	0.14
GDP (Eurostat Million Euro)	1,202,193	1,245,331	1,257,784	1,269,104	1,279,765	1,289,747	1,299,033	1,307,607	1,315,452	1,323,345	1,331,285	1,339,273	1,347,309
GDP growth (%) real—European Commission		1.90	1.00	0.90	0.84	0.78	0.72	0.66	0.60	0.60	0.60	0.60	0.60
Debt (Million Euro)	1,173,340	1,204,235	1,223,824	1,236,108	1,260,056	1,283,556	1,306,568	1,329,052	1,350,970	1,369,662	1,388,531	1,410,254	1,432,189
Debt to GDP (%) European Commission	97.6	96.7	97.3	97.4	98.46	99.52	100.58	101.64	102.7	103.5	104.3	105.3	106.3
Amount to protect in case of default													
Debt-GDP	–	–	–	–	–	–	7,534	21,445	35,517	46,317	57,245	70,981	84,880
Interest rate flat 0.4%		0.40%	0.40%	0.40%	0.40%	0.40%	0.40%	0.40%	0.40%	0.40%	0.40%	0.40%	0.40%
u		1.00	0.99	0.99	0.98	0.98	0.98	0.97	0.97	0.96	0.96	0.96	0.95
Single premium protection amount	550	–	–	–	–	–	13	38	58	85	121	122	113
Regular premium protection amount	47												
Annuity in advance PV $\ddot{a}_{x:\overline{n}\vert}$	11.66	1	1.00	0.99	0.99	0.98	0.98	0.97	0.96	0.96	0.95	0.95	0.94
Interest rate EIOPA 12.2018		−0.33%	−0.28%	−0.18%	−0.05%	0.10%	0.24%	0.37%	0.50%	0.62%	0.73%	0.82%	0.91%

(continued)

Table 1.8b (continued)

Spain/Year—adverse	*2018*	*2019*	*2020*	*2021*	*2022*	*2023*	*2024*	*2025*	*2026*	*2027*	*2028*	*2029*	*2030*
u		100.33%	100.55%	100.53%	100.18%	99.51%	98.58%	97.43%	96.10%	94.61%	93.02%	91.39%	89.71%
Single premium protection amount	532	–	–	–	–	–	13	38	58	83	117	117	107
Regular premium protection amount	46												
Annuity in advance PV $\ddot{a}_{x:\overline{n}\vert}$	11.65	1	1.00	1.00	1.00	1.00	0.99	0.98	0.97	0.95	0.93	0.92	0.90

Source Author calculations based on debt and GDP projections by the European Commission (2020) and cumulative default rates by S&P Global (2019)

Table 1.9 Default protection cost—European Commission debt projections until 2030—Ireland

Ireland/Year	*2018*	*2019*	*2020*	*2021*	*2022*	*2023*	*2024*	*2025*	*2026*	*2027*	*2028*	*2029*	*2030*
Cumulative probability of default A+		0.05	0.09	0.20	0.33	0.43	0.53	0.64	0.76	0.89	1.03	1.17	1.31
Annual probability of default A+		0.05	0.04	0.11	0.13	0.1	0.1	0.11	0.12	0.13	0.14	0.14	0.14
GDP (Eurostat Million Euro)	324,038	347,215	359,368	370,868	382,068	392,919	403,370	413,374	422,881	431,762	439,965	448,105	456,171
GDP growth (%) real—European Commission		5.60	3.50	3.20	3.02	2.84	2.66	2.48	2.30	2.10	1.90	1.85	1.80
Debt (Million Euro)	206,088	204,857	193,699	195,076	189,506	185,065	181,517	178,164	176,342	174,432	172,906	172,072	171,520
Debt to GDP (%) European Commission	63.6	59	53.9	52.6	49.6	47.1	45	43.1	41.7	40.4	39.3	38.4	37.6
Amount to protect in case of default													
Debt-GDP	–	–	–	–	–	–	–	–	–	–	–	–	–
Interest rate flat 0.08%		0.08%	0.08%	0.08%	0.08%	0.08%	0.08%	0.08%	0.08%	0.08%	0.08%	0.08%	0.08%
u		1.00	1.00	1.00	1.00	1.00	1.00	0.99	0.99	0.99	0.99	0.99	0.99
Single premium protection amount	–	–	–	–	–	–	–	–	–	–	–	–	–

(continued)

Table 1.9 (continued)

Ireland/Year	*2018*	*2019*	*2020*	*2021*	*2022*	*2023*	*2024*	*2025*	*2026*	*2027*	*2028*	*2029*	*2030*
Regular premium protection amount	–												
Annuity in advance PV $\ddot{a}_{x:\overline{n}\rceil}$	11.89	1	1.00	1.00	1.00	0.99	0.99	0.99	0.99	0.99	0.98	0.98	0.98
Interest rate EIOPA 12.2018		−0.33%	−0.28%	−0.18%	−0.05%	0.10%	0.24%	0.37%	0.50%	0.62%	0.73%	0.82%	0.91%
u		100.33%	100.55%	100.53%	100.18%	99.51%	98.58%	97.43%	96.10%	94.61%	93.02%	91.39%	89.71%
Single premium protection amount	–	–	–	–	–	–	–	–	–	–	–	–	–
Regular premium protection amount	–												
Annuity in advance PV $\ddot{a}_{x:\overline{n}\rceil}$	11.66	1	1.00	1.00	1.00	1.00	0.99	0.98	0.97	0.95	0.94	0.92	0.90

Source Author calculations based on debt and GDP projections by the European Commission (2020) and cumulative default rates by S&P Global (2019)

(rounded to two decimals). The bill per taxpayer is shaped to 29 Euro and 28 Euro (assuming that taxpayers are roughly 50% of the population), respectively, for the lump sum and to 2 Euro (for both curves) for the periodic cost (rounded to the Euro) (Table 1.12a). If France wants to be protected even for this adverse scenario, then it can examine the aforementioned financing routes.

1.5.8 Belgium

Belgium is very similar to France in terms of its evolution of debt to GDP as per the baseline scenario. It remains below 100%, although it can be (or has been) very close to it (even above it in the recent past). If the adverse scenario is realized, then it may exceed it. We work as we did in France; we start with a GDP of 428,220 in 2019 (Eurostat database [Eurostat, 2020]), we consider a credit rating of AA—constant throughout the years, and we examine two interest rate curves—a flat yielding 0.04% and the EIOPA risk-free one. The lump sum needed on January 1, 2019 to protect against future default turns out to be 156 Million Euro and 149 Million Euro, respectively, and the annual amount is in both cases 13 Million Euro (Table 1.11). This corresponds to 0.04 and 0.03% of the GDP for the lump sum and 0.00% for the periodic amount. The cost per taxpayer (assuming that taxpayers are 50% of the population of the country) is 27 Euro and 26 Euro for the lump sum, respectively, and 2 Euro for the periodic under both scenarios (rounded to the Euro) (Table 1.12a). This can be funded with the means that have been illustrated for the other countries.

1.5.9 Other Countries

The remaining European Union countries, Austria, Bulgaria, Croatia, Czech Republic, Denmark, Estonia, Finland, Germany, Hungary, Latvia, Lithuania, Luxembourg, Malta, Netherlands, Poland, Romania, Slovakia, Slovenia, and Sweden, as well as the UK (which withdraw in 2020) seem to have a projected debt to GDP ratio below 100% under all scenarios, even the adverse one. This means that the replication of the aforementioned process would yield a lump sum and annual amount equal to zero (Table 1.12a and 1.12b).

Table 1.10 Default protection cost—European Commission debt projections until 2030—France (adverse)

France/Year—adverse	*2018*	*2019*	*2020*	*2021*	*2022*	*2023*	*2024*	*2025*	*2026*	*2027*	*2028*	*2029*	*2030*
Cumulative probability of default AA		0.02	0.03	0.08	0.22	0.36	0.48	0.60	0.71	0.80	0.89	0.97	1.03
Annual probability of default AA		0.02	0.01	0.05	0.14	0.14	0.12	0.12	0.11	0.09	0.09	0.08	0.06
GDP (Eurostat Million Euro)	2,353,090	2,418,997	2,438,349	2,455,417	2,471,623	2,486,947	2,501,372	2,514,879	2,527,453	2,541,354	2,556,602	2,573,220	2,591,233
GDP growth (%) real—European Commission		1.30	0.80	0.70	0.66	0.62	0.58	0.54	0.50	0.55	0.60	0.65	0.70
Debt (Million Euro)	2,315,441	2,392,388	2,428,596	2,470,150	2,506,720	2,542,655	2,577,914	2,612,456	2,646,244	2,676,046	2,707,442	2,743,053	2,780,393
Debt to GDP (%) European Commission	98.4	98.9	99.6	100.6	101.42	102.24	103.06	103.88	104.7	105.3	105.9	106.6	107.3
Amount to protect in case of default													
Debt-GDP	–	–	–	14,733	35,097	55,708	76,542	97,577	118,790	134,692	150,840	169,833	189,160
Interest rate flat 0.07%		0.07%	0.07%	0.07%	0.07%	0.07%	0.07%	0.07%	0.07%	0.07%	0.07%	0.07%	0.07%
u		1.00	1.00	1.00	1.00	1.00	1.00	1.00	0.99	0.99	0.99	0.99	0.99
Single premium protection amount	975	–	–	7	49	78	91	117	130	120	135	135	113
Regular premium protection amount	82												
Annuity in advance PV $\ddot{a}_{x:\overline{n}|}$	11.90	1	1.00	1.00	1.00	1.00	0.99	0.99	0.99	0.99	0.99	0.98	0.98
Interest rate EIOPA 12. 2018		−0.33%	−0.28%	−0.18%	−0.05%	0.10%	0.24%	0.37%	0.50%	0.62%	0.73%	0.82%	0.91%
u		100.33%	100.55%	100.53%	100.18%	99.51%	98.58%	97.43%	96.10%	94.61%	93.02%	91.39%	89.71%

France/Year—adverse	*2018*	*2019*	*2020*	*2021*	*2022*	*2023*	*2024*	*2025*	*2026*	*2027*	*2028*	*2029*	*2030*
Single premium protection amount	931	–	–	7	49	78	91	114	126	115	126	124	102
Regular premium protection amount	80												
Annuity in advance PV $\ddot{a}_{x:\overline{n}|}$	11.67	1	1.00	1.01	1.00	1.00	0.99	0.98	0.97	0.95	0.94	0.92	0.91

Source Author calculations based on debt and GDP projections by the European Commission (2020) and cumulative default rates by S&P Global (2019)

Table 1.11 Default protection cost—European Commission debt projections until 2030—Belgium (adverse)

Belgium/Year—adverse	*2018*	*2019*	*2020*	*2021*	*2022*	*2023*	*2024*	*2025*	*2026*	*2027*	*2028*	*2029*	*2030*
Cumulative probability of default AA		0.02	0.03	0.08	0.22	0.36	0.48	0.60	0.71	0.80	0.89	0.97	1.03
Annual probability of default AA		0.02	0.01	0.05	0.14	0.14	0.12	0.12	0.11	0.09	0.09	0.08	0.06
GDP (Eurostat Million Euro)	430,372	430,372	432,524	434,687	436,773	438,782	440,713	442,564	444,334	445,889	447,227	449,016	451,261
GDP growth (%) real—European Commission		1.10	0.50	0.50	0.48	0.46	0.44	0.42	0.40	0.35	0.30	0.40	0.50
Debt (Million Euro)	430,372	428,220	433,822	440,772	444,548	448,260	451,907	455,487	458,997	465,508	471,824	478,651	486,008
Debt to GDP (%) European Commission	100	99.5	100.3	101.4	101.78	102.16	102.54	102.92	103.3	104.4	105.5	106.6	107.7
Amount to protect in case of default													
Debt-GDP	–	–	1298	6086	7775	9478	11,194	12,923	14,663	19,619	24,597	29,635	34,747
Interest rate flat 0.04%		0.04%	0.04%	0.04%	0.04%	0.04%	0.04%	0.04%	0.04%	0.04%	0.04%	0.04%	0.04%
u		1.00	1.00	1.00	1.00	1.00	1.00	1.00	1.00	1.00	1.00	1.00	1.00
Single premium protection amount	156	–	0	3	11	13	13	15	16	18	22	24	21
Regular premium protection amount	13												
Annuity in advance PV $\ddot{a}_{x:\overline{n}\rceil}$	11.92	1	1.00	1.00	1.00	1.00	0.99	0.99	0.99	0.99	0.99	0.99	0.99
Interest rate EIOPA 12.2018		−0.33%	−0.28%	−0.18%	−0.05%	0.10%	0.24%	0.37%	0.50%	0.62%	0.73%	0.82%	0.91%
u		100.33%	100.55%	100.53%	100.18%	99.51%	98.58%	97.43%	96.10%	94.61%	93.02%	91.39%	89.71%

Belgium/Year—adverse	*2018*	*2019*	*2020*	*2021*	*2022*	*2023*	*2024*	*2025*	*2026*	*2027*	*2028*	*2029*	*2030*
Single premium protection amount	149	–	0	3	11	13	13	15	15	17	21	22	19
Regular premium protection amount	13												
Annuity in advance PV $\ddot{a}_{x:\overline{n}|}$	11.67	1	1.00	1.01	1.00	1.00	0.99	0.98	0.97	0.95	0.94	0.92	0.91

Source Author calculations based on debt and GDP projections by the European Commission (2020) and cumulative default rates by S&P Global (2019)

Table 1.12a Default protection cost and split per taxpayer—European Commission debt projections until 2030—All countries

Flat rate (10-yr yield)							*EIOPA risk-free rate*					
Contribution	*Lump sum*			*Periodic amount*			*Lump sum*			*Periodic amount*		
Country	*Million Euro*	*% of GDP*	*Euro/taxpayer*	*Million Euro*	*% of GDP*	*Euro/taxpayer*	*Million Euro*	*% of GDP*	*Euro/taxpayer*	*Million Euro*	*% of GDP*	*Euro/taxpayer*
Austria	0	0	0	0	0	0	0	0	0	0	0	0
Belgium (adverse)	*156*	*0.04*	*27*	*13*	*0.00*	*2*	*149*	*0.03*	*26*	*13*	*0.00*	*2*
Bulgaria	0	0.00	0	0	0.00	0	0	0.00	0	0	0.00	0
Croatia	0	0.00	0	0	0.00	0	0	0.00	0	0	0.00	0
Cyprus	0	0.00	0	0	0.00	0	0	0.00	0	0	0.00	0
Czech Republic	0	0.00	0	0	0.00	0	0	0.00	0	0	0.00	0
Denmark	0	0.00	0	0	0.00	0	0	0.00	0	0	0.00	0
Estonia	0	0.00	0	0	0.00	0	0	0.00	0	0	0.00	0
Finland	0	0.00	0	0	0.00	0	0	0.00	0	0	0.00	0
France (adverse)	*975*	*0.04*	*29*	*82*	*0.00*	*2*	*931*	*0.04*	*28*	*80*	*0.00*	*2*
Germany	0	0.00	0	0	0.00	0	0	0.00	0	0	0.00	0
Greece (base)	*13,502*	*7.20*	*2700*	*1342*	*0.72*	*268*	*14,290*	*7.62*	*2858*	*1343*	*0.72*	*269*
Hungary	0	0.00	0	0	0.00	0	0	0.00	0	0	0.00	0
Ireland	0	0.00	0	0	0.00	0	0	0.00	0	0	0.00	0
Italy (base)	*24,071*	*1.35*	*802*	*2196*	*0.12*	*73*	*25,568*	*1.43*	*852*	*2215*	*0.12*	*74*
Latvia	0	0.00	0	0	0.00	0	0	0.00	0	0	0.00	0
Lithuania	0	0.00	0	0	0.00	0	0	0.00	0	0	0.00	0

Flat rate (10-yr yield)							*EIOPA risk-free rate*					
Contribution	*Lump sum*			*Periodic amount*			*Lump sum*			*Periodic amount*		
Country	*Million Euro*	*% of GDP*	*Euro/taxpayer*	*Million Euro*	*% of GDP*	*Euro/taxpayer*	*Million Euro*	*% of GDP*	*Euro/taxpayer*	*Million Euro*	*% of GDP*	*Euro/taxpayer*
Luxembourg	0	0.00	0	0	0.00	0	0	0.00	0	0	0.00	0
Malta	0	0.00	0	0	0.00	0	0	0.00	0	0	0.00	0
Netherlands	0	0.00	0	0	0.00	0	0	0.00	0	0	0.00	0
Poland	0	0.00	0	0	0.00	0	0	0.00	0	0	0.00	0
Portugal (base)	*427*	*0.20*	*85*	*37*	*0.02*	*7*	*433*	*0.20*	*87*	*37*	*0.02*	*7*
Romania	0	0.00	0	0	0.00	0	0	0.00	0	0	0.00	0
Slovakia	0	0.00	0	0	0.00	0	0	0.00	0	0	0.00	0
Slovenia	0	0.00	0	0	0.00	0	0	0.00	0	0	0.00	0
Spain (adverse)	*550*	*0.04*	*23*	*47*	*0.00*	*2*	*532*	*0.04*	*23*	*46*	*0.00*	*2*
Sweden	0	0.00	0	0	0.00	0	0	0.00	0	0	0.00	0
United Kingdom	0	0.00	0	0	0.00	0	0	0.00	0	0	0.00	0

Source Author calculations based on debt and GDP projections by the European Commission (2020) and cumulative default rates by S&P Global (2019)

Table 1.12b Default protection cost and split per taxpayer—IMF debt projections until 2027 and until 2060—Greece

Flat rate (10-yr yield)							*EIOPA risk-free rate*					
Contribution	*Lump sum*			*Periodic amount*			*Lump sum*			*Periodic amount*		
Country	*Billion Euro*	*% of GDP*	*Euro/taxpayer*	*Billion Euro*	*% of GDP*	*Euro/taxpayer*	*Billion Euro*	*% of GDP*	*Euro/taxpayer*	*Billion Euro*	*% of GDP*	*Euro/taxpayer*
Greece (IMF 2027)	16.54	8.74	3309	1.64	0.87	329	17.54	9.27	3508	1.65	0.87	330
Greece (IMF 2060)	18.62	9.84	3725	1.85	0.98	370	19.78	10.45	3955	1.86	0.98	372

Source Author calculations based on debt and GDP projections by the IMF (2018) and cumulative default rates by S&P Global (2019)

1.5.10 A Note on the Interest Rates

In our analysis, we used the ten-year government bond yields of the countries of interest as of December 30, 2019 and the EIOPA risk-free term structure. These interest rates are nominal, and may be (or should have been) replaced by the real interest rates, as real GDP growth has been used in our numerical illustration. Our model can practically work for any interest rate hypothesis, model or forecast; the output will change accordingly.

However, (we trust that) such a change would marginally influence the result and we will briefly include it here. In addition, the use of such real interest rates incorporates two additional forecasts; the inflation rate and the interest rate forecast. By looking at the projections of the Debt Sustainability Monitor prepared by the European Commission (2020) we realize that the latter has been set to the targeted inflation of 2.0% after 2026 for all countries. This is exogenously defined and somehow reduces the trustworthiness of any real interest rate forecast, which is on its own a risk.

Furthermore, by looking at the projections of the Debt Sustainability Monitor prepared by the European Commission (2020), we find (at least for the countries of interest) that the implicit interest rate averages could have a wide range depending on the assumptions made. In addition, at least one of these averages is not much different from the interest rates we used. This can be seen in the following Table 1.13.

For Greece there are no such estimates; however, the IMF has produced a range of scenarios (IMF, 2018) and the interest rate we used is not far from the long-term average. In addition, according to an earlier IMF country report (IMF, 2015), the real long-term interest rates for Greece (post 2021) are forecasted to be between approximately 1.4 and 1.8%, depending on the review.

We use the combined historical scenario average for the years after 2021 to produce the relevant figures. For the years prior to 2021, we estimate the real implicit interest rate as the difference between the nominal implicit interest rate and the inflation rate. We find that

- For Italy, the lump sum increases to 24.386 Billion Euro from 24.071 Billion Euro; the periodic amount increases to 2.205 Billion Euro from 2.196 Billion Euro.

Table 1.13 Real implicit interest rates

Country	*Baseline no-policy change scenario Average 2021–30*	*Combined historical scenario average (2021–30)*	*Average of averages*	*10-yr government bond yield*
Italy	0.4	1.2	0.8	1.2
Cyprus	0	0.7	0.35	0.5
Portugal	0.3	1	0.65	0.4
Spain	−0.1	0.8	0.35	0.4
Ireland	−0.5	0.8	0.15	0.08
France	−0.9	0	−0.45	0.07
Belgium	−0.6	0.2	−0.2	0.04

Source Created by the authors with data from European Commission (2020) and World Government Bonds (2020) and own calculations
Note "The implicit interest rates are derived endogenously in the debt projection model based on certain assumptions on market interest rates, on the maturity structure of government debt and on projected financing needs." European Commission (2020)

- For Cyprus, both amounts remain zero as the country did not post any risk of having its debt exceeding its GDP.
- For Portugal, the lump sum amount drops to 418 Million Euro from 427 Million Euro; the periodic amount does not change (in Million Euro).
- For Spain (adverse scenario), the lump sum amount drops to 529 Million Euro from 550 Million Euro; the periodic amount drops to 46 Million Euro from 47 Million Euro.
- For Ireland, both amounts remain zero as Ireland did not post any risk of having its debt exceeding its GDP.
- For France (adverse scenario), the lump sum increases to 980 Million Euro from 975 Million Euro; the periodic amount remains as is (in Million Euro).
- For Belgium (adverse scenario), the lump sum amount becomes 154 Million Euro compared with 156 Million Euro; the periodic amount does not change (in Million Euro).

We realize that the difference is rather small for all countries.

1.6 Global Evaluation of the Approach

The building of the model and the numerical application allow some observations and remarks; more specifically

- We realize that the contribution of a country tends to be more sensitive to the debt to GDP ratio rather than the interest rate—at least at the current interest rate levels.
- The very existence of such a reserve could be perceived by the investors as a safety net; as a result, they may be willing to receive a lower interest rate as a compensation. This could apply to the part of debt that is protected by such mechanism or the overall lending interest rate of the country. In both cases, this would further reduce the debt burden of the country. It could thus be beneficial in reducing the debt to GDP ratio. This is an advantage that should be carefully considered.
- The approach could be financed with a dedicated asset with a covenant that would not allow its use for any other purpose. A dedicated asset could also be used for the placement of the relevant contributions so that they are preserved. This rationale favors and at the same time is facilitated by the idea of the one safe asset.
- Although policymaking is not in the immediate targets of this chapter, the EU or any other institution could launch such a mechanism in order to protect a country from future defaults.
- The creation of a pool at an EU level is expected to have a funding and/or maintenance expense. This cost has to be embedded in the overall cost per country as described above.

1.7 Future Research

Some of the limitations mentioned earlier could be considered for future research. We used global corporate (not sovereign) credit ratings and assumed that they remain constant over time. We made the same assumption for the sovereign bond yields of the countries, as well as for the EIOPA risk-free term structure. Consequently, a next step could be (i) to find sovereign credit ratings and default rates, that could change over time (following the debt sustainability of the countries); and (ii) to let interest rate term structures that also move as time passes (realizing though that the forecasting of interest rates can be notoriously bad).

We did not really enter deeply into the funding alternatives of such a reserve although we drafted some potential directions of how a country could collect the necessary contributions. The policymaking proposals are simple as such; as a result, future research venues could be dedicated to the indication of directions of how this could be achieved at a European level. They could also emphasize in the actual creation of the reserve, the split of the contribution per country—even by those that do not seem to need such a reserve.

1.8 Conclusions

Countries experience increased agony to avoid defaults as we just entered a period of increased uncertainty due to a pandemic and have the experience of the recent global financial crisis that started in 2007–2008. Following this new era, we recommend an assessment of the debt with the use of actuarial techniques that take into account the probability of default. We treat the probability of default as the probability of death and estimate the contributions—similar to a pure premium—that the interested countries need to make so as to avoid future defaults by the creation of a reserve. We perform the relevant calculations for the EU countries and propose basic ideas of how it could work in practice. The EU has an important role to play, as this mechanism can be set under its auspices for practical but also for reputational purposes. The competent authorities can easily implement this approach, which could prevent the risk of sovereign defaults in the future.

References

Aizenman, J., Binici, M., & Hutchinson, M. M. (2013). *Credit ratings and the pricing of sovereign debt during the euro crisis* (National Bureau of Economic Research, Working Paper 19125). https://www.nber.org/papers/w19125. Last accessed 21 May 2020.

Babbel, D. F., & Bertozzi, S. (1996). *Insuring sovereign debt against default: Annotated bibliography on external debt capacity* (World Bank Discussion Papers, WDP328, pp. 1–22). Washington, DC: The World Bank. http://documents.worldbank.org/curated/en/473531468739174194/Insuring-sovereign-debt-against-default-annotated-bibiliography-on-external-debt-capacity. Last accessed 21 May 2020.

Beirne, J., & Fratzscher, M. (2013). *The pricing of sovereign risk and contagion during the European sovereign debt crisis* (European Central Bank, Working

Paper Series, No. 1625). https://www.ecb.europa.eu/pub/pdf/scpwps/ecbwp1625.pdf. Last accessed 21 May 2020.

Bi, H., & Traum, N. (2012). Estimating sovereign default risk. *American Economic Review, 102*(3), 161–166. https://doi.org/10.1257/aer.102.3.161.

Bicksler, J. L., & Chen, A. H. (1992). Pricing corporate debt with event-risk provisions. *International Review of Financial Analysis, 1*(1), 51–63.

Blanc-Brude, F., & Yim, J-L. (2019). *The pricing of private infrastructure debt—A dynamic approach and comparison with corporate debt* (pp. 1–82). A Publication of the EDHEC Infrastructure Institute-Singapore. https://edhec.infrastructure.institute/wp-content/uploads/2019/04/blanc-brude_yim_2019_web_light.pdf. Last accessed 21 May 2020.

Blundell-Wignall, A., & Slovik, P. (2011). A market perspective on the European sovereign debt and banking crisis. *OECD Journal: Financial Market Trends, 2010*(2), 1–28. www.oecd.org. Last accessed 21 May 2020.

Bouabdallah, O., Checherita-Westphal, C., Warmedinger, T., de Stefani, R., Drudi, F., Setzer, R., & Westphal, A. (2017). *Debt sustainability analysis for euro area sovereigns: A methodological framework, European Central Bank* (Occasional Paper Series, No. 185). www.ecb.europa.eu. Last accessed 21 May 2020.

Bradley, M., de Fontenay, E., de Lira Salvatierra, I. A., & Gulati, M. (2018). Pricing sovereign debt: Foreign versus local parameters. *European Financial Management, 24,* 261–297. https://doi.org/10.1111/eufm.12161.

Bruche, M., & Naqvi, H. (2010). A structural model of debt pricing with creditor determined liquidation. *Journal of Economic Dynamics and Control, 34*(5), 951–967. https://doi.org/10.1016/j.jedc.2010.01.005.

Camba-Méndez, G., Kostrzewa, K., Marszal, A., & Serwa, D. (2016). *Pricing sovereign credit risk of an emerging market, European Central Bank* (Working Paper Series, No. 1924). https://www.ecb.europa.eu/pub/pdf/scpwps/ecbwp1924.en.pdf. Last accessed 21 May 2020.

Claessens, S., & van Wijnbergen, S. (1990). *An option-pricing approach to secondary market debt: Applied to Mexico* (Policy, Planning and Research Department Working Papers, pp. 1–21). Washington, DC: World Bank, WPS 333. http://documents.worldbank.org/curated/en/995481468753020520/An-option-pricing-approach-to-secondary-market-debt-applied-to-Mexico. Last accessed 21 May 2020.

Colla, P., Ippolito, F., & Wagner, H. F. (2012). Leverage and pricing of debt in LBOs. *Journal of Corporate Finance, 18,* 124–137.

Constâncio, V. (2018). *Why EMU requires more financial integration.* European Central Bank, Keynote Speech. https://www.ecb.europa.eu/press/key/date/2018/html/ecb.sp180503_1.en.html. Last accessed 13 Nov 2019.

Cruces, J. J., & Trebesch, C. (2013). Sovereign defaults: The price of haircuts. *American Economic Journal: Macroeconomics, 5*(3), 85–117.

Datta, S., Iskandar-Datta, M., & Patel, A. (1999). Bank monitoring and the pricing of corporate public debt. *Journal of Financial Economics, 51*, 435–449.

EIOPA. (2018). Risk-free interest rate term structures for December 2018. *EIOPA tools and data*. https://www.eiopa.europa.eu/tools-and-data/risk-free-interest-rate-term-structures-0_en. Last accessed 4 Apr 2020.

English, W. B. (1996). Understanding the costs of sovereign default: American state debts in the 1840's. *The American Economic Review, 86*(1), 259–275.

European Commission. (2018, July). Compliance report ESM stability support programme for Greece. *Fourth Review*. https://ec.europa.eu/info/sites/info/files/economy-finance/compliance_report_4r_2018.06.20.docx.pdf. Last accessed 4 Apr 2020.

European Commission. (2020). *Debt Sustainability Monitor 2019* (European Economy, Institutional Paper 120). https://ec.europa.eu/info/publications/economic-and-financial-affairs-publications_en. Last accessed 4 Apr 2020.

European Stability Mechanism. (2020). *Lending toolkit*. https://www.esm.europa.eu. Last accessed 4 Apr 2020.

Eurostat. (2020). GDP and main aggregates—Selected international annual data. *Eurostat Products Datasets*. https://ec.europa.eu/eurostat/en/web/products-datasets/-/NAIDA_10_GDP. Last accessed 4 Apr 2020.

Gumus, I., & Koeda, J. (2018). *Model-based estimation of sovereign default* (Working Paper). Available at SSRN: https://ssrn.com/abstract=3056539. Last accessed 21 May 2020.

International Monetary Fund. (2015). *Greece—Preliminary draft debt sustainability analysis* (IMF Country Report No. 15/165). http://www.imf.org. Last accessed 4 Apr 2020.

International Monetary Fund. (2018). *Greece—2018 Article IV consultation and proposal for post-program monitoring-press release; staff report; and statement by the executive director for Greece* (IMF Country Report No. 18/248). http://www.imf.org. Last accessed 4 Apr 2020.

International Monetary Fund. (2020, April). *World economic outlook: The great lockdown*. https://www.imf.org/en/Publications/WEO. Last accessed 3 May 2020.

Kletzer, K. (2005). *Sovereign debt, volatility and insurance* (Federal Reserve Bank of San Francisco, Working Paper Series, Working Paper 2006-05, pp. 1–26). http://www.frbsf.org/publications/economics/papers/2006/wp06-05bk.pdf. Last accessed 21 May 2020.

McGregor, T. (2019). *Pricing sovereign debt in resource-rich economies* (IMF Working Paper, WP/19/240, pp. 1–30). https://www.imf.org/en/Publications/WP/Issues/2019/11/08/Pricing-Sovereign-Debt-in-Resource-Rich-Economies48708. Last accessed 21 May 2020.

Merton, R. C. (1974). On the pricing of corporate debt: The risk structure of interest rates. *Journal of Finance, 29*(2), 449–470.

Monti, M. (2010). A new strategy for the single market—At the service of Europe's economy and society. *Report to the President of the European Commission José Manuel Barroso.* https://ec.europa.eu/. Last accessed 13 Nov 2019.

Norges Bank Investment Management. (2020). *The fund.* https://www.nbim.no/en/. Last accessed 17 May 2020.

O'Kane, D. (2012). *The link between Eurozone sovereign debt and CDS prices* (pp. 1–16). EDHEV-Risk Institute. www.edhec-risk.com. Last accessed 21 May 2020.

Ortiz-Molina, H. (2006). Top management incentives and the pricing of corporate public debt. *Journal of Financial and Quantitative Analysis, 41*(2), 317–340.

Reneby, J. (1998). *Pricing corporate debt, Stockholm school of economics.* Ph.D. Dissertation. https://ex.hhs.se/dissertations/221754-FULLTEXT01.pdf. Last accessed 21 May 2020.

Soytas, M. A., & Volkan, E. (2016). A new estimation technique of sovereign default risk. *Central Bank Review, 16,* 119–125.

S&P Global Ratings. (2019). Default, transition and recovery: 2018 annual global corporate default and rating transitions study. *Ratings Direct.* www.spratings.com. Last accessed 4 Apr 2020.

SWFI. (2020). *Top 91 largest sovereign wealth fund rankings by total assets.* https://www.swfinstitute.org/fund-rankings/sovereign-wealth-fund. Last accessed 17 May 2020.

World Government Bonds (2020). Bond Historical Data. http://www.worldgovernmentbonds.com/bond-historical-data/. Accessed Apr 2020.

Yamarthy, R. S. (2017). *Essays on asset pricing, debt valuation, and macroeconomics.* Ph.D. Dissertation, University of Pennsylvania, Publicly Accessible Penn Dissertations, 2650. https://repository.upenn.edu/edissertations/2650. Last accessed 21 May 2020.

CHAPTER 2

The Impact of Quantitative Easing Policy on the Government Debt and the NPLs of the Eurozone Periphery Countries

Dionysios Chionis, Fotios Mitropoulos, and Antonios Sarantidis

2.1 Introduction

After the outbreak of the crisis, in 2008, the central banks were focused to find an exit path in that great recession. The consequences of the financial crisis have become more apparent in the South European countries of the eurozone. In order to assist these economies to face the negative consequences of the recession and the low levels of inflation or deflation, the European Central Bank (hereafter called ECB) announced in 2015

D. Chionis (✉) · F. Mitropoulos
Department of Economics, Democritus University of Thrace, Komotini, Greece
e-mail: dchionis@ierd.duth.gr

F. Mitropoulos
e-mail: fmitropo@econ.duth.gr

A. Sarantidis
School of Social Sciences, Hellenic Open University, Patras, Greece
e-mail: antonis.sarantidis@ac.eap.gr

T. Poufinas (ed.), *Debt in Times of Crisis*,
https://doi.org/10.1007/978-3-030-74162-4_2

the implementation of an expansionary monetary policy, the Quantitative Easing (QE) program. Since then and in addition to the monetary expansion, Central banks developed a new wave of unconventional monetary policy so as to further stimulate the economy and to compress the spread of the government bonds (Varghese & Zhang, 2018).

ECB was not the first central bank which has implemented Asset Purchase Programs to tackle the recession and deflation in its member countries. The Bank of Japan (2001), the Federal Reserve System in US (2008) and Bank of England (2009) have first implemented large-scale asset purchase programs as policy possible measures. The ECB was the last central bank that introduced this kind of program as policy measures in March 2015. For less than 4 years (from March 2015 until the end of December 2018), the ECB has spent more than €2.6 trillion, buying up mostly government and corporate debt. To execute quantitative easing, ECB increases the supply of money by buying private, government bonds and other securities. By increasing the supply of money, it is possible to have a positive impact in order to lower the cost of money. A lower cost of money means that the interest rates are low, and banks can lend with easier terms. However, inflation remains subdued and the procedure of bond buying has a negative impact on European banks' profitability.

In September of 2019, the ECB announced a new round of QE. The central bank's quantitative easing program entails an asset purchase program of €20 billion per month starting from November and lasting until the ECB deems necessary. Apart from that, ECB decreased its main deposit rate by 10 basis points to −0.5%, a record low but in line with the market expectations. On the other side, the scope of the new program is on a smaller scale. From April 2016 until March 2017 the average monthly amount was €80 billion, while it was €60 billion from March 2015 until March 2016.

2.2 Literature Review

The unconventional monetary policy has a real effect on the economy (Joyce et al., 2012) and various authors (inter alia Aßhoff et al., 2020; Dell'Ariccia G et al., 2018) had assessed the impact of Quantitative Easing and other unconventional monetary policies that are followed by central banks in the wake of the financial crisis that began in 2008. There are various topics in the literature, which examine the impact of QE on real economic variables (Baumeister & Benati, 2013; Chen et al., 2012; Hesse et al., 2017; Hohberger et al., 2017; Weale & Wieladek, 2016), on the long-term bond yields and spillovers through portfolio reallocation (Altavilla et al., 2015; Andrade et al., 2016; De Santis, 2016) and on the expansion of Central banks' balance sheets by purchasing assets (Gambacorta et al., 2012; Curdia & Woodford, 2009). Altavilla et al. (2015), suggested that the decrease in bond yields following Outright Monetary Transactions (OMT) announcements supports a significant increase in real activity, credit and prices in periphery economies of the euro area. Another strand of the literature (Gagnon et al., 2017; Tillmann, 2016) has examined the effects of unconventional monetary policy and the spillovers to different markets. In a recent study, Varghese and Zhang (2018) found that the recent ECB QE program shows signs of supporting inflation expectations but the positive impact on bank profitability is seen during the pre-period of QE. Furthermore, Kenourgios et al. (2019) analyzed the cross-markets correlations, among the four programs which were implemented by the ECB (SMP, OMT, CBPP3 and PSPP) and claimed that CBPP3 was the program with the most prominent impact. On the other side, many authors (Bahmani & Toms, 2015; MacDonald, 2017; Suh & Koo, 2016) examine the effects of US unconventional monetary policy on developed and emerging economies.

In this study, we investigate the effects of ECBs QE implementation in seven European countries. A previous paper (Sarantidis et al., 2019), examined the relationship of quantitative easing policy programs, government bond yields and banking stock price returns for EU periphery countries. The results supported the idea that the implementation of QE has positive effects, by decreasing the bond yields for the periphery countries that participated in the program. In contrast, the findings noted that there were no effects on banking returns. However, in this research, we describe the effects of ECBs QE implementation in seven European countries, namely the GIPSI countries of South Europe, plus Germany and France.

This study focuses on the government debt and the Non-Performing Loans (hereafter NPL). So, the aim is to examine the possible effects that ECB's QE implementation policy has on the government debt and on the NPL of the EU periphery countries. NPLs are still putting the European Banking Union at risk (Macchiarelli et al., 2019). The high accumulation of NPLs in Europe continues to be an important challenge that needs to be tackled (Grasmann et al., 2019). Many countries across Europe suffer from high levels of non-performing loans (NPLs), in particular in Cyprus, Greece, Portugal, Ireland, Italy and some Central and Eastern European countries. NPLs across the euro area peaked at eight percent of total loans in 2013 and have fallen only gradually in some countries since then. The NPLs to total loans dispersion across euro area countries is also considerable, the amplitude ranges from 0.8% (Luxembourg) to 42.2% (Greece), (Source: European Banking Authority July 2019).

We employ the Changes-in-Changes approach, which is a very popular tool that has not been widely used and applied to economics and other social sciences, in order to estimate the effects that are caused by a possible policy or intervention in a specific time period (Angrist & Pischke, 2008). We use monthly panel data for seven (7) EU countries from 2008 until 2018 (the end of the first round of QE). We include in our analysis the additional macroeconomic variables of Central Bank assets to GDP, 10-year government bond, foreign direct investments, bank deposit to GDP and industrial production index. Furthermore, we separate our data into three categories; one for the periphery countries that are participating in the QE of ECB, one for the country that did not participate (Greece) and one for France. Greece was the only country of Europe's periphery that did not participate in the QE, due to its higher debt rates and non-investment grades. Only when the debt rates decrease, the structural reforms are implemented and the debt becomes sustainable, then Greece could have the opportunity to participate in the QE program.

This research introduces a new methodological approach, namely the Changes-in-Changes approach in the area of NPLs and government debt for the peripheral countries of the Eurozone. We examine the dominant role of Germany and France. Moreover, we investigate the role of France as a benchmark for countries of the periphery as France may be considered as a country closer to them in terms of its government debt levels (as a percent of GDP). Nowadays, France tries to play a significant role in the convergence of Eurozone and its actions and interventions are showing that it could act as a rival of Germany in Europe.

2.3 The Dataset

The variables included in our analysis are the government debt as percentage of GDP, the Non-Performing Loans, and a variable that reflects the quantitative easing policy of ECB. Data are collected for seven different Eurozone countries. These countries are Germany, France, Greece, Ireland, Italy, Portugal and Spain. In the meantime, Germany and France are both used as a control group in the Changes-in-Changes (hereafter CIC) estimation procedure. In the aforementioned method (CIC) the specification of the control group is of crucial importance. This is because the control group is the group that is not exposed to the intervention or was exposed the least (QE policy).

There are many reasons for choosing Germany as a control group. Germany plays a dominant role in the eurozone and has the largest national economy in Europe. However, the main reasons are that Germany has had the lowest bond yields among the European countries during the chosen sample period, that its economy was the most stable in Europe and that the bond yields of Germany are used as a basis point for the estimation of bond spreads. We also choose France as a control group because we would like to expand our research and to have so comparable results. Apart from that, the role of France has increased dramatically in the recent years. The main reasons for France are that its economy is stable but reacts to the revival of Germany's power, and understands better the problems that the periphery countries are facing. France started to show similar fiscal imbalances with the periphery countries and the government debt increased rapidly, near the level of the national GDP. Finally, IMF in a recent study (IMF, 2019) urged the government of France to implement structural reforms in order to limit its debt. The sample consists of monthly panel data covering the period from January 2008 until December 2018.

In this study, we first attempt to answer the hypothesis of whether the QE implementation policy of ECB has affected positively the economies of Ireland, Italy, Portugal and Spain by reducing their government debt as well as the Non-Performing Loans. We also included Greece in our analysis to find possible differences that exist among these two variables, as Greece is a totally different case because it never managed to join the QE program. Second, we try to find out the differences that exist among these two variables between the two countries we use as control groups, namely Germany and France.

Furthermore, except for the variables of the government debt (as a percentage of GDP) and the Non-Performing Loans (as percentage of the total loans) that are used as dependent variables, we also included a set of other macroeconomic variables. Several studies are using these macroeconomic variables to assess the impact they have on government debt and

Table 2.1 Sample period and source of Variables

Variable description	*Source*	*Sample period*
Gross Government Debt (% of GDP)	Thomson Reuters Datastream	2008m1–2018m12
Non-perfoming Loans (% total gross loans)	Thomson Reuters Datastream	2008m1–2018m12
Central Bank Assets to GDP	Thomson Reuters Datastream	2008m1–2018m12
Bank Deposits to GDP	Thomson Reuters Datastream	2008m1–2018m12
FDI (% of GDP)	Thomson Reuters Datastream	2008m1–2018m12
Industrial Production Index	Thomson Reuters Datastream	2008m1–2018m12

Source Created by the Authors

Non-Performing Loans (Baker et al., 2004; Bekaert et al., 2013; Grammatikos & Vermeulen, 2012; Jensen et al., 1989; Kumar & Baldacci, 2010; Loungani et al., 1990). According to these studies, our estimation includes the variables of the central bank assets to GDP, the bank deposits to GDP, the Foreign Direct Investments and the industrial production index. For the estimation results, the industrial production Index has been normalized to an interval from zero (0) to one (1). Moreover, we set a dummy variable that shows the period after the ECB's QE implementation policy. This dummy variable takes the value 0 for the period before the QE and 1 for the period after the QE. The QE was first implemented in January 2015 by the ECB (Belke & Gros, 2019).

The sources of the variables and the sample periods are presented in Table 2.1.

2.4 Methodology

This study examines the possible effects that the ECBs QE had on the government debt as well as on the Non-Performing Loans of the EU periphery countries. In the empirical part, we are first testing for the existence of possible correlations among the variables and then employ the CIC methodological approach. Before we test our variables for possible correlations, we first normalize the industrial production index to an interval from zero to one. The following equation has been used:

$$X' = \frac{X - MIN(X)}{MAX(X) - MIN(X)} \tag{2.1}$$

where, X indicates the initial value, MIN the minimum value, MAX the maximum value and X' the normalized value. After that, we proceed with the correlations among all the variables, where we do not find any correlated pairs. These results are not going to be presented here but are available upon request by the authors.

Next, we employ the CIC (Athey & Imbens, 2006) method to capture and to estimate the possible effects that are caused by a "treatment" in a specific time (Angrist & Pischke, 2008). The CIC method is a generalized version of the Difference-in-Differences (hereafter called DID). We employ this methodology instead of the DID due to some limitations that the latter has. According to Bertrand et al. (2004), the estimation of DID shows a possible serial correlation problem. They concluded that because of three parameters. These parameters are that the method requires long time series, that the dependent variables are positively serially correlated and that the standard errors are inconsistent because the treatment group variable changes itself little over time. To address these problems, Bertrand et al. (2004) propose a four-step procedure. Namely, they propose the method of aggregating the data into pre- and post-treatment, to allow the method for unrestricted covariance structure, to use simple parametric corrections and finally to employ the block bootstrapping methodology.

To address those limitations, Athey and Imbens (2006) proposed and developed the *CIC* approach. This method is applied by using either panel data or repeated cross-sections and it allows time and treatment effects to differ systematically across individuals. In contrast to the *DID* approach, the *CIC* approach can address the question of what the effect of a treatment would be if it were applied to the control group (Asteriou et al., 2019). Moreover, they mention that the CIC relies heavily on linearity and additivity and requires multiple groups and periods. Finally, we use the methodology of bootstrapping to address possible problems that may exist in the estimation of our data (Asteriou et al., 2019; MacKinnon, 2002).

The CIC uses two groups, the control group and the treatment group. The control group is the group that is not exposed to the intervention and the treatment group is the group that is exposed to the intervention. Both groups should have a similar reaction if they do not receive the intervention. In our case, the treatment group consists of the government debt and the Non-Performing Loans of the periphery countries and the control group consists of the same variables for the countries of Germany and France. Specifically, Germany and France are used as a control group, while Greece, Ireland, Italy, Portugal and Spain as treatment groups. The intervention in our analysis is the ECB's QE policy that was implemented in January 2015. We estimate the CIC two times for each country in our control group, and for each of our dependent variables; An estimation that did not include the macroeconomic variables and an estimation that does include them.

The econometric procedure for CIC that Athey and Imbens (2006) propose is that they hypothesize that in the absence of the intervention the outcome satisfies the following relationship:

$$Y^{pre} = h(U_i, T_i) \tag{2.2}$$

with $h(u, t)$ increasing in u. The random variable U_i is an underlying unobserved effect of individual i and T_i is the time (the QE implementation period). Moreover, the outcome of an individual with $U_i = u$ will be the same in a given time period. U_i is allowed to vary across groups, but not over time, so that, $U_i \perp T_i | G$. The CIC also requires that the changes over time in the distribution of each group's outcome arise from the fact that $h(u, 0)$ differs from $h(u, 1)$. The function $h(u, t)$ is strictly increasing in u for $t \in \{0, 1\}$. If U is either continuous or discrete, then the distribution function of Y^{pre} can be written as:

$$F_{Y^{pre},11}(y) = F_{Y,10}\left(F^{-1}_{Y,00}\left(F_{Y,01}(y)\right)\right) \tag{2.3}$$

$h(u, t)$ is invertible in u; denote this inverse by $h^{-1}(y; t) then,$

$$F_{Y^{pre},gt}(y) = Pr(h(U, t) \leq y | G = g, T = t)$$

$$= Pr\left(U \leq h^{-1}(y; t) | G = g, T = t\right)$$

$$= Pr\left(U \leq h^{-1}(y; t) | G = g\right) \tag{2.4}$$

$$= Pr\left(U_g \leq h^{-1}(y; t)\right) = F_{u,g}\left(h^{-1}(y; t)\right).$$

If letting $(g, t) = (0, 0)$ and substitute $y = h(u, 0)$, then

$$F_{Y,00}(h(u, 0)) = F_{U,0}\left(h^{-1}(h(u, 0); 0)\right) = F_{U,0}(u). \tag{2.5}$$

By applying to each side $F_{Y,00}^{-1}$ for all $u \in \mathbb{U}_0$, then:

$$h(u,0) = F_{Y,00}^{-1}\big(F_{U,0}(u)\big) \tag{2.6}$$

By applying $(g,t) = (0,1)$ using that $h^{-1}(y;1) \in \mathbb{U}_0$ for all $y \in \mathbb{Y}_{01}$ and applying the transformation $F_{U,0}^{-1}(\cdot)$ to both sides,

$$F_{U,0}^{-1}\big(F_{Y,01}(y)\big) = h^{-1}(y;1), \, forally \in \mathbb{Y}_{01} \tag{2.7}$$

Combining the two equations for all $y \in \mathbb{Y}_{01}$,

$$h\Big(h^{-1}(y;1),0\Big) = F_{Y,00}^{-1}\big(F_{Y,01}(y)\big). \tag{2.8}$$

$h\big(h^{-1}(y;1),0\big)$ is the period 0 outcome for an individual with the realization of u that corresponds to outcome y in group 0 and period 1. By applying $(g,t) = (1,0)$ and substituting $y = h(u,0)$ then:

$$F_{Y,10}(h(u,0)) = F_{U,1}(u). \tag{2.9}$$

After the combination of the two equations with $(g,t) = (1,1)$ for all $y = \mathbb{Y}_{01}$ then:

$$F_{Y^{pre},11}(y) = F_{U,1}\Big(h^{-1}(y;1)\Big) = F_{Y,10}\Big(h\Big(h^{-1}(y;1),0\Big)\Big) = F_{Y,10}\Big(F_{Y,00}^{-1}\big(F_{Y,01}(y)\big)\Big) \tag{2.10}$$

Under all the above, the identification result can be interpreted by the transformation,

$$k^{CIC}(y) = F_{Y,01}^{-1}\big(F_{Y,00}(y)\big). \tag{2.11}$$

The second-period outcome for a group with an unobserved component u, $h(u,0) = y$ is given from the above transformation, then the distribution of $Y_{11}^{pre} = k^{CIC}(Y_{10})$. The average treatment effect from the *CIC* approach can be written as,

$$\tau^{CIC} \equiv \mathbb{E}\Big[Y_{11}^{post} - Y_{11}^{pre}\Big] = \mathbb{E}\Big[Y_{11}^{post}\Big] - \mathbb{E}\Big[k^{CIC}(Y_{10})\Big] =$$

$$= \mathbb{E}\Big[Y_{11}^{post}\Big] - \mathbb{E}\Big[F_{Y,01}^{-1}\big(F_{Y,00}(Y_{10})\big)\Big] \tag{2.12}$$

where Υ is a random variable with distribution $D = (Y|G = g, t)$. Given random samples from each subgroup, a generally consistent estimator of τ^{CIC} is

$$\tau^{CIC} = N_{11}^{-1} \sum_{i-1}^{N_{11}} Y_{11,i} - N_{10}^{-1} \sum_{i-1}^{N_{10}} F_{01}^{-1}\left(F_{00}\left(Y_{10,i}\right)\right), \tag{2.13}$$

where F_{00} and F_{01} are the control groups in the initial and latter time periods, $Y_{11,i}$ is a random draw on the observed outcome for the $g = 1, t = 1$ group and similarly for the $Y_{10,i}$.

According to *CIC* explanations, the model takes the following form:

$$\tau_{ct}^{CIC} = \mathbb{E}\left[Y_{ct}^{treatgroup} - Y_{ct}^{controlgroup}\right] = \Delta^{CIC} + \boldsymbol{\gamma}'\boldsymbol{Z} \tag{2.14}$$

where τ is the average treatment effect in country c and time t, Δ represents the CIC coefficient (treatment), and $\boldsymbol{Z}$ represents a vector of macroeconomic variables.

In our analysis, the CIC model takes the previous form, where again τ is the average treatment effect (ATE) in country c and in time t. The CIC coefficient is represented by Δ, showing the difference between our treatment (periphery countries) and control groups (Germany and France). Finally, the macroeconomic variables of the central bank assets to GDP, the bank deposits to GDP, the Foreign Direct Investments and the industrial production index are represented by Z. The contribution of our work in the field lies precisely in the use of CIC in the investigation of the determinants of NPLs and the government debt level of the countries under investigation. The advantages of this method are that the groups and the time periods are treated asymmetrically in contrast to that of the DID. Moreover, the CIC estimates nonparametrically the change that occurred on the control group over time in the second period, it includes covariates, and allows for discrete outcomes.

2.5 Empirical Results

In this section, we present the estimation results of the possible effects that the QE period has on the government debt and the Non-Performing Loans on the EU periphery countries. In the first part, we analyzed the estimation results of CIC for all the periphery countries in order to capture the average change they have in contrast to Germany and to

France. In the second part, we analyzed the estimation results for each periphery country by examining whether the QE affected positively or negatively the government debt and the Non-Performing Loans. Greece is a country in our analysis that did not participate in ECB's QE program. Beyond that, we included Greece in our study to have so the possibility to compare the possible percentage loss due to its inability to participate in the specific program.

Table 2.2 presents the overall CIC estimation results for all the countries of our sample with Germany as a control group, where columns 1 and 2 present the results for government debt while columns 3 and 4 present Non-Performing Loans. This Table gives us a first result about the possible effects that QE has on these two variables. The Average Treatment Effect (ATE) in the first column shows us no significant results.

Table 2.2 Estimation results for EU periphery countries with Germany as control group

	Gross Government Debt		*Non-perfoming Loans*	
Variables	*(1)*	*(2)*	*(3)*	*(4)*
CIC (ATE)	0.326	**−2.272****	**17.731****	**7.067****
	(−1.20)	(−6.75)	(20.05)	(6.46)
Gross Government Debt				0.114
				(0.79)
Non-performing Loans		0.004		
		(0.79)		
Central Bank Assets		**−0.134****		**0.994****
		(−9.74)		(14.49)
Bank Deposits		−0.013		−0.027
		(−0.46)		(−0.19)
Foreign DirectInvestments		**−0.026****		**−0.123****
		(−6.27)		(−5.77)
Industrial Production		**−1.480****		**−7.251****
		(−11.25)		(−10.60)
Observations	1320	1320	1320	1320

Source Authors' calculations

Notes Bold figures indicate statistical significant coefficients, ** denotes statistical significance at the 1% level ($p < 0.01$), * denotes statistical significance at the 5% level ($p < 0.05$), + denotes statistical significance at the 10% level ($p < 0.1$). The CIC (ATE) variable refers to the average treatment effect. Also, it refers to the quantitative easing implementation period (2015m01 and onwards) and takes the value 1 for that specific period. In all the estimations, the standard errors are block-bootstrapped, and the z-statistics are reported in the parentheses. The results are given in percentage points

By including the macroeconomic variables, the ATE is negative and significant showing that during the QE period, the debt rate decreases by 2.272% in contrast to that of Germany. The Central Bank Assets (−0.134), the FDI (−0.026) and the Industrial Production (−1.148%) show to decrease the debt rates. Regarding the Non-Performing Loans, column three gives us positive and significant results at the 1% level. The NPLs increased during the QE period in the periphery countries by 17.731%, while including the macroeconomic variables, the ATE continues to be significant by 7.067%. Moreover, the Central Bank Assets (0.994) have a positive impact on NPLs while the FDI (−0.123) and the Industrial Production (−7.251) have a negative and significant impact.

The estimation results where France is set as a control group are presented in Table 2.3. The ATE in the first column is negative and

Table 2.3 Estimation results for EU periphery countries with France as a control group

	Gross Government Debt		*Non-perfoming Loans*	
Variables	*(1)*	*(2)*	*(3)*	*(4)*
CIC (ATE)	**−0.796****	−0.708	**12.101****	**7.862****
	(−3.02)	(−1.39)	(13.23)	(7.09)
Gross Government Debt				0.055
				(0.83)
Non-performingLoans		0.010		
		(0.83)		
Central Bank Assets		**−0.134****		**0.935****
		(−4.61)		(14.50)
Bank Deposits		**−0.895****		−0.202
		(−12.21)		(−1.09)
Foreign DirectInvestments		**0.026****		**−0.091****
		(2.98)		(−4.35)
Industrial Production		**−1.390****		**−9.989****
		(−4.14)		(−13.20)
Observations	1320	1320	1320	1320

Source Authors' calculations

Notes Bold figures indicate statistical significant coefficients, ** denotes statistical significance at the 1% level ($p < 0.01$), * denotes statistical significance at the 5% level ($p < 0.05$), + denotes statistical significance at the 10% level ($p < 0.1$). The CIC (ATE) variable refers to the average treatment effect. Also, it refers to the quantitative easing implementation period (2015m01 and onwards) and takes the value 1 for that specific period. In all the estimations, the standard errors are block-bootstrapped, and the z-statistics are reported in the parentheses. The results are given in percentage points

significant (−0.796) showing that the debt rates during the QE period decreased. In the second column, the ATE is not significant, while the macroeconomic variables of Central Bank Assets (−0.134), Bank Deposits (−0.895) and Industrial Production (−1.390) are negative and significant, reducing so the debt levels of the periphery countries. Only the FDI shows to affect positively (0.026) the debt rates. The NPLs in the third column are positive and significant (12.101), showing an increase during the implementation period of QE. In the fourth column, the NPLs continue to be positive and significant (7.862). The variable of Central Bank Assets (0.935) shows to increase the NPLs, while FDI (−0.091) and Industrial Production (−9.989) decreases them. If we contrast the estimation results that Germany and France as control groups are giving us, then we conclude that in both countries the debt rates after the QE implementation are decreasing. Also, the variables of Central Bank Assets, Bank Deposits and Industrial Production show to play an important role in order to reduce the debt rates. Moreover, the period after the QE shows that the NPLs are increasing. The Central Bank Assets have also a positive impact on NPLs, while the FDI and the Industrial Production show to have a negative impact.

Table 2.4 presents the CIC estimation results for each periphery country with Germany set as control group. Greece, although did not participate in the QE, shows to reduce its government debt by −0.900 (column 1) and −4.547(column 2). The NPLs (0.056) show to increase the debt rates, while Central Bank Assets (−0.872), Bank Deposits (−0.247) and Industrial Production (−1.810) show to reduce it. The participation of Ireland in the QE shows not to affect the debt rates. The NPLs have in Ireland the same impact as in Greece by increasing the debt rates by 0.249. Bank Deposits (−0.188), FDI (−0.188) and Industrial Production (−1.311) have a negative impact, decreasing so Irelands debt rates. The ATE in Italy is positive by 0.619 (column 5), the only variable that shows to decrease the debt rate in Italy is Industrial Production (−1.053). In Portugal and Spain, the ATE shows no significant results after the QE implementation. In both countries the NPLs (0.077 and 0.102) have positive effects on their debt rates, while the Industrial Production has negative. Bank deposits affected negatively (−0.167) only the debt of Portugal.

The results where France was set as a control group are presented in Table 2.5. The ATE is negative in Ireland (−2.987), Portugal (−0.572) and Spain (−0.928), showing that the QE decreased their debt rates. The

Table 2.4 Estimation results for Gross Government Debt as dependent variable and Germany as control group

	Greece		*Ireland*		*Italy*		*Portugal*		*Spain*	
Variables	*(1)*	*(2)*	*(3)*	*(4)*	*(5)*	*(6)*	*(7)*	*(8)*	*(9)*	*(10)*
CIC (ATE)	**−0.900****	**−4.547****	−0.536	−1.163	**0.619***	0.024	−0.129	−0.262	0.225	−1.062
	(−4.76)	(−2.97)	(−0.98)	(−0.34)	(2.16)	(0.03)	(−0.43)	(−0.33)	(0.74)	(−1.16)
Non-performing Loans		**0.056****		**0.249****		−0.036		**0.077****		**0.102+**
		(2.76)		(10.71)		(−1.32)		(3.02)		(1.89)
Central Bank Assets		**−0.872****		−0.019		0.143		−0.027		0.165
		(−3.61)		(−0.80)		(1.54)		(−0.18)		(1.07)
Bank Deposits		**−0.247****		**−0.188****		−0.028		**−0.167****		−0.041
		(−3.92)		(−4.32)		(−0.60)		(−5.44)		(−1.66)
Foreign DirectInvestments		−0.018		**−0.022****		−0.085		0.044		−0.045
		(−0.09)		(−3.22)		(−1.15)		(1.46)		(−1.16)
Industrial Production		**−1.810****		**−1.311****		**−1.053****		**−1.295****		**−1.239****
		(−3.77)		(−5.66)		(−4.09)		(−8.84)		(−9.53)
Observations	264	264	264	264	264	264	264	264	264	264

Source Authors' calculations

Notes Bold figures indicate statistical significant coefficients, ** denotes statistical significance at the 1% level ($p < 0.01$), * denotes statistical significance at the 5% level ($p < 0.05$), + denotes statistical significance at the 10% level ($p < 0.1$). The CIC (ATE) variable refers to the average treatment effect. Also, it refers to the quantitative easing implementation period (2015m01 and onwards) and takes the value 1 for that specific period. In all the estimations, the standard errors are block-bootstrapped, and the *z*-statistics are reported in the parentheses. The results are given in percentage points

Table 2.5 Estimation results for Gross Government Debt as dependent variable and France as control group

	Greece		*Ireland*		*Italy*		*Portugal*		*Spain*	
Variables	*(1)*	*(2)*	*(3)*	*(4)*	*(5)*	*(6)*	*(7)*	*(8)*	*(9)*	*(10)*
CIC (ATE)	−0.074	−0.636	**−2.987****	−2.101	−0.140	−0.196	**−0.572+**	−0.066	**−0.928****	−1.318
	(−0.39)	(−0.29)	(−5.23)	(−0.83)	(−0.49)	(−0.13)	(−1.91)	(−0.05)	(−3.06)	(−0.95)
Non-performing Loans		**0.057+**		**0.249****		0.043		−0.056		0.039
		(1.77)		(3.77)		(0.56)		(−0.60)		(0.23)
Central Bank Assets		0.141		−0.007		0.028		0.064		0.092
		(0.85)		(−0.11)		(0.13)		(0.23)		(0.32)
Bank Deposits		**−1.739****		**−0.517****		**−1.261****		**−1.003****		**−1.467****
		(−16.29)		(−3.08)		(−7.02)		(−4.81)		(−7.87)
Foreign DirectInvestments		−0.375		−0.021		−0.251		0.082		**−0.334+**
		(−1.53)		(−1.12)		(−0.93)		(0.85)		(−1.84)
Industrial Production		1.158		−0.874		0.328		−1.284		0.269
		(1.44)		(−0.80)		(0.27)		(−1.25)		(0.22)
Observations	264	264	264	264	264	264	264	264	264	264

Source Authors' calculations

Notes Bold figures indicate statistical significant coefficients, ** denotes statistical significance at the 1% level ($p < 0.01$), * denotes statistical significance at the 5% level ($p < 0.05$), + denotes statistical significance at the 10% level ($p < 0.1$). The CIC (ATE) variable refers to the average treatment effect. Also, it refers to the quantitative easing implementation period (2015m01 and onwards) and takes the value 1 for that specific period. In all the estimations, the standard errors are block-bootstrapped, and the z-statistics are reported in the parentheses. The results are given in percentage points

NPL variable is positive in Greece (0.057) and Ireland (0.249), meaning that the debt rates in that countries increased during the QE period. The Bank deposits variable is negative in all countries, showing that the debt rates are decreasing. Specifically, in Greece, the variable records a decrease of 1.739, in Ireland 0.517, in Italy 1.261, in Portugal 1.003 and in Spain 1.467. Only in Spain, the FDI shows to also decrease the debt rates by 0.334.

The estimation results for the Non-Performing Loans as a dependent variable with Germany as a control group are presented in Table 2.6. That table shows that the ATE is positive in all countries. In Greece, the ATE is positive at 39.371 (column 1), in Ireland 14.214 (column 3), in Italy 15.261 and 4.352 (column 5 and 6), in Portugal 14.403 and 6.856 (column 7 and 8) and in Spain 5.406 and 4.966 (column 9 and 10). That mean that the NPLs increased during the period of QE in the periphery countries in contrast to Germany. The Gross Government Debt has a positive impact increasing so the dependent variable in Greece (0.521), Ireland (0.919), Portugal (0.227) and Spain (0.054). The Central Banks Assets are negative in Greece (−6.793), Ireland (−0.561), Italy (−2.308), Portugal (−0.519) and Spain (−2.293), decreasing so the NPLs in these countries. Furthermore, the FDI is also negative in Greece (−3.197), Italy (−0.385), Portugal (−0.308) and Spain (−0.079). Industrial Production shows also to decrease the NPLs in Greece (−6.137), Ireland (−3.635), Italy (−2.325), Portugal (−2.475) and Spain (−0.982).

The results differ slightly when France is used as a control group. The ATE is positive in Greece (33.451 and 26.729), in Ireland (3.433), in Italy (7.943 and 2.726), in Portugal (10.25 and 7.456) and in Spain (2.122), increasing so the NPLs in the period of the QE implementation. From the additional macroeconomic variables, the Gross Government Debt is positive in Greece (0.069) and in Ireland (0.213), while the Central Bank Assets are also positive in Greece (1.423), in Ireland (0.698), in Italy (1.460) and in Spain (0.986). The FDI shows to decrease the NPLs in Greece (−2.832) and in Spain (−0.137). The Industrial Production decreases the NPLs in all periphery countries. In Greece, the decrease is 12.914, in Ireland 7.427, in Italy 5.800, in Portugal 5.992 and in Spain 4.384 (Table 2.7).

The estimation results between Germany and France as control groups are showing us that during the QE implementation period the debt rates of the periphery countries are decreasing, while the NPLs are increasing.

Table 2.6 Estimation results for Non-performing Loans as dependent variable and Germany as control group

	Greece		*Ireland*		*Italy*		*Portugal*		*Spain*	
Variables	*(1)*	*(2)*	*(3)*	*(4)*	*(5)*	*(6)*	*(7)*	*(8)*	*(9)*	*(10)*
CIC (ATE)	**39.371****	8.283	**14.214****	0.725	**15.261****	**4.352***	**14.403****	**6.856****	**5.406****	**4.966****
	(47.27)	(1.15)	(17.12)	(0.19)	(22.25)	(2.01)	(23.81)	(6.06)	(13.78)	(5.18)
Gross Government Debt		**0.521****		**0.919****		−0.191		**0.227****		**0.054+**
		(2.76)		(10.71)		(−1.32)		(3.02)		(1.89)
Central Bank Assets		**−6.793****		**−0.561****		**−2.308****		**−0.519+**		**−2.293****
		(−10.92)		(−15.41)		(−14.72)		(−1.98)		(−34.95)
Bank Deposits		0.193		−0.094		−0.100		−0.015		0.019
		(0.98)		(−1.11)		(−0.94)		(−0.29)		(1.03)
Foreign DirectInvestments		**−3.197****		−0.021		**−0.385***		**−0.308****		**−0.079****
		(−5.73)		(−1.60)		(−2.28)		(−6.16)		(−2.82)
Industrial Production		**−6.137****		**−3.635****		**−2.325****		**−2.475****		**−0.982****
		(−4.22)		(−8.58)		(−3.91)		(−10.02)		(−10.58)
Observations	264	264	264	264	264	264	264	264	264	264

Source Authors' calculations

Notes Bold figures indicate statistical significant coefficients, ** denotes statistical significance at the 1% level ($p < 0.01$), * denotes statistical significance at the 5% level ($p < 0.05$), + denotes statistical significance at the 10% level ($p < 0.1$). The CIC (ATE) variable refers to the average treatment effect. Also, it refers to the quantitative easing implementation period (2015m01 and onwards) and takes the value 1 for that specific period. In all the estimations, the standard errors are block-bootstrapped, and the z-statistics are reported in the parentheses. The results are given in percentage points

Table 2.7 Estimation results for Non-performing Loans as dependent variable and France as control group

	Greece		*Ireland*		*Italy*		*Portugal*		*Spain*	
Variables	*(1)*	*(2)*	*(3)*	*(4)*	*(5)*	*(6)*	*(7)*	*(8)*	*(9)*	*(10)*
CIC (ATE)	**33.451****	**26.729****	**3.433****	−3.245	**7.943****	**2.726***	**10.25****	**7.456****	**2.122****	1.189
	(40.72)	(29.21)	(4.22)	(−1.57)	(11.58)	(2.01)	(16.32)	(10.43)	(4.76)	(1.63)
Gross Government Debt		**0.069+**		**0.213****		0.028		−0.025		0.005
		(1.77)		(3.77)		(0.56)		(−0.60)		(0.23)
Central Bank Assets		**1.423****		**0.698****		**1.460****		−0.187		**0.986****
		(8.13)		(16.75)		(9.70)		(−1.01)		(10.98)
Bank Deposits		0.007		0.188		−0.185		0.031		−0.031
		(0.05)		(1.19)		(−1.16)		(0.22)		(−0.41)
Foreign DirectInvestments		**−2.832****		0.016		0.224		0.103		**−0.137***
		(−11.32)		(0.96)		(1.03)		(1.61)		(−2.03)
Industrial Production		**−12.914****		**−7.427****		**−5.800****		**−5.992****		**−4.384****
		(−17.00)		(−8.30)		(−6.23)		(−10.36)		(−12.07)
Observations	264	264	264	264	264	264	264	264	264	264

Source Authors' calculations

Notes Bold figures indicate statistical significant coefficients, ** denotes statistical significance at the 1% level ($p < 0.01$), * denotes statistical significance at the 5% level ($p < 0.05$), + denotes statistical significance at the 10% level ($p < 0.1$). The CIC (ATE) variable refers to the average treatment effect. Also, it refers to the quantitative easing implementation period (2015m01 and onwards) and takes the value 1 for that specific period. In all the estimations, the standard errors are block-bootstrapped, and the z-statistics are reported in the parentheses. The results are given in percentage points

The macroeconomic variable that increased the debt rates during the QE period was only the NPL variable, while the Central Bank Assets, Bank Deposits, FDI and Industrial Production variables have decreased the debt rates in the periphery countries. The ATE for the NPLs as a dependent variable was positive for both Germany and France as a control group, increasing so the NPLs during that specific period (QE). The Gross Government debt when used as independent variable showed to increase the NPLs, while the Central Bank Assets, FDI and Industrial Production showed to decrease it.

To conclude, our estimation results are showing that the countries that participated in the QE policy reduced its debt rates and increased their NPLs. Surprisingly, the debt rates of Greece are reduced, which was not expected because of Greece's nonparticipation in the QE. Also, its NPLs are increasing to a greater extent in contrast to the rest of the periphery countries. The macroeconomic variables of Central Bank Assets, Bank Deposits and Industrial Production show to have a possible negative effect on government debt (by reducing it), while the Foreign Direct Investments and the Industrial Production show to have also a negative effect on NPLs (by reducing it). When the Government Debt and the NPLs are included in the CIC as independent variables then they increase the NPLs and the Government Debt, respectively. These findings can be possibly used to draft proposals to the policymakers in the sense that would a country want to influence the level of NPLs and government debt it could steer appropriately the relevant determinants. However, making such recommendations lies beyond the scope of this research and is thus left for future research.

2.6 Conclusion

In this study, we empirically examined the impact of ECB's QE policy program on the government debt and NPLs of the Eurozone periphery countries for a period spanning from 2008 to 2018. We employed the CIC approach and investigated the impact that unconventional monetary policy has among the periphery countries and the reaction of additional macroeconomic variables. We run our estimations with two control groups (Germany and France). We follow this line of research because we tended to examine the divergence in eurozone and the creation of a union with countries at different speed.

The estimation results show that Germany and France as control groups are giving us similar results, in both countries, the debt rates after the QE implementation are decreasing but not with the same intensity. The NPLs are positive showing an increase during the implementation period of QE. Also, the variables of Central Bank Assets, Bank Deposits and Industrial Production show to reduce the debt and NPLs rates.

After that, we estimated the CIC approach for each periphery country with Germany and France set as control groups. The estimation results of Germany and France as control groups are showing us that the QE period has had positive effects on the periphery countries by decreasing their debt rates. The macroeconomic variable that increased the debt rates was only the NPL variable (when used as an independent variable), while the Central Bank Assets, Bank Deposits, FDI and Industrial Production decreased the debt rates in the periphery countries. Similar results hold true for the NPLs as dependent variable. The ATE in all countries for both control groups was positive, increasing so the NPLs during the QE period. The Gross Government debt when used as independent variable showed to increase the NPLs, while the Central Bank Assets, FDI and Industrial Production decreased the NPLs.

Greece is a totally different situation, as it did not participate in the QE program, and has still the highest rate of government debt and NPLs. In the QE period, the government debt of Greece shows to fractionally decline but on the other side, the NPLs increased rapidly.

References

Altavilla, C., Carboni, G., & Motto, R. (2015). *Asset purchase programmes and financial markets: Lessons from the euro area*. ECB Working Paper, 1864.

Andrade, Ph., Breckenfelder, J., De Fiore, F., Karadi, P., & Tristani, O. (2016). *The ECB's asset purchase programme: An early assessment*. ECB Working Paper, 1956.

Angrist, J. D., & Pischke, J. S. (2008). *Mostly harmless econometrics: An empiricist's companion*. Princeton University Press.

Aßhoff, S., Belke, A., & Osowski, T. (2020). Unconventional monetary policy and inflation expectations in the euro area. *Ruhr Economic Papers, 837*, RWI - Leibniz-InstitutfürWirtschaftsforschung, Ruhr-University Bochum, TU Dortmund University, University of Duisburg-Essen.

Asteriou, A., Pilbeam, K., & Sarantidis, A. (2019). The behaviour of banking stocks during the financial crisis and recessions. Evidence from changes-in-changes panel data estimations. *Scottish Journal of Political Economy, 66*(1), 154–179.

Athey, S., & Imbens, G. W. (2006). Identification and Inference in nonlinear difference-in-differences models. *Econometrica, 74*(2), 431–497.

Bahmani, S., & Toms, J. (2015). Assessing the effect of quantitative easing on foreign direct investment in Brazil. *The American Economist, 60*(2), 176–182.

Bekaert, G., Hoerova, M., & Duca, M. L. (2013). Risk, uncertainty and monetary policy. *Journal of Monetary Economics, 60*(7), 771–788.

Baker, M. C., Foley, F., & Wurgler, J. (2004). *The stock market and investment: Evidence from FDI flows*. NBER Working Paper, 10559.

Baumeister, C., & Benati, L. (2013). Unconventional monetary policy and the great recession: Estimating the macroeconomic effects of a spread compression at the zero lower bound. *International Journal of Central Banking, 9*(2), 165–212.

Belke, A., & Gros, D. (2019). QE in the euro area: Has the PSPP benefited peripheral bonds? *Ruhr Economic Papers, 803*, RWI - Leibniz-InstitutfürWirtschaftsforschung, Ruhr-University Bochum, TU Dortmund University, University of Duisburg-Essen.

Bertrand, M., Duflo, E., & Mullainathan, S. (2004). How much should we trust differences-in-differences estimates? *The Quarterly Journal of Economics, 119*(1), 249–275.

Chen, H., Cúrdia, V., & Ferrero, A. (2012). The macroeconomic effects of large-scale asset purchase programmes. *The Economic Journal, 122*(564), F289–F315.

Curdia, V., & Woodford, M. (2009). *Conventional and unconventional monetary policy* (p. 7514). CEPR Discussion Paper: CEPR.

Dell'Ariccia, G., Rabanal, P., & Sandri, D. (2018). Unconventional monetary policies in the euro area, Japan, and the United Kingdom. *Journal of Economic Perspectives, 32*(4), 147–172.

De Santis, R. (2016). *Impact of the asset purchase programme on euro area government bond yields using market news*. ECB Working Paper, 1939.

Gagnon, J., Bayoumi, T., Londono-Yarce, J. M., Saborowski, C., & Sapriza, H., (2017). *Direct and spillover effects of unconventional monetary and exchange rate policies*. IMF Working Paper, 17/56.

Gambacorta, L., Hofmann, B., & Peersman, G. (2012). The effectiveness of unconventional monetary policy at the zero lower bound: A cross-country analysis. *Bank of International Settlements, 384*.

Grammatikos, T., & Vermeulen, R. (2012). Transmission of the financial and sovereign debt crises to the EMU: Stock prices, CDS spreads and exchange rates. *Journal of International Money and Finance, 31*(3), 517–533.

Grasmann, P., Aspegren, M., & Willems, N. (2019). Tackling non-performing loans in Europe. SUERF Policy Note, Issue No. 107, October 2019.

Hesse, H., Hofmann, B., & Weber, J. (2017). *The macroeconomic effects of asset purchases revisited*. BIS Working Paper, 680.

Hohberger, S., Priftis, R., & Vogel, L. (2017). *The macroeconomic effects of quantitative easing in the Euro Area: Evidence from an estimated DSGE model*. European University Institute, Working Paper ECO 2017/04.

International Monetary Fund. (2019). *France: Staff concluding statement of the 2019 Article IV, mission*. https://www.imf.org/en/News/Articles/2019/06/03/.

Jensen, M. C., Kaplan, S. N., & Stiglin, L. (1989). Effects of LBOs on tax revenues of the U.S. treasury. *Tax Notes, 42*(6), 1–18.

Joyce, M., Miles, D., Scott, A., & Vayanos, D. (2012). Quantitative easing and unconventional monetary policy—An introduction. *The Economic Journal, 122*(564), F271–F288.

Kenourgios, D., Drakonaki, E., & Dimitriou, D. (2019). ECB's unconventional monetary policy and cross-financial-market correlation dynamics. *The North American Journal of Economics and Finance, 50*, 101045.

Kumar, M. S., & Baldacci, E. (2010). *Fiscal deficits, public debt, and sovereign bond yields*. IMF Working Papers 10/184.

Loungani, P., Rush, M., & Tave, W. (1990). Stock market dispersion and unemployment. *Journal of Monetary Economics, 25*(3), 367–388.

Macchiarelli, C., Giacon, R., Georgosouli, A., & Monti, M. (2019). Why non-performing loans are still putting the European Banking Union at risk. *LSE EUROPP—European Politics and Policy*, 27 March.

MacDonald, M. (2017). International capital market frictions and spillovers from quantitative easing. *Journal of International Money and Finance, 70*, 135–156.

MacKinnon, J. G. (2002). Bootstrap inference in econometrics. *Canadian Journal of Economics/Revue Canadienne D'économique, 35*(4), 615–645.

Sarantidis, A., Mitropoulos, F., & Kollias, K. (2019). Quantitative easing and government bonds: Evidence from the EU. *International Journal of Financial Engineering and Risk Management, 3*(1), 79–94.

Suh, S., & Koo, B. (2016, March 22). *Spillovers from U.S. unconventional monetary policy and its normalization to emerging markets: A capital flow perspective*. Bank of Korea, Working Paper 2016–4.

Tillmann, P. (2016). Unconventional monetary policy and the spillovers to emerging markets. *Journal of International Money and Finance, 66*, 136–156.

Varghese, R., & Zhang, Y. S. (2018). *A new wave of ECB's unconventional monetary policies: Domestic impact and spillovers*. International Monetary Fund. IMF Working Paper No. 18/11, https://www.imf.org/en/Publications/WP/Issues/2018/01/24/A-New-Wave-of-ECBs-Unconventional-Monetary-Policies-Domestic-Impact-and-Spillovers-45577. Accessed Feb 2020.

Weale, M., & Wieladek, T. (2016). What are the macroeconomic effects of asset purchases?. *Journal of Monetary Economics, 79*, 81–93.

CHAPTER 3

Tariffs and Debt

George Galanos, Thomas Poufinas, and Charalampos Agiropoulos

3.1 Introduction

Tariffs influence trade, production, consumption patterns and welfare of not only the countries that impose them, but also the welfare of their trading partners. They do so through both the absolute levels of protection they impart and through distortions associated with their structure. Tariffs create a wedge between domestic and world prices pushing demand toward domestically produced substitutes. A large body of empirical research indicates that countries with low policy-induced trade barriers tend to enjoy rapid growth. On the other hand, theoretical models suggest that the relationship between trade barriers and growth may be contingent on the level of development. One of the current US president's most prominent policy actions since taking office has been

G. Galanos (✉) · C. Agiropoulos
Department of International and European Studies,
University of Piraeus, Piraeus, Greece
e-mail: galgeorg@unipi.gr

T. Poufinas
Department of Economics, Democritus University of Thrace, Komotini, Greece

T. Poufinas (ed.), *Debt in Times of Crisis*,
https://doi.org/10.1007/978-3-030-74162-4_3

to raise tariffs. Most of his administration's recent trade policy proposals focus on implementing a set of new tariffs and quotas on selected imports from selected countries. The president promised to eliminate the entire national debt by the end of his second term by using tariffs in order to increase government revenue. The natural question is thus whether it is possible to use tariffs in order to contain debt (Reinsch, 2018).

Tariff rates vary a lot among the countries; their contribution to total or tax revenues covers also a wide range (The World Bank, 2020; World Trade Organization, 2019). In the United States, tariff was the largest single source of revenue for the federal government until World War I, with a contribution ranging between approximately 90 and 50% for the period 1830–1910. The at-the-time approved federal income tax eliminated it. For the greatest part of the American history the tariff policy characterized the corresponding tax policy (Hansen, 1990). The countries that nowadays seem to depend on tariff revenue have much less developed economies than the United States and large informal sectors. For them, tariffs on goods entering the country from abroad represent an easier way to raise revenue than tracking every citizen's income. On the other hand, it is well known that several developed countries have implemented a tariff policy, hoping to balance their external debt, which has not been achieved so far. The aim of this chapter is to investigate whether tariffs affect the public and private debt of a country and this is the primary novelty in the area. Additional contributions of this present research are identified in that it considers a set of countries (and not a single one) as well as a series of econometric models at the same time.

3.2 Literature Review

The literature that is related to this study is categorized in three parts; the first presents the research that treats public debt; the second shows the papers that tackle private debt; and the third the studies that deal with tariffs along with public and private debt.

3.2.1 Public Debt

"In order to increase the average maturity and partial indexation of public debt, the strategy for managing it should be optimized." This conclusion has been approached for the first time by Giavazzi and Pagano (1990) and

Calvo and Guidotti (1990) who have detected the problem of the difference between several fiscal policies and they have modelized it adequately. However, Barro (2003), on the other hand, has been led to the same conclusion by trying to structure the public debt so that tax revenue could be appropriately reduced as public expenditure operates externally in an appropriate environment.

In addition, Missale et al. (2002) and Giavazzi and Missale (2004) emphasized to encounter the stability of the public debt over Gross Domestic Product. Georges (2006) proposes a short-term public debt maturity because the cheaper it is the lower the risk to the public budget. Georges (2006) analyzed the effect of various maturity frameworks on interest rate and primary surplus for Canada and found that these two effects reduce cost and risk offsetting.

Wolswijk and de Haan (2006) recorded—since the creation of the euro area—a blend of currency risk reduction, the increase in public debt maturity, the use of derivatives (swaps) and government bonds linked to inflation. While this strategy was not enough to prevent the damaging effects of the 2007 crisis in European countries, Anderson et al. (2010) relied on a sample of 24 emerging economies to point out that improving debt management (in particular, the increase in the duration of public debt) has reduced the impact of the crisis on these countries.

3.2.2 *Private Debt*

According to Myers (1984), firms facing high costs of asymmetric information will use external funds only when internally generated funds are not adequate. If external funds are required, the firm will issue the "safest" security first—the one whose value changes least when inside information is revealed to the market—first debt and then, only as a last resort, equity. Because private debt lenders are better informed through monitoring and screening, and are usually senior (Welch, 1997) and collateralized (Rajan & Winton, 1995), it is hypothesized that private debt will be a safer instrument than arm's length debt, holding constant the degree of information asymmetry between the firm and the outside market. Thus, firms with higher levels of asymmetric information, and a higher probability of default, will issue private debt before public debt. As the degree of asymmetric information decreases, the scale of safety becomes less important, and the debt choice for firms with lower asymmetry will be determined by other factors—e.g. transactions costs, the flexibility of covenants

(Gilson & Warner, 1997), credit quality (Diamond, 1991) and the possibility of rent extraction by banks (Rajan, 1992).

Bank debt and non-bank private debt differ in terms of regulatory requirements, maturity, placement structure, and the concentration and identity of debt holders. This regulation allows companies to market debt directly to private institutional investors rather than going through the more time-consuming public securities issuance process. Carleton and Kwan (1995) describe non-bank private loans as tightly held and relatively illiquid. In addition, non-bank private loans tend to have lower flotation costs than public issues and have custom-designed covenants.

3.2.3 Tariffs

More than a century ago, Schumpeter (1918) published an exceptional essay on the fiscal state. Schumpeter (1918) argued that the ability to tax lies at the very heart of political power and that the rise of the modern political state was shaped by fiscal evolution in medieval and postmedieval times. Although he did not provide a framework to determine potential interactions shaping the revenue systems, he clearly recognized that there are three types of influences—economic, political and administrative, perhaps because he had not yet formed an economic theory of political action.

In late 60s a few studies by Hinrichs (1966) and Musgrave (1969) fall into Schumpeter's category. Hinrichs was mainly interested in linking stages of economic and fiscal development, while Musgrave emphasized the role of changing opportunities to tax and of administration costs (so-called tax handles) in the evolution of tax structure. Some further contributions were made in the 1970s and 1980s. Kau and Rubin (1981) highlighted the economic limits to fiscal development and the effects of changes in such limits on the growth of revenue systems. A study by Hansen (1983) focused on the impact of political factors on the tax system while a separate literature grew up around selected revenue sources such as the tariff (Baldwin, 1986; Caves, 1976; Helleiner, 1977; Magee et al., 1989) and debt (Barro, 1979, 1986).

While there is a host of evidence about the impact of trade policies on trade flows, less attention to date has been given to the assessment of the effect of trade policies on foreign direct investment (FDI). The theoretical models of the multinational enterprise suggest that trade policies exert an important role as a determinant of FDI (Bergstrand & Egger, 2007;

Markusen & Maskus, 2002). Indeed, trade policies may have different impacts depending upon the nature of FDI. Recent international trade models with heterogeneous firms show that tariffs may also affect the number of firms involved in FDI and the number of affiliates established in the foreign country (e.g. Antràs & Foley, 2009).

In the empirical literature on the determinants of FDI, trade policies are commonly considered by means of dummies aimed at capturing the impact of regional trade agreements (e.g. Baltagi et al., 2008; Stein & Daude, 2007) however, dummies may be inappropriate, as they implicitly assume that trade protection across countries and industries is all the same, while this is not the case. Many papers include proxies for overall trade costs, such as the index of the openness to trade or indices measuring the perceived trade costs by firms (e.g. Blonigen & Piger, 2011; Blonigen et al., 2007; Carr et al., 2001). However, these indices capture trade frictions other than trade policies and, in addition, we frequently observe wide differences in the degree of openness in countries sharing a common trade policy as, for example, the EU member states. A direct measure of trade protection therefore might be better able to capture the impact of trade policy on FDI.

Interestingly enough the attempts to link tariff with debt directly (and not through revenue) are limited, and none of them focuses on the impact that tariffs may have on debt. The first one studies the development of the revenue structure in Canada from 1871 to 1913 (Winer & Hettich, 1991). The choice of the period is justified by the fact that the major revenue sources during these years were tariff, debt and excises. The ratio of revenue ex tariffs over tariffs and the ratio of deficit over tariffs are linked with a series of economic, political and administrative variables. As a matter of fact they all contribute in shaping the revenue structure. The authors conclude that in the nineteenth century Canada debt and tariffs were sources of revenue—competing to each other as they say—and were both employed by the government as fiscal tools.

On another direction Carey (1999) investigates the relationship between debt and tariffs as represented by bond prices on one hand and Smoot Hawley Tariffs in the 1930s. He finds that the sovereign bond market did not feel the introduction of tariffs in a way that justifies a mild concern. As a matter of fact the contribution of tariffs in the price movement in 1930 is perceived to be small. This is justified by the gradual drop in the bond market instead of a sharp drop that should have happened on any single day would this not be the case. There are additional explanations offered, such as that: the market imperfections prevented the tariff form being reflected by the bond prices immediately or that the events caused by the tariff were too complex to be captured by the bond prices. He concludes that the marginal contribution of tariffs to the Great Depression is quite small.

Finally, Reinsch (2018) realizes that although tariffs are a source of revenue for the government they do not suffice to pay down the debt. Moreover, he states that they will not eliminate the federal budget deficit and thus they will not contribute to the reduction of the government debt.

3.3 Problem Description and Theoretical Background

The intuition behind the investigation of the influence of tariffs on debt stems from the effort of countries to contain their government debt at levels that can be sustained by their economic activities in total and in particular by their GDPs. High public debt to GDP can lead to distressed economies and can create problems to other aspects of the economic (and not only) lives of the countries. However, the same holds true with the private debt; high private debt to GDP may result in distressed households and enterprises, which can also lead to further problems for the interested parties, including the country as a whole.

The question that the countries try to answer is what measures to take so as to maintain primarily their public and secondarily their private debt (as a portion of their GDP) at amounts that they can serve. One such approach was offered by the United States as the last couple of years it brought forward the belief that imposing or increasing tariffs will assist in reducing public debt.

In our research we try to find evidence of the link between public and private debt (as a percent of GDP) and the tariff rates for the countries of interest. We do that with the use of certain econometric models that will be presented in the following sections. At the same time we incorporate in our models other macroeconomic metrics that are known or believed to also influence the public and private debt.

Revealing this relationship can be beneficial to the respective authorities and policymakers, as they can decide on the tariff rates they may want to apply or which other country figures they may want to improve so as to maintain the public and private debt at the desired levels. Countries that have suffered the most during the latest economic crisis may have experienced higher debt levels compared to countries that have managed to weather the crisis more successfully. As a matter of fact high public and private debt compared to GDP could have been among the causes of heavier suffering. Consequently, tackling or avoiding a potential (new) crisis is in their interest; knowing in advance what to do is of key importance and it requires a global approach rather than the management of one or a few determinants—variables.

3.4 Data, Variables and Methodology

3.4.1 Data

Our dataset consists of tariff Argentina, Australia, Brazil, Canada, China, European Union (EU), India, Indonesia, Japan, South Korea, Mexico, Russia, Saudi Arabia, South Africa, Turkey and the United States. These are essentially the G20 countries with the European Union substituting for the four EU countries participating in it. These are Germany, France, Italy and the United Kingdom. We replaced them with the EU as tariff rates are the same within the European Union countries, which is reflected in our databases, hence would add no value in our model.

Our data source is the World Bank for the unemployment (rate—% of labor force), the inflation (rate—%), the GDP per capita (current USD), the exports of goods and services (% of GDP), the imports of goods and services (% of GDP), the foreign direct investment - FDI (net inflows, current USD), the GDP growth (annual %), the gross fixed capital formation (annual % growth), the tariff rate (weighted mean, all products—%), the public debt (total central government debt —% of GDP) and the private debt (private debt, loans and debt securities—% of GDP).

Our time series extends from 1991 to 2018, which is deemed a sufficient period for allowing us to draw reliable results.

3.4.2 Descriptive Statistics

The descriptive statistics of our dataset, i.e. the mean, the 50th percentile, the standard deviation, the variance, the number of observations, the range, the minimum value and the maximum value of the relevant metric are summarized in Table 3.1.

Table 3.1 Descriptive statistics

stats	*PRDEBT*	*PDEBT*	*EXP*	*lFDI*	*GDP*	*GFC*	*IMP*	*INF*	*TARIFF*	*UNEMP*
Mean	92.87	58.27	24.95	23.36	3.467	3.890	23.28	23.59	6.302	7.577
p50	67.65	48.88	24.15	23.33	3.196	4.461	23.07	3.977	4.810	6.030
sd	65.31	42.95	11.44	1.921	3.946	9.785	9.017	154.0	5.234	5.676
Variance	4265	1845	130.9	3.690	15.57	95.76	81.30	23,707	27.40	32.22
N	428	375	446	430	448	408	446	418	375	363
Range	284.1	235.6	55.72	13.13	29.54	79.67	48.17	2077	31.28	31.43
Min	8.197	1.562	6.598	15.03	−14.53	−41.50	6.078	−1.401	0.890	2.048
Max	292.3	237.1	62.32	28.16	15.01	38.17	54.25	2076	32.17	33.47

Source Authors' calculations

We observe that the gross fixed capital formation exhibits the biggest standard deviation compared with its mean (1.15 times), whereas the inflation exhibits the smallest (0.17 times) (Table 3.2).

The biggest correlation is that of the gross fixed capital formation with the GDP growth with a correlation coefficient of 0.866, whereas the smallest is the one of the tariff rate with private debt with a correlation coefficient of -0.393.

3.4.3 *Variables*

As the purpose of our work is to find potential evidence of the relation between debt and tariffs, the variables that are used as measures of debt are the public debt (total central government debt—% of GDP) and the private debt (private debt, loans and debt securities—% of GDP). These are our dependent variables. The tariff is measured by the tariff rate (weighted mean, all products—%) and is our independent variable. However, as the level of both public and private debt depends on other variables we use as control variables the unemployment (rate—% of labor force), the inflation (rate—%), the GDP per capita (current USD), the exports of goods and services (% of GDP), the imports of goods and services (% of GDP), the foreign direct investment - FDI (net inflows, current USD) and the GDP growth (annual %), the gross fixed capital formation (annual % growth), which all go on the independent variable side (Table 3.3).

In our models below we use the following notation:

3.4.4 *Methodology*

We regressed the public debt and private debt with the tariff rate as well as the aforementioned macroeconomic variables to identify the potential impact of tariff on debt and find potential evidence of whether the introduction (or the increase) of tariffs can contribute to the reduction of debt.

For that we employed four models. The first one is the ordinary least squares (OLS) regression, whereas the remaining three are panel data models, namely, the fixed, effects the random effects and finally a linear dynamic panel data model—that of Arellano Bond GMM (generalized method of moments).

Table 3.2 Correlation matrix

Correlation table	*PRDEBT*	*PDEBT*	*EXP*	*lFDI*	*GDP*	*GFC*	*IMP*	*INF*	*TARIFF*	*UNEMP*
PRDEBT	1									
PDEBT	0.260	1								
EXP	0.0625	−0.255	1							
lFDI	0.405	0.00740	0.0879	1						
GDP	−0.109	−0.298	−0.0287	0.0551	1					
GFC	−0.164	−0.152	−0.00860	−0.0100	0.866	1				
IMP	0.176	−0.247	0.878	0.172	−0.0158	−0.0182	1			
INF	−0.0370	−0.137	−0.103	−0.145	−0.0695	−0.0411	−0.134	1		
TARIFF	−0.345	−0.141	−0.235	−0.328	0.226	0.0492	−0.303	0.144	1	
UNEMP	−0.214	−0.0694	0.0191	−0.238	−0.148	−0.0222	0.0453	−0.00910	−0.0649	1

Source Authors' calculations

Table 3.3 Notation

Variable	*Indicator*	*Variable*	*Indicator*
Unemployment	UNEMP	GDP growth	GDP
Inflation	INF	gross fixed capital formation	GFC
Exports of goods and services	EXP	tariff	TARIFF
Imports of goods and services	IMP	public debt	PDEBT
Foreign direct investment	FDI	private debt	PRDEBT

Source Created by the Authors

Before proceeding to unit root and cointegration tests we test for cross-section dependence. We use the cross-section dependence test (CD test) proposed by Pesaran (2004). CD test strongly rejects the null hypothesis of cross-section independence for all the sample variables. In face of this evidence, we proceed to test for unit roots using the so-called "second-generation" tests for unit roots in panel data that are robust to cross-section dependence (see Pesaran, 2015). To examine the stationarity properties of the variables in our models we use the second-generation panel unit root tests developed by Maddala and Wu (1999) and Pesaran (2003) both suitable for unbalanced panel dataset and cross-section dependence. The null hypothesis of a unit root (non-stationarity) cannot be rejected for all the sample variables. This means that the variables contain a unit root (e.g. integrated of order one) as expected by the visual inspection of their time series. In order to investigate whether a long-run equilibrium relationship exists among the sample variables we implement Pedroni's (1999) ADF-based and PP-based cointegration tests as well as Kao's (1999) ADF-based tests. Both tests suggest the rejection of the null hypothesis of no cointegration null at any significance level.

3.4.4.1 OLS

We used a multivariate OLS regression on our data using Stata to calculate the coefficients and error terms for public debt and private debt.

$$
\begin{aligned}
PDEBT = a &+ \beta_1 \cdot EXP + \beta_2 \cdot LogFDI + \beta_3 \cdot GDP + \beta_4 \cdot GFC \\
&+ \beta_5 \cdot IMP + \beta_{6.} \cdot INF + \beta_7 \cdot TARIFF + \beta_8 \cdot UNEMP
\end{aligned}
$$

and

$$PRDEBT = a + \beta_1 \cdot EXP + \beta_2 \cdot LogFDI + \beta_3 \cdot GDP + \beta_4 \cdot GFC + \beta_5 \cdot IMP + \beta_{6.} \cdot INF + \beta_7 \cdot TARIFF + \beta_8 \cdot UNEMP$$

3.4.4.2 *Fixed Effects*

The fixed effects model is simply a linear regression model in which the intercept terms vary over the individual units *i*, i.e.

$$y_{it} = a_i + x_{it}^{'}\beta + \varepsilon_{it}, \quad \varepsilon_{it} \sim IID\left(0, \sigma_{\varepsilon}^2\right)$$

where it is usually assumed that all x_{it} are independent of all ε_{it}. We can write this in the usual regression framework by including a dummy variable for each unit i in the model (Verbeek, 2008). That is,

$$y_{it} = \sum_{j=1}^{N} a_j d_{ij} x_{it}^{'}\beta + \varepsilon_{it}$$

where $d_{ij} = 0$ when $i = j$ and 0 elsewhere. We have also assumed the strictly exogenous regressors case in the conditional moments, (see Wooldridge, 2015). We have not assumed equal-sized groups in the panel. The vector β is a set of parameters of primary interest, α_i is the group-specific heterogeneity. We have included time-specific effects but, they are only tangential in what follows. Since the number of periods is usually fairly small, these can usually be accommodated simply by adding a set of time-specific dummy variables to the model. Our interest here is in the case in which N is too large to do likewise for the group effects.

3.4.4.3 *Random Effects*

It is commonly assumed in regression analysis (Verbeek, 2008) that all factors that affect the dependent variable, but that have not been included as regressors, can be appropriately summarized by a random error term. In our case, this leads to the assumption that the α_i are random factors, independently and identically distributed over individuals. Thus we write the random effects model as

$$y_{it} = \mu + a_i + x_{it}^{'}\beta + \varepsilon_{it}, \varepsilon_{it} \sim IID\left(0, \sigma_{\varepsilon}^2\right); \alpha_i \sim IID\left(0, \sigma_{\alpha}^2\right)$$

where $a_i + \varepsilon_{it}$ is treated as an error term consisting of two components: an individual specific component, which does not vary over time, and a remainder component, which is assumed to be uncorrelated over time. It is also assumed that a_i and ε_{it} are mutually independent and independent of x_{js} (for all j and s).

3.4.4.4 Dynamic Panel Data

Following the non-parametric techniques this study employs parametric techniques organized around the instrumental variables estimators (GMM) developed in Arellano and Bond (1991) and Blundell and Bond (1998) respectively (Difference GMM estimators and System GMM estimators). Furthermore, this study considers a dynamic panel data model in the sense that it contains at least one lagged dependent variable.

With the intention to examine the dynamic aspects we use dynamic panel data techniques such as Difference Generalized Method of Moments (DIF-GMM) estimators attributed to Arellano and Bond (1991) and System Generalized Method of Moments (SYS-GMM) estimators proposed by Arellano and Bover (1995) and Blundell and Bond (1998), respectively. The use of the latter is mainly justified as it improves significantly the estimates' accuracy and enlarges efficiency when the lagged dependent variables are considered as poor instruments as in the first-differenced regressors (Baltagi & Li, 2002). As a consequence, the SYS-GMM gives more robust results than the first-differenced GLS and GMM estimation methods (Blundellet al., 2001).

3.5 Regression Summary

The particulars of the regressions we ran appear in Tables 3.4 and 3.5 for the public and private debt, respectively. The output of all four models, i.e. OLS, fixed effects, random effects and Arellano–Bond GMM is shown per dependent variable for comparison purposes also.

In Tables 3.4 and 3.5 for each of the independent variables the first row indicates the coefficients, whereas the second row, where the numbers are put in the parentheses, indicates the standard deviation.

Their explanation is given in the next section and their implications are drafted in the section that follows it.

Table 3.4 Public debt regression results

PDEBT	*OLS*	*Fixed effects*	*Random effects*	*Arellano–Bond GMM*
Exports of goods *a* ~ %	−1.301***	−0.0540	−0.104	−1.036***
	(0.34)	(0.76)	(0.61)	(0.09)
Log of Foreign dir ~ *t*	−2.844*	2.264	2.339	6.554***
	(1.66)	(5.41)	(4.99)	(0.38)
GDP growth (annual ~)	−5.726***	−2.264*	−2.358*	−0.882***
	(1.80)	(1.20)	(1.25)	(0.29)
Gross fixed capita ~ *a*	0.833	0.657	0.655	0.342***
	(0.62)	(0.46)	(0.47)	(0.10)
Imports of goods *a* ~ %	−0.0240	1.746	1.492	−0.619***
	(0.44)	(1.61)	(1.32)	(0.11)
Inflation, consume ~ *u*	−1.063***	0.547	0.471	0.407***
	(0.37)	(0.54)	(0.45)	(0.10)
Tariff rate, appli ~ *m*	−2.976***	0.306	0.262	−1.141***
	(0.78)	(0.74)	(0.65)	(0.22)
Unemployment, tota ~	−1.078***	3.485	2.489	4.664***
	(0.30)	(2.37)	(1.77)	(0.27)
Constant	202.879***	−64.20	−52.05	−84.862***
	(47.20)	(166.26)	(134.97)	(10.53)
R-sqr	0.299	0.185		
dfres	225	13		
BIC	2432	2105		

$^{*}p < 0.10$, $^{**}p < 0.05$, $^{***}p < 0.01$
Source Authors' calculations

3.5.1 Results

3.5.1.1 Public Debt

The OLS regression indicates that the public debt is negatively correlated at all levels with the tariff rate, the inflation rate, the unemployment, the exports and the GDP growth and at the 10% level with the logarithm of the FDI. The remaining variables show no statistical significance.

Table 3.5 Private debt regression results

PRDEBT	*OLS*	*Fixed effects*	*Random effects*	*Arellano–Bond GMM*
Exports of goods *a* ~ %	−1.280**	−0.884	−0.894	−1.882***
	(0.53)	(0.73)	(0.70)	(0.13)
Log of Foreign dir ~*t*	7.932**	4.205	4.321	11.148***
	(3.15)	(3.82)	(3.85)	(0.55)
GDP growth (annual ~)	−0.528	−0.328	−0.357	−1.524***
	(2.43)	(1.12)	(1.10)	(0.43)
Gross fixed capita ~ *a*	−1.367	−0.123	−0.123	−0.0620
	(0.86)	(0.28)	(0.27)	(0.15)
Imports of goods *a* ~ %	1.957**	0.734	0.770	2.689***
	(0.81)	(0.84)	(0.83)	(0.16)
Inflation, consume ~ *u*	0.00500	0.0420	0.042*	−0.046***
	(0.05)	(0.02)	(0.02)	(0.01)
Tariff rate, appli ~ *m*	−4.526***	−1.075	−1.109	−1.205***
	(1.04)	(0.94)	(0.96)	(0.31)
Unemployment, tota ~	−2.172***	−1.979	−1.904	−0.746*
	(0.52)	(1.68)	(1.59)	(0.40)
Constant	−46.51	36.08	28.54	−154.014***
	(85.98)	(105.29)	(114.54)	(15.68)
R-sqr	0.237	0.214		
dfres	255	13		
BIC	2966	2307		

$^*p < 0.10$, $^{**}p < 0.05$, $^{***}p < 0.01$
Source Authors' calculations

The fixed effects and random effects models show that the public debt is negatively correlated with the GDP growth only at the 10% level, with the rest of the variables having no statistical significance.

The Arellano–Bond GMM yields that the public debt is negatively correlated with the tariff rate, the exports, the imports and the GDP growth at all significance levels, whereas it is positively correlated at all levels with the (logarithm of the) FDI, the inflation, the unemployment rate and the gross fixed capital formation.

The difference in the results of the four models explored, and in particular the outcome of the fixed effects and random effects models, is attributed to the fact that the static behavior of the regressors cannot interpret the dependent variable, whereas in Arellano–Bond GMM a dynamic panel data analysis is performed, which means that even the dependent variable provides information and enhances the model's interpretative capability.

3.5.2 Private Debt

The OLS regression indicates that the private debt is negatively correlated at all levels with the tariff rate, the exports and the unemployment. It is positively correlated with the (logarithm of the) FDI and the imports at the 5% significance level. The remaining variables exhibit no statistical significance.

The random effects model shows that the private debt is positively correlated with the inflation rate at the 10% significance level. The other variables seem to have no statistical significance. No variable posts any statistical significance when the fixed effects model is used.

The Arellano–Bond GMM yields that the private debt is negatively correlated with the tariff rate, the exports, the inflation rate and the GDP growth at all significance levels. It is negatively correlated with unemployment at the 10% significance level. It is positively correlated with the logarithm of the FDIand the imports at all significance levels. The rest of the variables post no statistical significance.

In a way similar to public debt, the difference in the results that the four models produce, and in particular the outcome of the fixed effects and random effects models, can be explained by the fact that the static behavior of the regressors cannot interpret the dependent variable, whereas in Arellano–Bond GMM a dynamic panel data analysis is performed, which means that even the dependent variable provides information and enhances the model's interpretative capability.

Due to the limited available data, the independent characteristics do not seem to vary over time thus the fixed effects estimators have adequate statistical power. Although, this study does consider power and efficiency as the primary criterium for selecting the appropriate model, the authors believe that the amount of data is crucial and as suggested a follow-up of this study when new data are available.

3.6 Result Interpretation and Implications

3.6.1 *Public Debt*

Looking at public debt it seems that both OLS and Arellano–Bond GMM subscribe to the point of view that tariffs can contribute to the reduction of debt (as a percent of GDP), as the higher the tariff rate the lowest the public debt (as a percent to GDP). Thus, assuming a constant GDP, the debt is reduced in absolute figures with the introduction and/or increase of tariffs.

Furthermore, both models consent to the impact of the exports; the highest the exports, the lowest the debt (as a percent of GDP). Therefore, for a flat GDP, the increase of exports may have beneficial results to the level of debt.

GDP growth seems to have a negative impact on public debt (as a percent of GDP) as per all approaches (OLS, Fixed Effects, Random Effects and Arellano Bond GMM). This is probably interpreted by the fact that as the GDP increases at a higher rate, then debt as a percent of GDP drops or increases at a lower rate. This outcome is most likely in line with expectations.

Going to unemployment, we see that the sign of the coefficients is the opposite. The Arellano–Bond GMM states that the lower the unemployment rate, the lower the debt (as a percent of GDP), which is probably the desired result. However, the result of OLS is not to be discarded as well; lower unemployment yields higher public debt to GDP ratio. One potential interpretation is that during periods of low unemployment, countries are in state of euphoria and public debt increases disproportionally to the GDP growth.

The OLS indicates that the higher the FDI, the lower the public debt to GDP ratio, which is the expected direction. The Arellano–Bond GMM model fosters that the higher the FDI, the higher the public debt to GDP ratio. Again the possible interpretation is that FDI contributes to GDP, thus the denominator increases; however, lending may become easier, thus the numerator, i.e. public debt, increases at a higher tempo. Gross fixed capital formation posts the same sign as per the Arellano–Bond only; this can be read in a similar manner as the sign of FDI.

The OLS model indicates that the higher the inflation, the lower the public debt to GDP ratio. This is most likely due to the fact that higher inflation means higher denominator or less lending, as interest rates go higher. The Arellano–Bond GMM, however, subscribes for a positive relationship, i.e. the higher the inflation the higher the public debt as a percent of GDP. A potential explanation can be offered by the fact that inflation in several countries has been negative in some of the years under investigation; this implies that the contribution of inflation has been negative; i.e. either the denominator increased more than public debt or public debt increased less than GDP. Overall, such a positive correlation could mean that as inflation grows, public debt becomes higher, as interest rates follow inflation; thus the numerator supersedes the denominator, i.e. GDP.

The Arellano–Bond model implies that higher imports coexist with lower public debt to GDP ratio, which is probably interpreted by the fact that when the state borrows less compared to GDP imports are not a showstopper and thus may find room to increase.

3.6.2 Private Debt

Going now to private debt, we realize that the increase or introduction of tariffs seems to lead to the reduction of the private debt as a percent of GDP, as verified by both OLS and Arellano–Bond GMM. This is most likely the desired result; individuals and enterprises tend to borrow less as they consume less foreign products.

The same holds true with the increase of exports. Consequently, for a level GDP, the increase of exports leads to a reduction of private debt; this comes probably as no surprise, since the exporting enterprises may need to borrow less as a result of the inflows they experience as a result of the increased exporting activity.

The two approaches agree that when unemployment increases the private debt decreases. This may be due to the realization that when unemployment becomes higher individuals and enterprises abstain from borrowing.

Both models indicate that the higher the FDI the higher the private debt as a percent of GDP. This is probably attributed to the fact that increased investments in the entrepreneurial world of a country make their borrowing easier and thus private debt increases; potentially at a higher rate than the GDP, since the latter may also increase when the FDI increases. Part of these investments could be as private debt.

The Arellano–Bond GMM posts that the higher the GDP growth, the lower the private debt to GDP ratio, which is probably anticipated as the denominator could be increasing at a higher pace than the numerator.

Arellano–Bond GMM shows that the increase of inflation reduces private debt as a percent of GDP; this is probably interpreted by the fact that individuals and enterprises can withstand less borrowed funds in a potentially higher interest rate environment (that goes together with higher inflation).

Finally, both OLS and Arellano–Bond GMM yield that the higher the imports as a percent of GDP the higher the private debt as a percent of GDP. This is probably anticipated as higher lending may be required to support the higher level of imports.

Our findings can be of value to the competent authorities and policy-makers that are looking for ways to control public or private debt. First of all, tariffs seem to assist in reducing the public and private debt as a portion of GDP. Consequently, the current (as of September 2019) president of the United States may have a valid story to tell, as evidenced by our results. However, we have to admit that our study does not investigate the impact of an increase in tariffs in other aspects of the economy. As a result, countries may want to consider the level of tariffs applied in better controlling the public and private debt, weighing at the same time the consequences of increased tariffs in their economy as a whole. Of course the latter can be done only in cases where agreements or treaties allow for a shift in the tariff rates.

Furthermore, the increase of exports seems to have a beneficial impact to both private and public debt as a percent of GDP. This means that countries have to pursue exports in order to reduce both debts. At the same time, as evidenced by at least two of the models, they need to achieve GDP growth, create the environment to attract FDI and reduce unemployment in order to contain public debt. In addition, they have to pay attention to imports to better steer private debt. These observations, next to the evidence found on the impact of tariffs on public and private debt, are probably no news to the ears of the interested parties; they are however confirmed by our work as well.

3.7 Conclusions

This study contributes to the investigation of the relationship among tariffs policy and debt in several ways. The empirical work is related clearly to Gaussian Mixture Models (GMM), the most appropriate theoretical framework presently available to analyze multidimensional economic issues. We characterize debt structure in a simple fashion that distinguishes the government debt from the private lending. This is accomplished in a time series context, allowing us to avoid the problems inherent in comparing policies across countries with differing tariffs. One should also note that the government tariffs policy is enforced through its choice and that the analysis contains explicit assumptions concerning the information upon which the government's decisions are based. We make a systematic attempt to formulate variables reflecting economic, political and administrative factors. The results demonstrate that a model of debt structure based on the tradition of political analysis can be implemented empirically and can be used successfully to explain important aspects of the growth and change of tariffs policies.

There is evidence that economic, political and administrative factors all play a role in shaping debt structure. More precisely the research undertaken in this chapter indicates that the increase or introduction of tariffs reduces the levels of both government and private debt. The exports and the GDP growth work in the same direction as well. Tackling unemployment may be beneficial for both debts. A reduction of imports seems to assist private debt. Consequently, focusing—in addition to tariffs—on exports, GDP growth and unemployment could be of interest to policymakers that wish to control public debt, as well as private debt (if desired). As to future research, the directional relationship of the debt versus tariffs can be tested using causality analysis seeking the direction of causality between debt and tariffs.

References

Anderson, J. L., Markides, C., & Kupp, C. (2010). The last frontier: Market creation in conflict zones, deep rural areas, and urban slums. *California Management Review, 52*(4), 6–28.

Antràs, P., & Foley, C. F. (2009). *Regional trade integration and multinational firm strategies*. National Bureau of Economic Research, Working Paper 14891. https://www.nber.org/papers/w14891. Accessed 21 Sept 2019.

Arellano, M., & Bond, S. (1991). Some tests of specification for panel data: Monte Carlo evidence and an application to employment equations. *Review of Economics and Statistics, 58*, 277–297.

Arellano, M., & Bover, O. (1995). Another look at the instrumental variable estimation of error-components models. *Journal of Econometrics, 68*(1), 29–51.

Baldwin, C. Y. (1986). *Competition in global industries*. Harvard Business Press.

Baltagi, B. H., Egger, P., & Pfaffermayr, M. (2008). Estimating regional trade agreement effects on FDI in an interdependent world. *Journal of Econometrics, 145*(1–2), 194–208.

Baltagi, B. H., & Li, D. (2002). Series estimation of partially linear panel data models with fixed effects. *Annals of Economics and Finance, 3*(1), 103–116.

Barro, R. J. (1979). On the determination of the public debt. *Journal of Political Economy, 87*(5, Part 1), 940–971.

Barro, R. J. (1986). US deficits since World War I. *The Scandinavian Journal of Economics*, 195–222.

Barro, R. J. (2003). Determinants of economic growth in a panel of countries. *Annals of Economics and Finance, 4*, 231–274.

Bergstrand, J. H., & Egger, P. (2007). A knowledge-and-physical-capital model of international trade flows, foreign direct investment, and multinational enterprises. *Journal of International Economics, 73*(2), 278–308.

Blonigen, B. A., Davies, R. B., Waddell, G. R., & Naughton, H. T. (2007). FDI in space: Spatial autoregressive relationships in foreign direct investment. *European Economic Review, 51*(5), 1303–1325.

Blonigen, B. A. & Piger, J. (2011). *Determinants of foreign direct investment.* National Bureau of Economic Research, Working Paper 16704. https://www.nber.org/system/files/working_papers/w16704/w16704.pdf. Accessed 21 Sept 2019.

Blundell, R., Bond, S., & Windmeijer, F. (2001). *Estimation in dynamic panel data models: Improving on the performance of the standard GMM estimator.* Emerald Group Publishing Limited.

Blundell, R., & Bond, S. (1998). Initial conditions and moment restrictions in dynamic panel data models. *Journal of Econometrics, 87*(1), 115–143.

Calvo, G., & Guidotti, P. (1990). Indexation and maturity of government bonds: An exploratory model. *Public debt management: Theory and history*, 52–93.

Carey, K. (1999). Investigating a debt channel for the Smoot-Hawley tariffs: Evidence from the sovereign bond market. *The Journal of Economic History, 59*(3), 748–761.

Carleton, W. T., & Kwan, S. H. (1995). *The role of private placement debt issues in corporate finance.* Federal Reserve Bank of San Francisco, Working Papers in Applied Economic Theory, 95-13.

Carr, D. L., Markusen, J. R., & Maskus, K. E. (2001). Estimating the knowledge-capital model of the multinational enterprise. *American Economic Review, 91*(3), 693–708.

Caves, R. E. (1976). Economic models of political choice: Canada's tariff structure. *Canadian Journal of Economics, 9*(2), 278–300.

Diamond, D. W. (1991). Monitoring and reputation: The choice between bank loans and directly placed debt. *Journal of Political Economy, 99*(4), 689–721.

Georges, P. (2006). Borrowing short- or long-term: Does the government really face a trade-off?. *Public Finance and Management, 6*(2), 206–243.

Giavazzi, F., & Pagano, M. (1990). Can severe fiscal contractions be expansionary? Tales of two small European countries. *NBER Macroeconomics Annual, 5*, 75–111.

Giavazzi, F., & Missale, A. (2004). *Public debt management in Brazil*. National Bureau of Economic Research, Working Paper 10394. https://www.nber.org/papers/w10394. Accessed 21 Sept 2019.

Gilson, S. C., & Warner, J. B. (1997). Junk bonds, bank debt, and financing corporate growth. *SSRN*. https://ssrn.com/abstract=47269. Accessed 21 Sept 2019.

Hansen, S. B. (1983). *The politics of taxation: Revenue without representation*. Praeger Publishers.

Hansen, J. M. (1990). Taxation and the political economy of the tariff. *International Organization, 44*(4), 527–551.

Helleiner, G. K. (1977). The political economy of Canada's tariff structure: An alternative model. *The Canadian Journal of Economics /revue Canadienne D'economique, 10*(2), 318–326.

Hinrichs, H. H. (1966). *A general theory of tax structure change during economic development*. Harvard Law School.

Kao, C. (1999). Spurious regression and residual-based tests for cointegration in panel data. *Journal of Econometrics, 90*, 1–44.

Kau, J. B., & Rubin, P. H. (1981). The size of government. *Public Choice, 37*(2), 261–274.

Maddala, G. S., & Wu, S. (1999). A comparative study of unit root tests with panel data and a new simple test. *Oxford Bulletin of Economics and Statistics, 61*, 631–652.

Magee, S. P., Brock, W. A., & Young, L. (1989). *Black hole tariffs and endogenous policy theory: Political economy in general equilibrium*. Cambridge University Press.

Markusen, J. R., & Maskus, K. E. (2002). Discriminating among alternative theories of the multinational enterprise. *Review of International Economics, 10*(4), 694–707.

Missale, A., Giavazzi, F., & Benigno, P. (2002). How is the debt managed? Learning from fiscal stabilizations. *Scandinavian Journal of Economics, 104*(3), 443–469.

Musgrave, R. A. (1969). Cost-benefit analysis and the theory of public finance. *Journal of Economic Literature, 7*(3), 797–806.

Myers, S. C. (1984). The capital structure puzzle. *The Journal of Finance, 39*(3), 574–592.

Pedroni, P. (1999). Critical values for cointegration tests in heterogeneous panels with multiple regressors. *Oxford Bulletin of Economics and Statistics, 61*, 653–670.
Pesaran, M. H. (2003). *A simple panel unit root test in the presence of cross section dependence*. Cambridge Working Papers in Economics 346, Faculty of Economics. University of Cambridge.
Pesaran, M. H. (2004). *General diagnostic tests for cross section dependence in panels*. IZA Discussion Paper, No. 1240, Bonn.
Pesaran, M. H. (2015). *Time series and panel data econometrics*. Oxford University Press, 1104 pp. https://doi.org/10.1007/s00362-016-0816-1. Accessed 23 Nov 2020.
Rajan, R. G. (1992). Insiders and outsiders: The choice between informed and arm's-length debt. *The Journal of Finance, 47*(4), 1367–1400.
Rajan, R., & Winton, A. (1995). Covenants and collateral as incentives to monitor. *The Journal of Finance, 50*(4), 1113–1146.
Reinsch, W. A. (2018). *Can we really pay down the national debt with tariffs?* Center for Strategic and International Studies. https://www.csis.org/analysis/can-we-really-pay-down-national-debt-tariffs. Accessed 21 Sept 2019.
Schumpeter, J.A. (1918). *Die Krise des Steuerstaats*. Leuschner &Lubensky.
Stein, E., & Daude, C. (2007). Longitude matters: Time zones and the location of foreign direct investment. *Journal of International Economics, 71*(1), 96–112.
The World Bank. (2020). Data. https://data.worldbank.org/. Accessed 23 Nov 2020.
Verbeek, M. (2008). *A guide to modern econometrics*. John Wiley & Sons.
Welch, I. (1997). Why is bank debt senior? A theory of asymmetry and claim priority based on influence costs. *The Review of Financial Studies, 10*(4), 1203–1236.
Winer, S. L., & Hettich, W. (1991). Debt and tariffs—An empirical investigation of the evolutions of revenue systems. *Journal of Public Economics, 45*, 215–242.
Wolswijk, G., & De Haan, J. (2006). Government debt management in Europe: recent changes in debt managers' strategies. *Public Finance and Management, 6*(2), 244–277.
Wooldridge, J. M. (2015). *Introductory econometrics: A modern approach*. South-Western Cengage Learning.
World Trade Organization. (2019). *World Tariff Profiles*. https://www.wto.org/english/res_e/booksp_e/tariff_profiles19_e.pdf. Accessed 23 Nov 2020.

CHAPTER 4

The Impact of Demographics on the Level of Tariffs

James Ming Chen, Thomas Poufinas, Charalampos Agiropoulos, and George Galanos

4.1 Introduction

Tariffs are customs duties on imports. They aim at giving a competitive advantage to domestic goods over similar imported goods. As such they serve as a source of revenue for a government (WTO, 2020). They are used as levers that can steer the level of imports and exports between two countries. They can be used to implement a trade policy that taxes foreign goods and privileges domestic production.

J. M. Chen (✉)
College of Law, Michigan State University, East Lansing, MI, USA
e-mail: chenjame@law.msu.edu

T. Poufinas
Department of Economics, Democritus University of Thrace, Komotini, Greece

C. Agiropoulos · G. Galanos
Department of International and European Studies, University of Piraeus, Piraeus, Greece

T. Poufinas (ed.), *Debt in Times of Crisis*,
https://doi.org/10.1007/978-3-030-74162-4_4

Besides being a source of income, tariffs can be used to protect local production and spur domestic output in place of imports. As a result they can contribute to the reduction of the trade deficit. It has recently been debated whether they can be used to reduce the government debt of a country (CSIS, 2018). Chapter 3 acknowledged a relation between tariffs and debt.

Demographic changes and forces seem to affect the debt of a country as they influence the labor force, the shift of manufacturing to certain countries, wages, membership in trade unions, inflation and interest rates (Goodhart & Pradhan, 2017). At the same time demographic factors affect the explicit and implicit tax flows (Hagist et al., 2009) that a government can secure in order to service its debt obligations.

Concurrently, certain demographic factors influence the tariffs imposed by governments. Tariff policy and its evaluation must account for the movement of labor, as well as the movement of goods and services. The European Union, for example, guarantees the free movement of labor. This commitment can be seen as an incentive to enter or exit from the EU. The EU also favors zero tariffs; in 2018 almost 70% of the imports in the EU bore zero tariffs (Eurostat, 2020).

The link between trade liberalization and labor market dynamics suggests that labor, especially in developing countries, may shift from industries that compete against imports to export industries (Turrini, 2002). Wealthier countries systematically impose higher tariffs on inelastically demanded goods where domestic producers exert greater market power (Broda et al., 2008). The prevalence of this effect prior to a country's accession to the World Trade Organization, and even afterward with respect to trade restrictions not addressed by the WTO Treaty, provides strong evidence that domestic producers with market power exert potent political influence over the formulation of noncooperative, anticompetitive trade policy (ibid.).

Moreover, there appears to be a positive correlation between trade openness and unemployment in OECD countries and a negative correlation in non-OECD countries (Turrini, 2002). There is further evidence that trade openness affects the labor market (WTO, 2017). The effect of the reversal of trade liberalization on employment has also been questioned (Ernst et al., 2019). These findings suggest that labor demographics may affect tariffs.

Migration could also affect the level of tariffs. The presence of a large number of immigrants in one country is often correlated with an increase in bilateral trade between the host and home countries of the migrants. Studies indicate that the impact of migration on merchandise trade tends to slightly favor the host country. This negative impact on the trade balance of the home country can be offset by remittances, trade in services and foreign direct investment (Migration Data Portal, 2019).

In Chapter 3 we realized that tariffs can have an impact on debt. Through a series of econometric models and machine learning techniques, this chapter examines whether demographics affect the level of tariffs. Depending on the model and the database, population and labor force may affect the level of tariffs. These findings align with the literature and our own intuitions. However, migration does not seem to influence tariffs. Furthermore, income per capita and consumption evidently affect the tariff rate. The relationship of the tariff rate to imports, exports and the tax rate is also established. Finding the link between tariff rates and demography can potentially explain some of the tariff moves, besides the exogenous decisions made by governments. This may be the most important contribution of our study.

4.2 Literature Review

"The ability to tax lies at the very heart of political power and the rise of the modern political state was shaped by fiscal evolution in medieval and postmedieval times." Joseph Schumpeter (1918) reached this conclusion at the dawn of modern macroeconomic science. Although he did not provide a framework to determine potential interactions shaping public revenue systems, he identified three distinct types of influences: (i) economic, (ii) political, and (iii) administrative. The clarity of Schumpeter's boundaries among these categories may have arisen from his failure, at least as of 1918, to form an economic theory of political action.

It was not until the late 1960s that other scholars started engaging Schumpeter's analysis in earnest. His essay was published in the German language and had little influence in the English-speaking scientific community. Hinrichs (1966) was mainly interested in linking stages of economic and fiscal development. He argued that the prime determinant of customs revenue was a country's openness to trade. Openness meant increased trade and therefore a rise in customs revenue if trade was being taxed at all. Another study by Hinrichs (1965) found that openness to trade also drove increases in total government revenue, particularly for low-income countries that drew a large share of revenue from taxes on foreign trade.

Musgrave (1969) argued that the lack of "tax handles," or administratively simple ways of collecting revenue, might limit revenue collection at low levels of income. He noted, however, that these limitations should become less severe as the economy develops. Most attempts to account for the share of tax revenue in GDP perform regression with proxies for possible tax handles.

Some further contributions were made in the 1970 and 1980s. Kau and Rubin (1981) highlighted the economic limits to fiscal development and the effects of changes in such limits on the growth of revenue systems. They also speculated whether collecting the taxes in urban areas may be less costly. Kau and Rubin (1981), Hettich and Winer (1988) similarly argued that "more efficient" taxation results in a larger government. Hansen (1983) focused on the impact of political factors on the tax system, while a separate literature examined selected revenue sources such as tariffs.

Caves (1976) and Helleiner (1977) analyzed Canadian tariffs. Conybeare (1978) applied a combination of the techniques employed by Caves and Helliener. Anderson (1980), proceeded along similar lines in investigating why some industries receive more government assistance than others. Both Anderson (1980) and Conybeare (1978) used cross-sectional data and multiple regression in their attempts to explain the structure of tariffs in Australia.

Magee et al. (1989) have identified three broad genres of economic theories seeking to explain the existence of protectionist trade policies. These scholars developed a complete general equilibrium theory that explains how well-organized groups manipulate government policies to exploit poorly organized rival groups. However, tariffs are usually a relatively inefficient means of achieving common policy objectives (Vousden, 1990).

Furthermore, Magee et al. (1989) have hypothesized that lobbying over tariffs would not damage welfare through high tariffs. They asserted that the political economy of trade would instead create a black hole threatening to engulf domestic productivity through the costs of bickering over tariffs and their levels. Later scholarship contested this conclusion, finding strong evidence that market power works in concert with political influence to raise tariffs on imports competing against domestically produced but inelastically demanded goods (Broda et al., 2008).

Additional contributions during the 1980s included Paul Krugman's (1987) model of learning-by-doing. Gene M. Grossman and Elhanan Helpman's (1991) endogenous growth models with research and development externalities highlighted the possibility that tariffs might be used to raise national income, provided that the appropriate industry is chosen for protection.

In the 1990s and 2000s, scholars contested the impact of tariffs on growth. Edwards (1992, 1998) and Clemens and Williamson (2004) found a negative impact, whereas Vamvakidis (2002), Yanikkaya (2003) and DeJong and Ripoll (2006) found a positive impact.

The most recent contributions have analyzed the theoretical effects of introducing a tariff. Mankiw (2020) described how a tariff decreases domestic consumption (by raising the price of imports), but increases domestic production (by raising the price that sellers can obtain). Tariffs therefore have three basic effects in the domestic economy: (i) to make consumers worse off; (ii) to make producers better off; and (iii) to raise revenue for the government. Despite the purely theoretical disadvantages of tariffs, Mankiw evaluated five arguments favoring their introduction; jobs, national security, infant industries, unfair competition and bargaining strategy.

The majority of academic economists oppose tariffs in principle (Worstall, 2016). However, this is not a unanimous view. For instance, Pettis (2018) has argued that most economic discussions of tariffs are more ideological than logical, and that what matters are the conditions under which trade intervention policies are made. The idea that all countries lose in a trade war is logically impossible, Pettis has asserted. Rather, tariffs can have a wide variety of economic effects.

Through empirical evaluation of the impact of demographic factors on tariff levels, this study seeks to harmonize observed tariff policy across 45 diverse countries with the competing, often contradictory predictions of the theoretical literature. Domestic factors such as per capita income and population will prove to carry greater weight than net migration or its impact on the labor force.

4.3 Data, Variables and Methodology

Our empirical analysis relies on two alternative theoretical pillars. The first pillar stands for the traditional econometric approach. More specifically, this study implements three econometric models: pooled OLS, fixed effects and random effects.

The second pillar uses machine learning techniques. Despite their interpretive clarity, generalized linear methods and other conventional econometric tools may not provide the most accurate description of relationships among economic variables or predict as yet unseen instances of a phenomenon. Certain machine learning methods excel in evaluating data that exhibit nonlinear relationships or arise from non-Gaussian stochastic processes (Breiman, 2001).

The "no free lunch" theorem of machine learning posits that data scientists cannot tell in advance which model is best suited to a particular dataset or predictive goal (Wolpert, 1996). A priori assumptions cannot supplant experimentation. Accordingly, we believe that it is prudent to reach beyond conventional econometrics and to apply multiple families of machine learning methods. We propose to apply algorithms based on decision trees and support vector machines.

4.3.1 Data

The panel dataset includes 45 countries (OECD and G20) for the period 2000–2018: Argentina, Australia, Austria, Belgium, Brazil, Canada, Chile, China, Colombia, Czech Republic, Denmark, Estonia, Finland, France, Germany, Greece, Hungary, Iceland, India, Indonesia, Ireland, Israel, Italy, Japan, Korea, Rep., Latvia, Lithuania, Luxembourg, Mexico, Netherlands, New Zealand, Norway, Poland, Portugal, Russian Federation, Saudi Arabia, Slovak Republic, Slovenia, South Africa, Spain, Sweden, Switzerland, Turkey, United Kingdom and the United States. The reason for choosing the specific period and the countries are strictly dictated by data availability.

4.3.2 Variables

This study uses the weighted mean applied tariff (TAR), which is the average of effectively applied rates weighted by the product import shares corresponding to each partner country, as the dependent variable for all three econometric models. The set of independent variables for the selected countries includes the natural logarithm of the adjusted net national Income (lINC) per capita, the total labor force (lLF), the net migration (lMIG) and the total population. We also include exports of goods and services (EXP), final consumption expenditures (CONS), net inflows of foreign direct investment (FDI) and imports of goods and services (IMP), each as a percentage of the relevant country's GDP.

All the above variables have been derived from the World Bank open access dataset.[1] Table 4.1 reports the main summary statistics of all variables used in the econometric approach.

From Table 4.1, it is evident that the sample data are well behaved showing controlled variability in relation to the mean of the population since the ratio of the standard deviation over the average is in most cases close to zero either between or within the panel dataset.

Figure 4.1 visualizes the dependent and independent variables through histograms and kernel density estimates.

One of the additional complications that arise when dealing with panel data, as opposed to time series, is the possibility that the sample variables or the random disturbances are correlated across the panel (Pesaran, 2015). The early literature on unit root and cointegration tests adopted the assumption of no cross-sectional dependence. However, it is common for macro-level data to violate this assumption, which will result in low power and size distortions of tests that assume cross-section independence (Polemis & Tsionas, 2019). For example, cross-section dependence in our data may arise as a result of common unobserved effects due to changes in countries' migration policies. We tackle this issue by employing the proper tests to investigate the existence of cross-sectional dependence in our sample (CD test).

To examine the stationarity properties of the variables in our models, we use the second-generation panel unit root tests developed by Maddala and Wu (1999) and Pesaran (2004). These tests are suitable for balanced panel dataset and cross-section dependence. The null hypothesis of a unit root (non-stationarity) cannot be rejected for all the sample variables. This means that the variables contain a unit root (e.g. integrated of order one) as expected by the visual inspection of their time series. In order to investigate whether a long-run equilibrium relationship exists among

[1] https://data.worldbank.org/.

Table 4.1 Descriptive statistics

Variable		*Mean*	*Std.Dev.*	*Min*	*Max*	*Observations*		
TAR	overall	3254	2857	0.49	26.51	N	=	855
	between		2299	1546	11.7	n	=	45
	within		1729	−3567	18.06	T	=	19
lINC	overall	9628	1039	5958	11.32	N	=	855
	between		0.981	6789	10.96	n	=	45
	within		0.372	8158	10.68	T	=	19
EXP	overall	43.96	29.62	9043	221.2	N	=	855
	between		28.88	11.52	179.3	n	=	45
	within		7787	3524	85.82	T	=	19
CONS	overall	73.73	8413	42.92	91.67	N	=	855
	between		8015	50.14	87.84	n	=	45
	within		2.81	57.91	87.49	T	=	19
FDI	overall	4632	9479	−58.32	86.59	N	=	855
	between		5288	0.253	23.44	n	=	45
	within		7905	−76.42	67.78	T	=	19
IMP	overall	41.42	25.26	9.195	187.2	N	=	855
	between		24.79	12.87	149	n	=	45
	within		6.026	7.667	79.63	T	=	19
lLF	overall	16.1	1764	12.04	20.48	N	=	855
	between		1781	12.14	20.46	n	=	45
	within		0.0799	15.69	16.48	T	=	19
lMIG	overall	12.15	1745	6159	15.52	N	=	622
	between		1.695	7774	15.45	n	=	38
	within		0.596	7828	14.23	T	=	16.37
lPOP	overall	16.83	1791	12.55	21.05	N	=	855
	between		1809	12.65	21.01	n	=	45
	within		0.0566	16.57	17.06	T	=	19
TAXC	overall	46.68	18.57	14.6	182.3	N	=	855
	between		17.12	15.14	110.9	n	=	45
	within		7612	23.97	165.8	T	=	19

Note TAR: Tariff rate, applied, weighted mean, all products (%), lINC: Adjusted net national income per capita (current US$), EXP: Exports of goods and services (% of GDP), CONS: Final consumption expenditure (% of GDP), FDI: Foreign direct investment, net inflows (% of GDP), IMP: Imports of goods and services (% of GDP), lLF: Labor force, total, lMIG: Net migration, lPOP: Population, total, TAXC: Total tax and contribution rate (% of profit)
Source Authors' calculations based on Eurostat and World Bank data, 2019

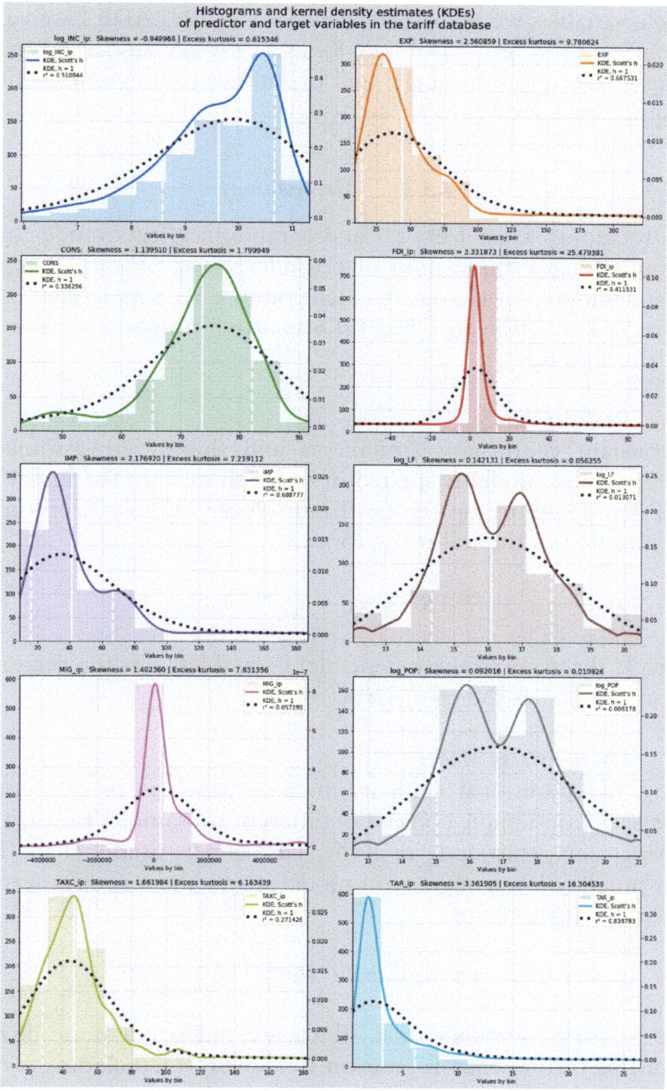

Fig. 4.1 Graphical visualization of the dependent and independent variables using histograms and density estimates (*Source* Authors' calculations)

the sample variables we implement Pedroni's (1999) ADF-based and PP-based cointegration tests as well as Kao's (1999) ADF-based tests. Both tests suggest the rejection of the null hypothesis of no cointegration null at any significance level.

4.3.3 Methodology

This study adopts a fixed effects and a random effects model to properly account for the imposition of possible effects on tariff rate due to structural demographic changes in each country. We supplement our analysis by using a traditional pooled OLS method in order to compare and contrast our findings.

4.3.3.1 Pooled OLS

When constant coefficients (intercepts and slopes) are assumed then Pooled regression model is applied in order to capture the initial dependance of demographics on the tariff rate. Pooled OLS regression model can be presented in the following form:

$$TAR_{it} = \beta_0 + x_{it}^{'}\beta + u_{it} \tag{4.1}$$

where, $x_{it}^{'}$ is the array of the independent variables, β is the vector of the coefficients and u_{it} is the error term.

4.3.3.2 Fixed Effects Model

Following the traditional OLS estimation, which is usually employed when the selection sample consists of different subsamples for each period of the panel data, this study uses the fixed effects model (FE). The FE model is simply a linear regression model where the intercept terms vary over the individual units *i*:

$$y_{it} = a_i + x_{it}^{'}\beta + \varepsilon_{it}, \varepsilon_{it} \sim IID\left(0, \sigma_\varepsilon^2\right) \tag{4.2}$$

where it is usually assumed that all x_{it} are independent of all ε_{it}. We can write this in the usual regression framework by including a dummy variable for each unit *i* in the model (Verbeek, 2008):

$$y_{it} = \sum_{j=1}^{N} a_j d_{ij} x_{it}^{'}\beta + \varepsilon_{it} \tag{4.2}$$

where $d_{ij} = 0$ when $i = j$ and 0 elsewhere.

We have also assumed the strictly exogenous regressors case in the conditional moments (Woolridge, 2009). We have not assumed equal-sized groups in the panel. The vector β is a set of parameters of primary interest. α_j is the group-specific heterogeneity. Although we have included time-specific effects, they prove to be only tangential. Since the number of periods is usually fairly small, these can usually be accommodated simply through the addition of a set of time-specific dummy variables. We are interested in the case in which N is too large to do likewise for group effects.

4.3.3.3 Random Effects Model

Fixed or random effects are employed when the panel dataset includes the same sample of countries (Woolridge, 2009). Because this study covers 45 countries from 2000 to 2018, the use of both fixed and random effects modeling is advised. In addition, it is commonly assumed in regression analysis (Verbeek, 2008) that all factors affecting the dependent variable, but that have not been included as regressors, can be appropriately summarized by a random error term. In our case, this leads to the assumption that the α_i are random factors, independently and identically distributed over individual observations.

Therefore, the random effects model can be written as:

$$y_{it} = \mu + a_i + x_{it}^{'}\beta + \varepsilon_{it}, \varepsilon_{it} \sim IID\left(0, \sigma_{\varepsilon}^2\right); \alpha_i \sim IID\left(0, \sigma_{\alpha}^2\right) \quad (4.3)$$

where $a_i + \varepsilon_{it}$ is treated as an error term consisting of two components: an individual specific component, which does not vary over time, and a remainder component, which is assumed to be uncorrelated over time. It is also assumed that a_i and ε_{it} are mutually independent and independent of x_{js} (for all j and s).

4.3.3.4 Machine Learning

Data Preparation

The supervised machine learning methods applied to this dataset required the splitting of data into randomized subsets for training and test. This practice, rarely followed in conventional econometrics, ensures that machine learning methods do not merely memorize labels or values associated with data to be predicted (Müller & Guido, 2016, pp. 17–18).

Holding out a fraction of the dataset for testing helps ensure the generalizability of any supervised machine learning model to data not seen during training (ibid.). In accordance with these recommended practices, we split our data into training and test subsets containing 75 and 25 percent, respectively, of the entire dataset and will report training and test results separately.

To ensure reproducible results, we set a seed of 1 for SciKit-Learn's pseudo-random number generator. This random seed governed not only the splitting of data into training and test subsets, but also the inherently stochastic processes underlying the random forest and extra trees algorithms.

Many machine learning algorithms perform more accurately when data is scaled (Müller & Guido, 2016, pp. 134–142). We applied standard scaling to training data. In other words, our machine learning methods evaluated all and reported all results in terms of Gaussian *z*-scores, or multiples of a dependent or independent variable's standard deviation from its mean. Care must be taken to withhold the test data while scaling the training data and then applying the scale of the training data to the test data, lest data leakage contaminates all predictive tests (ibid., pp. 138–140).

Bias, Variance, and Hyperparameter Tuning

Proper use of machine learning requires careful management of the *bias–variance* tradeoff. This dilemma arises from an intrinsic property of all supervised machine learning models: Greater inaccuracy, or bias, in the estimates of a model's parameters can reduce the variance among parameter estimates across samples (Kohavi & Wolpert, 1996). While excessive bias reduces a model's accuracy during training, excessive variance hampers efforts to apply supervised machine learning more generally beyond the data on which a machine learning algorithm has been trained (Geman et al., 1992).

Roughly speaking, *bias* refers to a method's overall accuracy, particularly in training. Excessive bias results in a model that *underfits* its data. Accurate as certain models may be during training, such as high-degree polynomial models, models overfit to training data do not provide reliable results unless they generalize well to new, unseen data. High-variance models tend to *overfit* training data. *Variance* therefore affects the generalizability and consistency of results with new data.

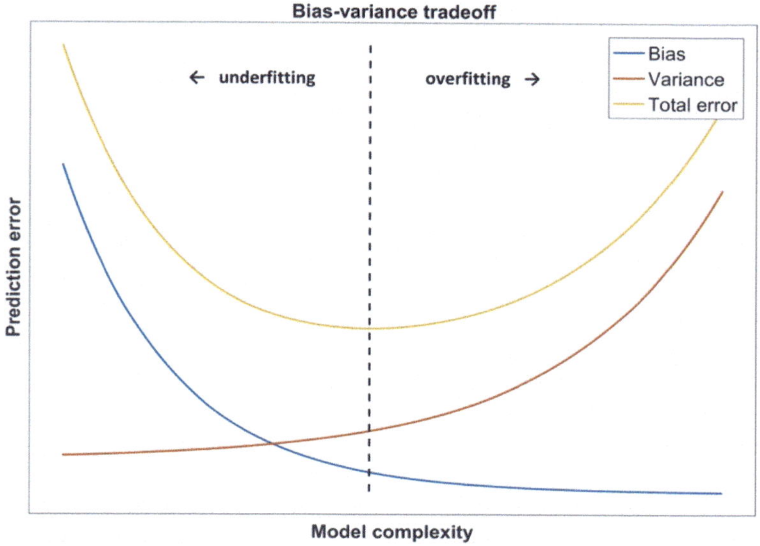

Fig. 4.2 Bias-variance tradeoff illustration (*Source* Kubben et al., 2019, p. 107, Fig. 8.3)

Figure 4.2 illustrates the bias–variance tradeoff as a quest to minimize prediction error (Kubben et al., 2019, p. 107, Fig. 8.3). At the optimal level of complexity, a model strikes the best attainable balance between under- and overfitting.

In practice, the problem is that most machine learning models offer a wide, sometimes daunting, list of adjustable hyperparameters (Géron, 2019, pp. 31–32). If these settings are not properly tuned, a machine learning model may fall far short of its predictive potential. We obtained all of our machine learning results through a grid search of each algorithm's hyperparameter space and *k*-folds cross-validation (Müller & Guido, 2016, pp. 258–282).

Trees, Forests, and Support Vector Machines

The classification and regression tree (CART) algorithm is the basis for a dazzling constellation of machine learning methods (Breiman et al., 1984; Loh, 2014). Decision trees and ensembles of decision trees often outperform linear regression. They are not limited to linear relationships. All decision tree-based algorithms are robust in the presence of outliers. These algorithms are also quite forgiving of misspecified models. The inclusion of weakly predictive or even wholly non-predictive variables generally does not weaken a decision tree or tree-based ensemble.

Among ensemble and boosting methods based on aggregations of decision trees, random forests are perhaps the simplest (Ho, 1995). Random forests require the tuning of only two hyperparameters: the maximum number of features that a randomized tree may contain, plus the maximum depth of each tree (or the number of splits we will allow within each tree). Randomizing the threshold for each predictor yields an even more diversified algorithm called ***extremely random trees***, or extra trees (Geurts et al., 2006).

The tuning of hyperparameters for these ensemble models can be visualized vividly in three dimensions (Figs 4.3 and 4.4):

One weakness of decision trees and tree-based ensemble methods is that they are not amenable to evaluation according to p-values and conventional tests of statistical significance. But the contribution of each predictive variable can be quantified. All tree-based methods in SciKit-Learn report "feature importances," a vector of values whose sum is 1 and whose individual values correspond to each regressor's contribution to the model's predictions (Géron, 2019, pp. 198–199). Specifically, feature importances in SciKit-Learn "is a weighted average, where each node's weight" in a decision tree or across all trees in a forest "is equal to the number of training samples that are associated with it" (ibid., p. 198).

We will also report results from support vector machine regression (Géron, 2019, pp. 153–174). This powerful and versatile class of machine learning algorithms has been applied to a wide range of regression tasks, including time series prediction of stock returns (Yang et al., 2002). Support vector machine regression performs especially well with complicated, "highly nonlinear objects" (Balabin & Lomakina, 2011, pp. 1710–1711). Although support vector machines do not report feature importances, they provide additional validation of results obtained through traditional econometric methods and through decision tree-based ensemble methods such as random forests and extra trees.

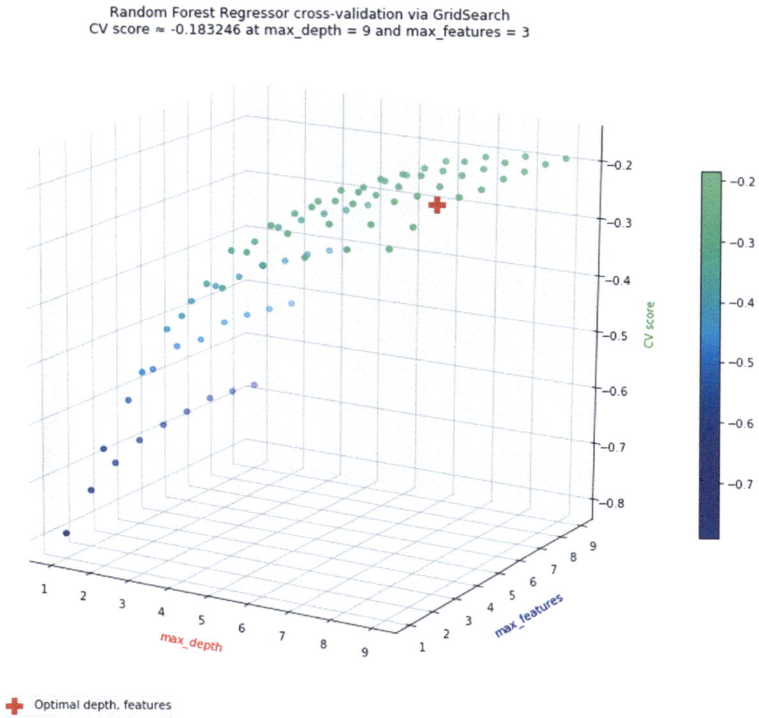

Fig. 4.3 Random Forest Regressor hyperparameters visualization in three dimensions (*Source* Authors' calculations)

4.4 Results and Result Interpretation

4.4.1 Econometric Models

The regressions reveal some of the relations as anticipated, whereas some others seem to run in a different direction. Tariffs appear to be negatively correlated with (the logarithm of adjusted national) income per capita at all significance levels in all three models (pooled OLS, fixed effects and random effects). Table 4.2 illustrates the correlation matrix of the dependent and independent variables. They exhibit a positive correlation with exports (as a percent of GDP) at the 5% significance level according to the pooled OLS approach. They appear to be positively correlated with

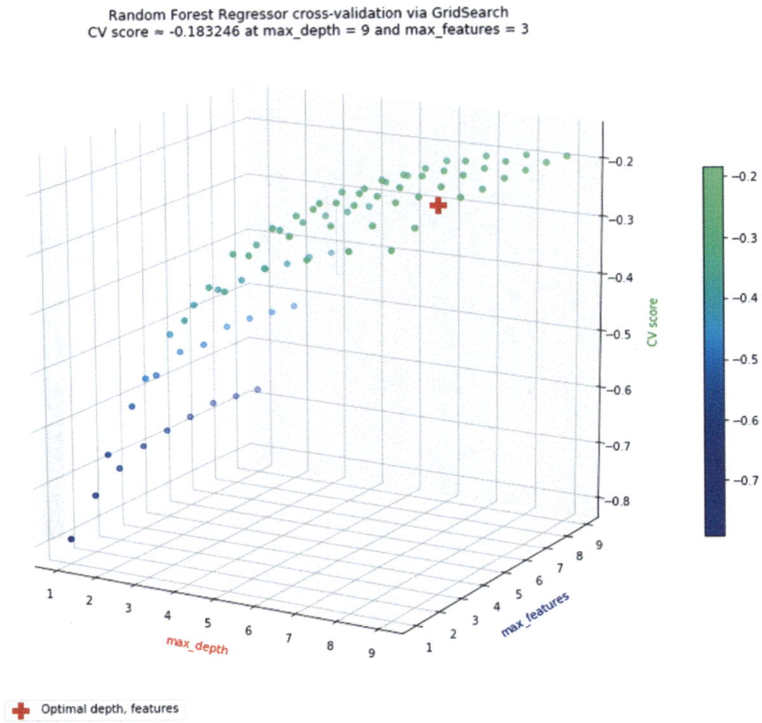

Fig. 4.4 Extra Trees Regressor hyperparameters visualization in three dimensions (*Source* Authors' calculations)

consumption (as a percent of GDP) at all significance levels in the fixed effects model.

Tariffs are negatively correlated with imports (as a percent of GDP) at all significance levels according to the pooled OLS method. They are negatively correlated with the (logarithm of the) population at all significance levels in the fixed effects model. They are positively correlated with the corporate tax rate at the 10% significance level within the pooled OLS method. The constant term seems to be statistically significant at all levels for all models. The rest of the variables exhibit no statistical significance. Nevertheless for robustness reasons this study has retained these variables to cross-check model's fit.

Table 4.2 Correlation table

Variables	*TAR*	*lINC*	*EXP*	*CONS*	*FDI*	*IMP*	*lLF*	*lMIG*	*lPOP*	*TAXC*
TAR	1									
lINC	−0.591[a]	1								
EXP	−0.303[a]	0.309[a]	1							
CONS	−0.0511	−0.0682	−0.551[a]	1						
FDI	−0.108[a]	0.137[a]	0.407[a]	−0.243[a]	1					
IMP	−0.347[a]	0.281[a]	0.974[a]	−0.415[a]	0.396[a]	1				
lLF	0.425[a]	−0.447[a]	−0.613[a]	0.0575	−0.213[a]	−0.648[a]	1			
lMIG	0.0383	0.023[a]	−0.404[a]	0.139[a]	−0.156[a]	−0.442[a]	0.712	1		
lPOP	0.436[a]	−0.469[a]	−0.608[a]	0.0618	−0.212[a]	−0.643[a]	0.998[a]	0.717	1	
TAXC	0.338[a]	−0.326[a]	−0.339[a]	0.241[a]	−0.109[a]	−0.320[a]	0.369[a]	0.114[a]	0.368[a]	1

Note [a]significant at 1%, TAR: Tariff rate, applied, weighted mean, all products (%), lINC: Adjusted net national income per capita (current US$), EXP: Exports of goods and services (% of GDP), CONS: Final consumption expenditure (% of GDP), FDI: Foreign direct investment, net inflows (% of GDP), IMP: Imports of goods and services (% of GDP), lLF: Labor force, total, lMIG: Net migration, lPOP: Population, total, TAXC: Total tax and contribution rate (% of profit)

Source Authors' calculations based on Eurostat and World Bank data, 2019

A possible interpretation of the negative relation of the level of tariffs with income is that when the citizens' income per capita increases, then the income tax collected is probably sufficient to cover the needs of the government. Consequently, the government does not have to levy tariffs to supplement its flows.

Alternatively, one might argue that low tariff rates are an artifact of high-income economies, in line with neoclassical predictions that free trade and a political commitment to comparative advantage should raise each nation's productivity and per capita income. Indeed, dissimilar social communities could react differently in the light of low tariff rates. It is still unclear and needs further investigation of the causality of the relationship among tariff rates and income per capita.

The positive relation of tariffs with consumption probably arises from the fact that when consumption increases, then the purchase of foreign goods and services rises relative to their domestic equivalents. Perhaps domestic production does not fully cover demand. Alternatively, consumers may favor imports because of their quality or stylishness. As a result, a government may impose tariffs in order to support or protect domestic products.

As it can be seen from Table 4.3, the negative relation of the level of tariffs with the population may be explained with an argument similar to the one offered for income. The bigger the population is, the more the taxes collected are. Hence, the government may rely more on direct and indirect taxes than on tariffs imposed on imports.

The aforementioned signs could be possibly expected as a matter of intuition. Nevertheless, the signs of the coefficients of exports, imports and taxes need more careful consideration. When exports increase, a country might increase tariffs to safeguard the benefit achieved through a positive balance of trade. Alternatively, another country might raise tariffs in response to increased trade. The latter interpretation is supported by observations within the pooled OLS approach.

As for imports, it appears that tariff rates increase when imports (as a percentage of GDP) decrease. This does not seem to be a paradox since an increase in tariff rates, imports are expected to drop too. Evidence for this relationship may appear in the pooled OLS approach. Alternatively, an increase or decrease of imports as a percentage of GDP might coincide with a decrease or increase on tariff rates (especially in the EU). This final possibility emerges in pooled OLS, but not in the other models.

Table 4.3 Regression summary

VARIABLES	*(1) (Pooled OLS)*	*(2) (Fixed Effects)*	*(3) (Random Effects)*
lINC_ip	-1.478^{***}	-1.621^{***}	-1.849^{***}
	(0.426)	(0.263)	(0.622)
EXP	0.0931^{**}	0.0133	0.0483
	(0.0389)	(0.0187)	(0.0426)
CONS	−0.0122	0.0920^{***}	0.0593
	(0.0450)	(0.0330)	(0.0514)
FDI_ip	0.00514	−0.00189	−0.00122
	(0.00764)	(0.00350)	(0.00266)
IMP	-0.125^{***}	−0.0183	−0.0696
	(0.0377)	(0.0237)	(0.0499)
lLF	−0.0804	4.998	−0.0856
	(1.880)	(3.297)	(4.741)
Perc_MIG_ip	2.986	−0.636	0.759
	(4.028)	(1.082)	(1.814)
lPOP	0.0987	-13.68^{***}	−0.0183
	(1.842)	(4.146)	(4.733)
TAXC_ip	0.0226^{*}	0.00665	0.00631
	(0.0117)	(0.00852)	(0.0110)
Constant	18.00^{***}	161.7^{***}	18.84^{**}
	(4.660)	(25.61)	(7.699)
Observations	855	855	855
R-squared	0.462	0.744	0.721
Country FE	YES	YES	YES
Number of Country Code			45

Robust standard errors in parentheses
$^{***}p < 0.01$, $^{**}p < 0.05$, $^{*}p < 0.1$
Note TAR: Tariff rate, applied, weighted mean, all products (%), lINC: Adjusted net national income per capita (current US$), EXP: Exports of goods and services (% of GDP), CONS: Final consumption expenditure (% of GDP), FDI: Foreign direct investment, net inflows (% of GDP), IMP: Imports of goods and services (% of GDP), lLF: Labor force, total, lMIG: Net migration, lPOP: Population, total, TAXC: Total tax and contribution rate (% of profit)
Source Authors' calculations based on Eurostat and World Bank data, 2019

Finally, positive correlation between tariff rates and domestic tax rates may be ascribed to the possibility that a country might elect to increase or decrease the two rates simultaneously. This positive correlation appears only within the pooled OLS model. A simultaneous increase of both rates may arise from an effort to exploit all sources of income at the same time.

In addition, countries with higher tax rates may tend to apply higher tariff rates, since tariffs also constitute a form of taxation.

Finally, we remark that migration seems to have no statistically significant impact on the level of tariffs. As we noted in the introduction, this is not necessarily paradoxical. Although the host country seems to benefit slightly more than a migrant's country of origin, financial flows returning to the home country compensate for its competitive disadvantage. Consequently, neither the host country nor the country of origin needs to change its tariffs: the host country most likely benefits upfront, whereas the country of origin benefits later.

4.4.1.1 Robustness Check

As a robustness check, we ran a series of regressions with each of the demographic variables separately in order to validate their impact on tariffs. We used the fixed effects model, as it exhibited the highest R^2 among the previously used models. We dropped the imports and exports from our control variables and we kept only the control variables that are closer to demography, such as income per capita and consumption. We also maintained the tax rate as relevant to the tariff rate (Table 4.4).

Our findings are in line with the discoveries of Table 4.3. The tariff rate is negatively correlated with income and positively correlated with consumption at all significance levels. The tax rate is positively correlated with the tariff rate at the 10% significance level only in the model that includes migration.

When the population is included, then it is negatively related with the tariff rate at all significance levels. If the labor force is used as an independent variable, then it is negatively correlated with the tariff rate at all significance levels. Migration seems to have no statistical significance.

The explanation is the same as the one offered above for the base model. The only variable that showed a statistical significance when inserted is the labor force. Its negative coefficient can be explained in a manner similar to the negative coefficient of the population: The higher the labor force becomes, the more taxes the government collects. Consequently, the government does not need to increase its tariff rate. Moreover, the productive capacity of such a country could increase (as the labor increases) and it needs to further foster its exports. As a result, such a country may even seek tariff reduction agreements with other countries so as to boost exports.

Table 4.4 Regression summary—robustness check

VARIABLES	*(2)* *(FE)*	*(4)* *(FE)*	*(6)* *(FE)*	*(8)* *(FE)*	*(10)* *(FE)*
lINC_ip	−1.526***	−2.047***	−1.592***	−2.084***	−1.491***
	(0.261)	(0.324)	(0.220)	(0.241)	(0.208)
CONS	0.079***	0.075***	0.035**	0.074***	0.084***
	(0.024)	(0.024)	(0.017)	(0.024)	(0.025)
TAXC_ip	0.005	0.004	0.013*	0.004	0.006
	(0.008)	(0.007)	(0.007)	(0.007)	(0.009)
lLF	−4.553***				
	(1.047)				
Perc_LF		−1.676			
		(6.905)			
lMIG_ip			−0.055		
			(0.071)		
Perc_MIG_ip				−0.711	
				(1.101)	
lPOP					−7.796***
					(1.334)
Constant	85.220***	18.090***	16.281***	17.668***	142.311***
	(15.770)	(3.135)	(2.880)	(2.816)	(21.913)
Observations	855	855	622	855	855
R-squared	0.734	0.723	0.802	0.723	0.742
Country FE	YES	YES	YES	YES	YES

Robust standard errors in parentheses
*** $p < 0.01$, ** $p < 0.05$, * $p < 0.1$

Note TAR: Tariff rate, applied, weighted mean, all products (%), lINC: Adjusted net national income per capita (current US$), EXP: Exports of goods and services (% of GDP), CONS: Final consumption expenditure (% of GDP), FDI: Foreign direct investment, net inflows (% of GDP), IMP: Imports of goods and services (% of GDP), lLF: Labor force, total, lMIG: Net migration, lPOP: Population, total, TAXC: Total tax and contribution rate (% of profit)

Source Authors' calculations based on Eurostat and World Bank data, 2019

4.4.2 *Machine Learning Techniques*

Our baseline machine learning model is a naked CART decision tree with a maximum depth of seven levels:

At least during training, this decision tree performed admirably in learning the relationships between tariffs and their predictor variables. It attained an r^2 value of 0.910506 on training data and an adjusted r^2 of 0.909229. When applied to the test data subset, however, the basic decision tree's performance fell to 0.731493 and 0.719647, respectively.

The application of two basic tree-based ensemble methods, random forests and extra trees, dramatically improved test set performance. The random forest and extra trees algorithms, respectively, raised r^2 to 0.817135 and 0.849846. Adjusted r^2 for the two algorithms remained above 0.8 at 0.809067 and 0.843221, respectively.

As with the basic decision tree, both tree-based ensembles exhibited some vulnerability to overfitting. Training set performance approached r^2 values of 1.00 in both instances (specifically, 0.962549 and 0.970420). The test set scores are more representative of these ensemble methods' generalizability to unseen data. We would therefore stand on firmer ground in asserting that tree-based ensembles for supervised machine learning can account for roughly 0.8–0.85 of the variance in tariff rates.

Of arguably greater importance to the interpretation of the predictive model are the vectors of feature importances for all three of these tree- or forest-based methods (Figs. 4.5, 4.6 and 4.7):

The three sets of feature importances confirm the linear methods' identification of statistically significant factors. The same four variables—the logarithm of per capita income, imports, the logarithm of population and the corporate tax rate—dominate all three vectors of feature importances. Among these four predictors, per capita income carries by far the most weight. Two other variables found to have statistical significance, consumption and exports, trail these four leading predictors. Finally, labor force, migration and foreign direct investment—the variables lacking statistical significance in the pooled OLS, fixed effects or random effects models failed to sway any of the tree-based machine learning models.

Among the three sets of feature importances, the vector associated with the extra trees method warrants closer attention, because that method outperforms the basic decision tree and random forests by a considerable margin. The extra trees vector suggests that per capita income outweighs the next most important feature, importance, by a ratio of roughly three to one.

Our support vector regression results are in line with the tree- and forest-based methods. Support vector regression reported an r^2 value of 0.930280 during training and an adjusted r^2 of 0.929286. Among machine learning methods applied in this study, the support vector machine proved most resistant to overfitting. It yielded a test set r^2 of 0.847865 and adjusted r^2 of 0.841153. Although the eponymous support vectors of this model do not bolster the interpretability of its

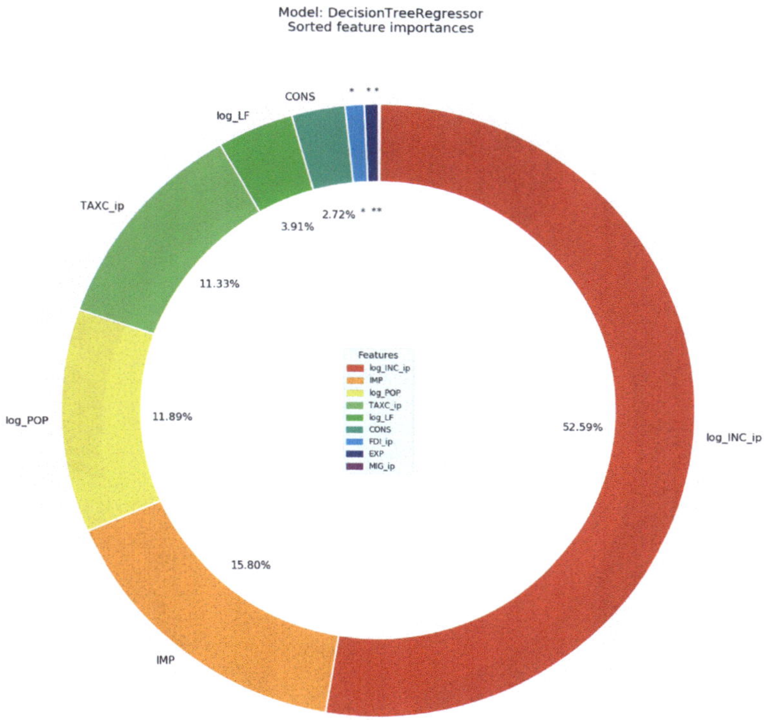

Fig. 4.5 Feature importances for Decision Tree Regressor model (*Source* Authors' calculation)

results, their dual coefficients and vector means can be computed and visualized as a three-dimensional plot where the x-axis assigns a unique integer value to each of the observations in the subset of training data (Fig. 4.8):

Table 4.5 reports training and test set results for each of the machine learning algorithms.

Figure 4.9 summarizes observed and fitted values for training and test sets for each of the four algorithms. No machine learning model performs particularly well in fitting extremely high tariff rates, whose z-scores approach or exceed $+4$.

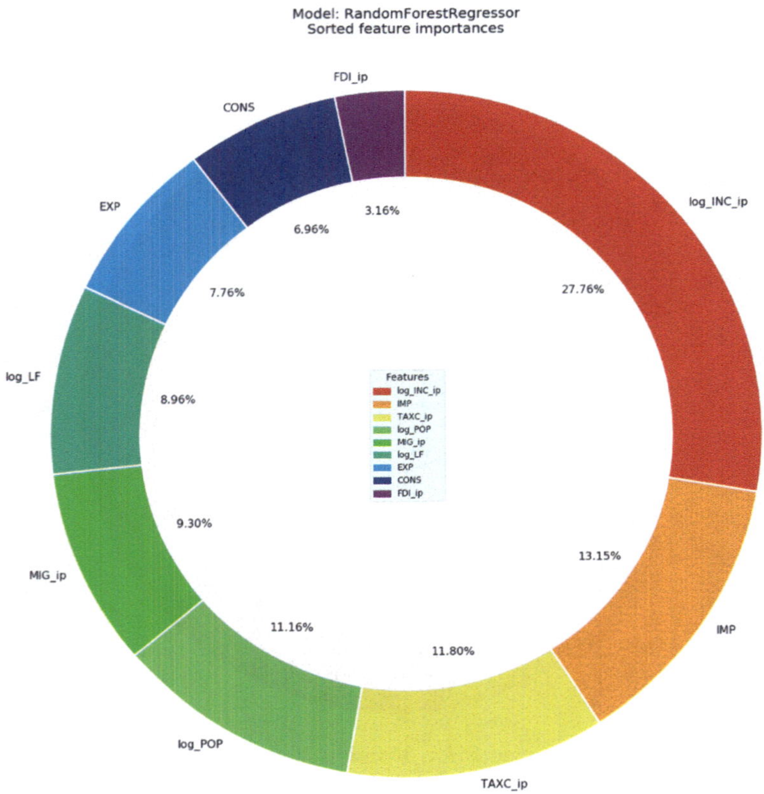

Fig. 4.6 Feature importances for Random Forest Regressor model (*Source* Authors' calculation)

4.5 Conclusion

"Taxes are what we pay for civilized society" (Supreme Court of the United States 1927) (Holmes, dissenting). As a special form of taxation, tariffs implicate a wide range of political, economic and demographic factors, at home and on the international stage. This study shows that

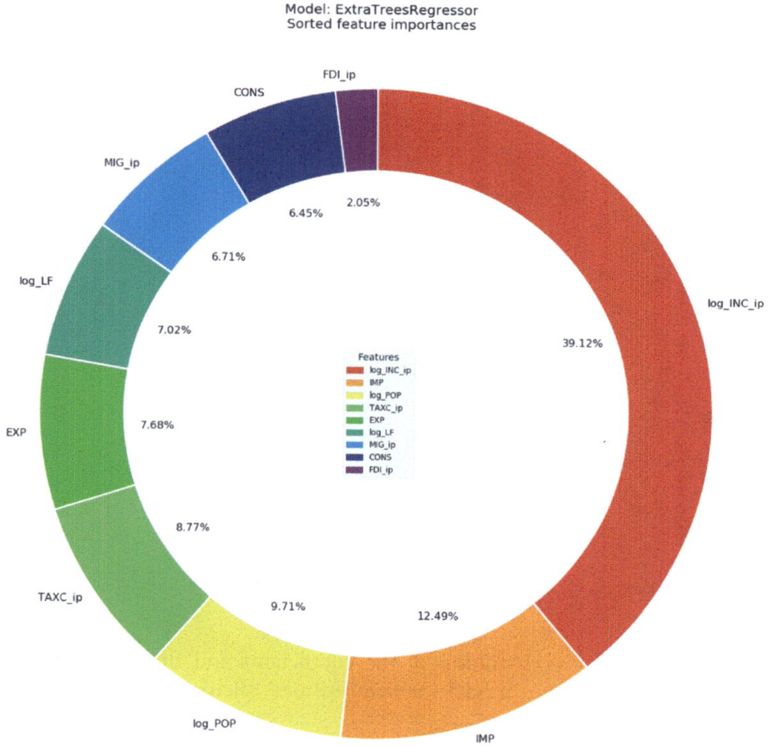

Fig. 4.7 Feature importances for Extra Tree Regressor model (*Source* Authors' calculation)

domestic factors, such as per capita income, population, imports and the domestic income tax rate, outweigh net migration and labor force effects. Machine learning techniques reinforce conclusions drawn from pooled OLS, fixed effects and random effects models based on traditional econometrics.

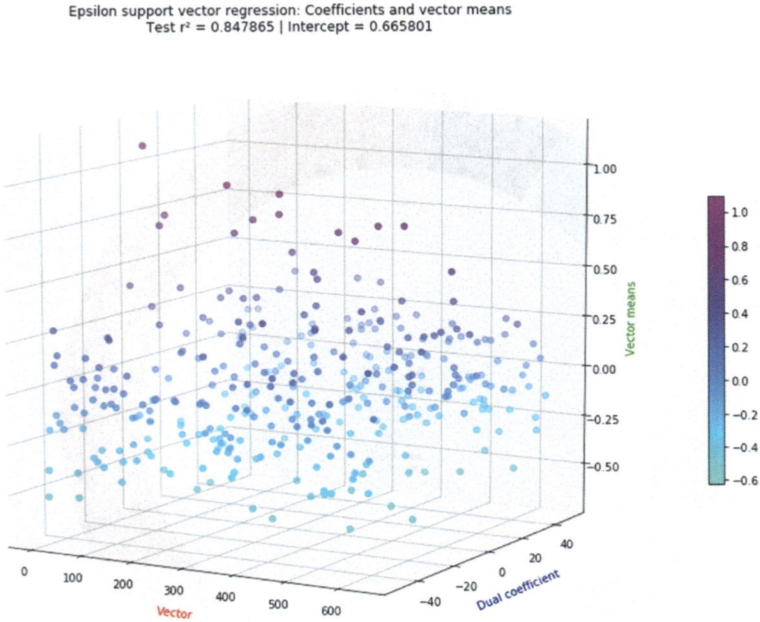

Fig. 4.8 Graphical representation of the coefficients and the vector means of the Epsilon Support Vector model (*Source* Authors' calculation)

Table 4.5 Summary of machine learning results

Model	r^2, *training set*	*Adjusted* r^2, *training set*	r^2, *test set*	*Adjusted* r^2, *test set*
Decision tree	0.910506	0.909229	0.731493	0.719647
Random forest	0.962549	0.962015	0.817135	0.809067
Extra trees	0.970420	0.969998	0.849846	0.843221
Support vector	0.944208	0.929286	0.847865	0.841153

Source Authors' calculations based on Eurostat and World Bank data, 2019

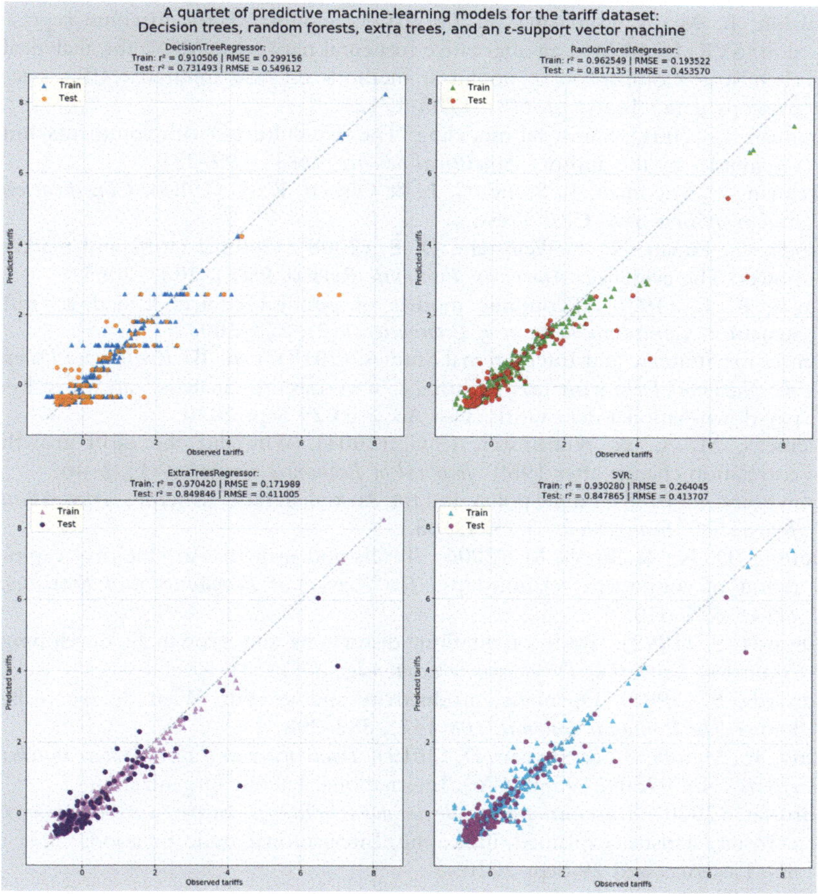

Fig. 4.9 Visualization of the training and the test sets for Decision Tree Regressor, Random Forest Regressor, Extra Trees Regressor and Support Vector Regressor model (*Source* Authors' calculation)

References

Anderson, K. (1980). The political market for government assistance to Australian manufacturing industries. *Economic Record, 56*(153), 132–144.

Balabin, R. M., & Lomakina, E. I. (2011). Support vector machine regression (SVR/LS-SVM)—an alternative to neural networks (ANN) for analytical chemistry? Comparison of nonlinear methods on near infrared (NIR) spectroscopy data. *Analyst, 136*(8), 1703–1712.

Breiman, L. (2001). Statistical modeling: The two cultures (with comments and a rejoinder by the author). *Statistical Science, 16*(3), 199–231.

Breiman, L., Friedman, J., Stone, C. J., & Olshen, R. A. (1984). *Classification and regression trees*. CRC Press.

Broda, C., Limao, N., & Weinstein, D. E. (2008). Optimal tariffs and market power: The evidence. *American Economic Review, 98*(5), 2032–2065.

Caves, R. E. (1976). Economic models of political choice: Canada's tariff structure. *Canadian Journal of Economics, 9*(2), 278–300.

Center for Strategic and International Studies. (2018). *Can We Really Pay Down the National Debt with Tariffs?* https://www.csis.org/analysis/can-we-really-pay-down-national-debt-tariffs. Last Accessed 29 Sept 2020.

Clemens, M. A., & Williamson, J. G. (2004). Why did the tariff–growth correlation change after 1950? *Journal of Economic Growth, 9*(1), 5–46.

Conybeare, J. (1978). Public policy and the Australian tariff structure. *Australian Journal of Management, 3*(1), 49–63.

DeJong, D. N., & Ripoll, M. (2006). Tariffs and growth: An empirical exploration of contingent relationships. *The Review of Economics and Statistics, 88*(4), 625–640.

Edwards, S. (1992). Trade orientation, distortions and growth in developing countries. *Journal of Development Economics, 39*(1), 31–57.

Edwards, S. (1998). Openness, productivity and growth: What do we really know? *The Economic Journal, 108*(447), 383–398.

Ernst, E., Merola, R., & Samaan, D. (2019). *Trade wars and their labour market effects* (No. 995045193502676). International Labour Organization.

Eurostat. (2020). *International trade in goods—Tariffs*. https://ec.europa.eu/eurostat/statistics-explained/index.php/International_trade_in_goods_-_tariffs. Last Accessed 29 Sept 2020.

Geman, S., Bienenstock, E., & Doursat, R. (1992). Neural networks and the bias/variance dilemma. *Neural Computation, 4*(1), 1–58.

Géron, A. (2019). *Hands-on machine learning with Scikit-Learn, Keras, and TensorFlow: Concepts, tools, and techniques to build intelligent systems*. O'Reilly Media.

Geurts, P., Ernst, D., & Wehenkel, L. (2006). Extremely randomized trees. *Machine Learning, 63*(1), 3–42.

Goodhart, C., & Pradhan, M. (2017). Demographics will reverse three multi-decade global trends.

Grossman, G. M., & Helpman, E. (1991). *Innovation and growth in the global economy*. MIT Press.

Hagist, C., Moog, S., Raffelhüschen, B., & Vatter, J. (2009). Public debt and demography-an international comparison using generational accounting. *CESifo DICE Report, 7*(4), 29–36.

Hansen, S. B. (1983). *The politics of taxation: Revenue without representation*. Praeger Publishers.

Helleiner, G. K. (1977). The political economy of Canada's tariff structure: An alternative model. *The Canadian Journal of Economics/Revue Canadienne D'Economique, 10*(2), 318–326.

Hettich, W., & Winer, S. L. (1988). Economic and political foundations of tax structure. *The American Economic Review, 78*(4), 701–712.

Hinrichs, H. H. (1965). Determinants of government revenue shares among less-developed countries. *The Economic Journal, 75*(29), 546–556.

Hinrichs, H. H. (1966). *A general theory of tax structure change during economic development*. Harvard Law School.

Ho, T. K. (1995, August). Random decision forests. In *Proceedings of 3rd international conference on document analysis and recognition* (Vol. 1, pp. 278–282). IEEE.

Kau, J. B., & Rubin, P. H. (1981). The size of government. *Public Choice, 37*(2), 261–274.

Kohavi, R., & Wolpert, D. H. (1996, July). Bias plus variance decomposition for zero-one loss functions. In *ICML* (Vol. 96, pp. 275–83).

Krugman, P. (1987). The narrow moving band, the Dutch disease, and the competitive consequences of Mrs. Thatcher: Notes on trade in the presence of dynamic scale economies. *Journal of Development Economics, 27*(1–2), 41–55.

Kubben, P., Dumontier, M., & Dekker, A. (2019). *Fundamentals of clinical data science* (p. 219). Springer Nature.

Loh, W. Y. (2014). Classification and regression tree methods. *Wiley StatsRef: Statistics Reference Online*.

Maddala, G. S., & Wu, S. (1999). A comparative study of unit root tests with panel data and a new simple test. *Oxford Bulletin of Economics and Statistics, 61*(S1), 631–652.

Magee, S. P., Brock, W. A., & Young, L. (1989). *Black hole tariffs and endogenous policy theory*. Cambridge Books.

Mankiw, N. G. (2020). *Principles of economics*. Cengage Learning.

Migration data portal. (2019). *Migration and trade*. https://migrationdataportal.org/themes/migration-and-trade. Last Accessed 29 Sept 2020.

Müller, A. C., & Guido, S. (2016). *Introduction to machine learning with Python: A guide for data scientists*. O'Reilly Media, Inc.

Musgrave, R. A. (1924). Fiscal Systems (New Haven, 1969). *He develops the approach of K. Wicksell, "A new principle of just taxation", in Classics in the theory of public finance, RA Musgrave & AT Peacock (eds) (London, 1967)*, 86–87.

Pedroni, P. (1999). Critical values for cointegration tests in heterogeneous panels with multiple regressors. *Oxford Bulletin of Economics and Statistics, 61*(S1), 653–670.

Pesaran, H. M. (2004). *General diagnostic tests for cross-sectional dependence in panels*. University of Cambridge, Cambridge Working Papers in Economics, 435.

Pesaran, M. H. (2015). *Time series and panel data econometrics*. Oxford University Press.

Pettis, M. (2018). *Tariffs and trade intervention*. Carnegie Endowment for International Peace.

Polemis, M. L., & Tsionas, M. G. (2019). Bayesian nonlinear panel cointegration: An empirical application to the EKC hypothesis. *Letters in Spatial and Resource Sciences, 12*(2), 113–120.

Schumpeter, J. (1918). 1991. The Crisis of the Tax State. *The Economics and Sociology of Capitalism*. Supreme Court of the United States, 1927. Compania General de Tabacos de Filipinas v. Collector of Internal Revenue. *United States Reports, 275*, 87–101.

Turrini, A. (2002). *International trade and labour market performance: Major findings and open questions*. UN.

Vamvakidis, A. (2002). How robust is the growth-openness connection? Historical evidence. *Journal of Economic Growth, 7*(1), 57–80.

Verbeek, M. (2008). *A guide to modern econometrics*. Wiley.

Vousden, N. (1990). *The economics of trade protection*. Cambridge University Press.

Wolpert, D. H. (1996). The lack of a priori distinctions between learning algorithms. *Neural Computation, 8*(7), 1341–1390.

Woolridge, J. M. (2009). Introductory econometrics: A modern approach 4 ed. *South-Western, Michigan State University, 378*, 57.

World Trade Organization (WTO). (2017). *World Trade Report*. https://www.wto.org/english/res_e/booksp_e/world_trade_report17_e.pdf. Last Accessed 29 Sept 2020.

World Trade Organization (WTO). (2020). *Trade Topics*. https://www.wto.org/english/tratop_e/tariffs_e/tariffs_e.htm. Last Accessed 29 Sept 2020.

Worstall, T. (2016). 100% of Economists Asked Said Import Tariffs Were Not a Good Idea, Forbes.

Yang, H., Chan, L., & King, I. (2002, August). Support vector machine regression for volatile stock market prediction. In *International Conference on Intelligent Data Engineering and Automated Learning* (pp. 391–396). Springer.

Yanikkaya, H. (2003). Trade openness and economic growth: A cross-country empirical investigation. *Journal of Development Economics, 72*(1), 57–89.

CHAPTER 5

Demographics as Determinants of Social Security

James Ming Chen, Thomas Poufinas, Charalampos Agiropoulos, and George Galanos

5.1 Introduction

Social security and more specifically pensions constitute important pillars of a country's economic and political framework. Participation by the state, employers and employees determines the level of contributions and, consequently, the level of benefits. When pensions are administered or guaranteed by the state, or when the state raises its contributions toward pension funding, retirement pensions can significantly affect a country's

J. M. Chen
College of Law, Michigan State University, East Lansing, MI, USA

T. Poufinas (✉)
Department of Economics, Democritus University of Thrace, Komotini, Greece
e-mail: tpoufina@econ.duth.gr

C. Agiropoulos · G. Galanos
Department of International and European Studies, University of Piraeus, Piraeus, Greece

T. Poufinas (ed.), *Debt in Times of Crisis*,
https://doi.org/10.1007/978-3-030-74162-4_5

debt levels. Chapter 4 provides evidence that social security and debt are linked to each other.

Demographic changes and forces can affect the debt of a country. They influence the labor force, the shift of manufacturing to certain countries, wages, membership in trade unions, inflation and interest rates (Goodhart & Pradhan, 2017). At the same time demographic factors affect the explicit and implicit tax flows (Hagist et al., 2009) that a government can secure in order to service its debt obligations.

Demographic changes also affect social security systems and pension schemes. (We refer to "social security in the broad sense of all forms of social insurance, rather than the narrow sense of a government-sponsored system of payments to the elderly.) Aging populations combined with a low fertility rate strain the capacity of social security and pension systems. Longevity, although desired, increases the portion of the population older than 65 and decreases the portion of the population between 15 and 64 years of age. In the European Union, for example, the current ratio of approximately 4 working-age people in the 15–64 age bracket for every person older than 65 is expected to move to a ratio of 2 to 1 by 2060 (European Parliament, 2015).

Pensions need to be adequate as well as sustainable. If pensions are inadequate, then increases in support may be required. Depending on the source of funding, either sustainability or debt will be affected. Unsustainable pension systems may collapse.

Migrant flows may increase the population of a country (or the EU as a whole). Although immigration can mitigate risks to the financial stability of social security and pension systems, it might give rise to other risks, such as potential social disruption, lack of infrastructure and insufficient or unstructured governance.

Increased integration within the EU could also contain threats to adequacy and sustainability. By the same token, EU integration and the political risks associated with immigration may invite skepticism about the impact of EU policies on social security (Baute et al., 2018).

We therefore hypothesize that population, the (un)employment rate, the fertility rate, the dependency ratio and migration may determine the ability of a state or a private scheme to collect the contributions that will secure the promised benefits.

Chapter 4 established the link between social security and debt. This chapter investigates the extent to which demographic factors are determinants of social security. Through econometric models and machine learning techniques, we find evidence that demographics do influence social security. Precise effects vary by model and the proxy used to measure social security or pension benefits. The novelty of this research lies within the use of a broad range of variables in a series of models, particularly models relying on machine learning techniques.

5.2 Literature Review

5.2.1 Social Security Development

From the earliest times, when people started to organize themselves in families, communities and societies, there has been a need for social security and protection against unforeseen situations. Although the concept of social security is generally associated with income maintenance and support programs, it also includes the concept of social protection. Compulsory savings provide social protection for individuals, not only for retirement pensions, but also for contingencies such as unemployment, disability and health problems (Connolly & Munro, 1999).

In the 1880s, Germany was the first nation to adopt a statutory social insurance system, thereby establishing the notion of benefits as a right and making it applicable to the industrial workforce as a whole (Börsch-Supan & Schnabel, 1997). Some years later, similar schemes were introduced in Latin America—specifically, Argentina, Brazil, Chile and Uruguay. Later, the worldwide economic crisis, which unfolded at the end of the 1920s and beginning of the 1930s, and the recovery policies adopted after that crisis, gave new impetus to the development of social security programs.

The 1930s witnessed a further expansion of social security schemes, mainly in Europe and the Americas. The first U.S. Social Security law came into effect in 1939 and is considered as one of the greatest social protection laws of all time (Miron & Weil, 1997). The Second World War and the postwar years saw significant developments in social security at the national, regional and international levels, with confirmation of social security as a human right. The Beveridge Report, published in the United Kingdom in 1942 and implemented from 1945 onward, had a considerable influence on Social Security (H.M. Stationery Office, 1969).

Nowadays, social security is recognized as a human right in fundamental human rights instruments, namely the Universal Declaration of Human Rights (United Nations, 1948). Despite important progress in the extension of social protection, the fundamental human right to social security remains unfulfilled for most of the world's population. ILO's World Social Protection Report 2017–2019 (2017) estimates that only 45% of the world's population are effectively protected by a social protection system mitigating at least one societal risk, with significant variation across regions.

5.2.2 *Social Security and Economic Growth*

Social security mitigates the risks of income losses from formal employment. Barr (2020) distinguished three types of cash benefits:

1. Social insurance: Compulsory insurance with benefits levels and durations, based on past contributions against a specific contingency.
2. Social assistance benefits: Means-tested benefits for specified contingencies (mostly tax-financed).
3. Universal benefits: Tax-financed benefits awarded on the basis of specific contingencies without a contribution or means test.

Global literature before the twenty-first century reached no consensus on the question whether a comprehensive system of social security impedes economic performance or, on the contrary, enhances economic activity (Borstlap, 1996). According to Okun (1975), social security expenditures are thrown in a leaky bucket because the welfare loss of those who pay social security premiums is larger than the welfare gain realized by social security beneficiaries.

Persson and Tabellini (1994), accounting for the results of the democratic correction mechanism, regarded inequality as harmful to economic growth. Kotlikoff (1998) argued that the substitution effect and income effect of social security depress savings and economic growth. Aghion et al. (1999) suggested that the relationship between inequality, poverty and economic growth is quite complicated. According to Pieters (1998), Social Security is a driver of economic growth and enhances labor productivity, fosters consumption and creates a stable economic environment for investment and innovation. In addition, Marimon and Zilibotti (1999), introduced a mechanism according to which a comprehensive Social Security System may enhance economic welfare and productivity growth.

Much of the twenty-first-century scholarship on the relationship between social security and economic growth has focused on the impact of social security on savings and investments. The most recent studies on the relationship between social security and economic growth have concentrated on endogenous growth theory. In classic endogenous growth theory, human capital plays an important role in technology progress and sustainable economic growth.

Scicchitano (2010) introduced the heterogeneity of human capital through both education and on-the-job training. Because of the importance of human capital, the impact of social security on human capital has caused wide public concern. The social security model of Mimoun and Raies (2009) links parents' pensions with the income of their children. The resulting increase in parents' investment in their children's education thereby improves human capital and public health throughout society. Pietro (2003) likewise posited that redistribution through social security can improve cultural experiences and basic educational conditions for low-income families. Therefore, social security increases labor productivity through human capital accumulation and fosters sustainable economic development.

By contrast, Lu and Liu (2017) argued that the expansion of social security leads to increase in government expenditures. Simultaneously, they found that excessive government intervention has an adverse impact on market efficiency and government spending has a "crowding-out effect" on private investment, which hinders economic growth.

5.2.3 *Second Demographic Transition*

Finally, we acknowledge the literature on the Second Demographic Transition even though the subject is not absolutely central to our study. At least since the Second World War, developed nations have shifted toward much higher rates of female participation in the paid workforce (Lesthaeghe, 2010, 2014). At the same time, fertility rates in developed countries have plummeted, and higher premiums on education and skilled labor have unraveled historical pathways to economic, social and even reproductive success.

Bitter divisions over the sociological consequences of the Second Demographic Transition have disrupted politics in the developed world, perhaps most strikingly in the United States (Lesthaeghe & Neidert, 2006, 2009). The political consequences of (reduced) fertility (increased) immigration, and rising instability in publicly funded or guaranteed pensions and other social security systems may be traced to the Second Demographic Transition.

5.3 Data Variables and Methodology

Similar to Chapter 4, this study explores the effect of several demographic variables on a country's social security model. Through the application of traditional econometric methods, this study estimates a pooled OLS, a Fixed Effects and a dynamic GMM model.

Additionally to the traditional econometric approach, this study uses state-of-the-art machine learning methods. Despite their interpretive clarity, generalized linear methods and other conventional econometric tools may not provide the most accurate description of relationships among economic variables or predict as yet unseen phenomena. Certain machine learning methods excel in evaluating data that exhibit nonlinear relationships or arise from non-Gaussian stochastic processes (Breiman, 2001).

The "no free lunch" theorem of machine learning posits that data scientists cannot tell in advance which model is best suited to a particular dataset or predictive goal (Wolpert, 1996). A priori assumptions cannot supplant experimentation. Accordingly, we believe that it is prudent to reach beyond conventional econometrics and to apply multiple families of machine learning methods. We will apply algorithms based on decision trees and support vector machines.

5.3.1 Data

Through empirical evaluation of the impact of demographic factors on social security, this study seeks to harmonize social security policies across 55 diverse countries with the competing, often contradictory predictions of the theoretical literature. The panel dataset includes 36 countries based on OECD and G20 subsets for 19 periods from 2000 to 2018. Based on data availability, we selected these countries: Australia, Austria, Belgium, Canada, Chile, Colombia, Czech Republic, Denmark, Estonia, Finland, France, Germany, Greece, Hungary, Iceland, Ireland, Israel, Italy, Japan, Korea, Rep., Lithuania, Luxembourg, Mexico, Netherlands, New Zealand, Norway, Poland, Portugal, Slovak Republic, Slovenia, Spain, Sweden, Switzerland, Turkey, United Kingdom, United States.

5.3.2 *Variables*

This study considered each of the following proxies for a country's fiscal commitment to its social security scheme:

- Pension funds (autonomous) assets as a share of GDP (PENSION_SHARE)
- Health spending as a percentage of GDP (HEALTH)
- Social spending as a percentage of GDP (SOC_SPEND)
- Pension spending (public) as a share of GDP (PENSION_SPEND).

The set of explanatory variables includes the natural logarithm of these indicators: the age dependency ratio (as a percentage of the working-age population) (lAGE_DEP), population (lPOP), net migration (lMIG) and autonomous pension fund assets in millions of dollars (lPENSION_MILLION). We also treated the fertility rate (FERT), inflation (INFL), the unemployment rate (UNEMP), social security contributions as a percentage of GDP (SOC_CONTR) and the replacement rate for males (REPL_M) and females (REPL_W) as independent variables. Depending on the response variable, the vector of explanatory variables might include only a subset of the available variables.

These variables were drawn from the World Bank open access dataset[1] and the OECD open archive data repository.[2] Table 5.1 reports the main summary statistics of all variables used in the econometric approach.

It is evident that the sample data is well behaved. Table 5.1 shows controlled variability in relation to the mean of the population, since the ratio of the standard deviation over the mean converges to zero. The following chart reports skewness and kurtosis for all variables (Fig. 5.1).

We have also used histograms and kernel density estimates to visualize all independent and dependent variables (Fig. 5.2).

Following an analogous approach with Chapter 4, this study employs tests in addition to cointegration and unit root tests to investigate the existence of cross-sectional dependence of the sample. All tests suggest the rejection of the null hypothesis at any level of significance.

Table 5.2 illustrates the correlation matrix between the variables. The correlation among the explanatory variables is moderate. The highest

[1] https://data.worldbank.org/.

[2] https://www.oecd-ilibrary.org/.

Table 5.1 Summary statistics

	(1)	*(2)*	*(3)*	*(4)*	*(5)*
VARIABLES	*N*	*mean*	*sd*	*min*	*max*
AGE_DEP	684	50.07	5.378	36.21	67.43
FERT	684	1.689	0.375	0.980	3.110
INFL	684	2.735	4.008	−4.478	54.92
POP	684	3.539e + 07	5.583e + 07	281,205	3.267e + 08
HEALTH	684	8.317	2.138	3.999	17.12
MIG	684	387,475	1.057e + 06	−4.769e + 06	5.516e + 06
REPL_M	647	68.70	32.03	28.40	206.4
REPL_W	647	69.22	34.41	26.20	223.0
PENSION_SHARE	684	29.85	38.11	0	184.3
PENSION_MILLION	684	545,284	1.950e + 06	0	1.666e + 07
PENSION_SPEND	665	7.206	3.718	0.769	17.09
SOC_CONTR	665	8.832	4.774	0	27.99
SOC_SPEND	665	19.56	5.797	4.391	32.21
UNEMP	684	7.661	3.987	1.900	27.49

Source Authors' calculations

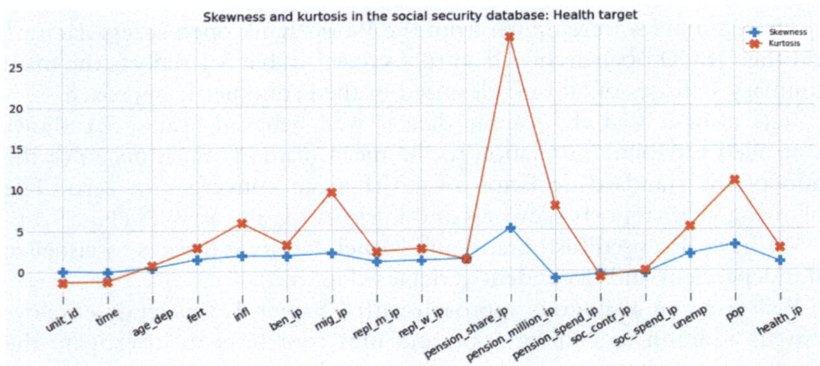

Fig. 5.1 Graphical representation of the skewness and kurtosis measures of the variables used (*Source* Authors' calculations)

Fig. 5.2 Graphical visualization of the dependent and independent variables using histograms and density estimates (*Source* Authors' calculations)

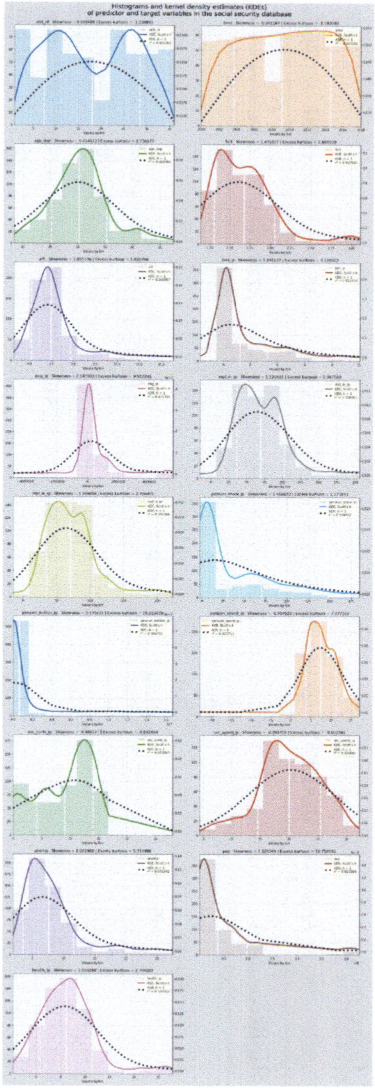

Table 5.2 Correlation matrix

	PENSION_SHARE	*lAGE DEP*	*FERT*	*INFL*	*lPOP*	*HEALTH*	*lMIGip*
PENSION_SHARE	1						
lAGE DEP	0.094	1					
FERT	0.225	0.603	1				
INFL	−0.108	0.011	0.184	1			
lPOP	−0.0454	0.117	0.022	0.0511	1		
HEALTH	0.371	0.231	−0.0225	−0.312	0.227	1	
lMIG	0.069	0.122	0.011	−0.086	0.784	0.398	1
REPL_M	−0.145	−0.124	−0.192	0.233	−0.075	−0.193	−0.080
REPL_W	−0.166	−0.154	−0.226	0.251	−0.065	−0.200	−0.093
lPENSION_MILLION	0.601	0.190	0.208	−0.254	0.539	0.505	0.606
PENSION_SPEND	−0.384	0.0553	−0.380	−0.139	0.128	0.225	0.140
SOC_CONTR	−0.409	−0.0956	−0.475	−0.125	0.0145	0.0551	−0.063
SOC_SPEND	−0.219	0.231	−0.238	−0.300	−0.0968	0.460	0.045
UNEMP	−0.278	−0.0541	−0.212	0.0455	0.0599	−0.126	−0.016

	REPL_M	*REPL_W*	*lPENSION_MILLION*	*PENSION_SPEND*	*SOC_CONTR*	*SOC_SPEND*	*UNEMP*
PENSION_SHARE							
lAGE DEP							
FERT							
INFL							
lPOP							
HEALTH							
lMIG							
REPL_M	1						
REPL_W	0.988	1					

	REPL_M	*REPL_W*	*lPENSION_MILLION*	*PENSION_SPEND*	*SOC_CONTR*	*SOC_SPEND*	*UNEMP*
lPENSION_MILLION	−0.243	−0.254	1				
PENSION_SPEND	0.324	0.338	−0.173	1			
SOC_CONTR	0.266	0.288	−0.328	0.615	1		
SOC_SPEND	0.186	0.192	−0.084	0.682	0.519	1	
UNEMP	0.273	0.297	−0.329	0.293	0.258	0.225	1

Source Authors' calculations

correlation of 0.682 is between social spending and pension public spending. Overall, the correlation matrix does not indicate any major concerns.

5.3.3 *Methodology*

This study adopts a dynamic GMM model along with a fixed effects model in order to explore the determinants of social security support based on demographic data for each country. We supplement our analysis using a traditional pooled OLS method in order to compare and contrast our findings. The theoretical framework of the pooled OLS in addition to the fixed effects models has been presented in previous chapters.

5.3.3.1 *Dynamic GMM*

Arellano and Bover (1995) developed a framework for efficient instrumental variable estimators of random effects models with information in levels which can accommodate predetermined variables. Blundell and Bond (1998) suggested a system estimator which uses moment conditions where lagged differences are illustrated as instruments for the level equation, while the moment conditions of lagged levels serve as instruments for the differenced equation. Based on the work of Arellano and Bover (1995), this estimator is used for datasets where T is relatively small and n is large. This method assumes that there is no autocorrelation in the idiosyncratic errors and requires the initial condition that panel-level effects be uncorrelated with the first difference of the first observation of the dependent variable (Tables 5.3a, 5.3b, 5.3c, and 5.3d).

We perform the Arellano–Bond test for serial correlation in the first-differenced errors at order m. The Arellano–Bond suggests no autocorrelation in linear dynamic panel models and no serial correlation in the first-differenced errors.

5.3.3.2 *Machine Learning*

Data Preparation

The supervised machine learning methods applied to this dataset required the splitting of data into randomized subsets for training and test. This practice, rarely followed in conventional econometrics, ensures that machine learning methods do not merely memorize labels or values associated with data to be predicted (Müller & Guido, 2017, pp. 17–18).

Table 5.3a Regression summary

	(1)	*(2)*	*(3)*
VARIABLES	*pooled_cl* *PENSION_SHARE*	*fixed* *PENSION_SHARE*	*GMM* *PENSION_SHARE*
lAGE_DEP	39.525	12.414	150.402***
	(0.464)	(0.272)	(0.009)
FERT	−11.869	−5.509	−23.545
	(0.411)	(0.291)	(0.460)
INFL	2.023**	−0.144	−0.034
	(0.017)	(0.550)	(0.976)
lPOP	−11.878**	91.667***	−32.948**
	(0.012)	(0.000)	(0.018)
HEALTH	5.609**	1.720	18.346**
	(0.032)	(0.111)	(0.015)
PENSION_SHARE	–	–	–
	–	–	–
lMIG	−3.519	−0.044	−8.090
	(0.191)	(0.950)	(0.286)
REPL_M	1.136	−0.336**	1.829
	(0.150)	(0.015)	(0.517)
REPL_W	−0.992	0.274**	−0.969
	(0.170)	(0.032)	(0.717)
lPENSION_MILLION	12.794***	1.492**	8.131
	(0.008)	(0.034)	(0.168)
PENSION_SPEND	−2.726	2.136*	2.619
	(0.293)	(0.066)	(0.547)
SOC_CONTR	0.585	0.134	−1.018
	(0.598)	(0.881)	(0.593)
SOC_SPEND	−1.854	−1.966**	−10.439**
	(0.104)	(0.016)	(0.018)
UNEMP	1.318	−0.115	2.955*
	(0.154)	(0.637)	(0.057)
Constant	−23.344	−1510.937***	–
	(0.905)	(0.000)	–
Observations	530	530	506
R-squared	0.698	0.953	
Country Cluster SE	Yes	Yes	Yes
Number of CountryCode			32

Robust pval in parentheses
*** $p < 0.01$, ** $p < 0.05$, * $p < 0.1$
Source Authors' calculations

Table 5.3b Regression summary

	(4)	(5)	(6)
VARIABLES	*pooled_cl* *HEALTH*	*fixed* *HEALTH*	*GMM* *HEALTH*
lAGE_DEP	−1.127	4.401***	−0.076
	(0.672)	(0.000)	(0.970)
FERT	0.611	0.875***	−0.364
	(0.511)	(0.006)	(0.767)
INFL	−0.115	−0.031	0.038
	(0.158)	(0.214)	(0.347)
lPOP	0.335	3.423***	0.190
	(0.169)	(0.000)	(0.706)
HEALTH	–	–	–
	–	–	–
PENSION_SHARE	0.022***	0.006*	0.020***
	(0.002)	(0.097)	(0.000)
lMIG	0.108	0.114**	0.239
	(0.501)	(0.024)	(0.309)
REPL_M	−0.109	−0.036**	−0.149
	(0.134)	(0.014)	(0.193)
REPL_W	0.094	0.040***	0.117
	(0.170)	(0.005)	(0.268)
lPENSION_MILLION	0.071	0.077**	0.098*
	(0.451)	(0.020)	(0.094)
PENSION_SPEND	0.098	−0.226***	0.043
	(0.352)	(0.002)	(0.749)
SOC_CONTR	−0.018	0.089	0.005
	(0.638)	(0.246)	(0.915)
SOC_SPEND	0.169***	0.335***	0.176
	(0.001)	(0.000)	(0.105)
UNEMP	−0.056	−0.022	0.014
	(0.125)	(0.377)	(0.783)
Constant	1.460	−74.483***	–
	(0.839)	(0.000)	–
Observations	530	530	506
R-squared	0.563	0.940	
Country Cluster SE	Yes	Yes	Yes
Number of CountryCode			32

Robust pval in parentheses

*** $p < 0.01$, ** $p < 0.05$, * $p < 0.1$

Source: Authors' calculations

Table 5.3c Regression summary

	(7)	(8)	(9)
VARIABLES	*pooled_cl* *SOC_SPEND*	*fixed* *SOC_SPEND*	*GMM* *SOC_SPEND*
lAGE_DEP	11.372*	−4.293***	−2.158
	(0.058)	(0.001)	(0.566)
FERT	−0.500	−0.248	1.580
	(0.812)	(0.576)	(0.255)
INFL	−0.101	0.014	−0.116*
	(0.488)	(0.633)	(0.059)
lPOP	−1.715***	2.486**	0.776
	(0.001)	(0.029)	(0.383)
HEALTH	0.650**	0.731***	0.993*
	(0.034)	(0.000)	(0.053)
PENSION_SHARE	−0.028	−0.015***	−0.007
	(0.174)	(0.009)	(0.725)
lMIG	0.467	−0.080	−0.270
	(0.201)	(0.376)	(0.342)
REPL_M	−0.123	−0.051***	−0.011
	(0.323)	(0.003)	(0.924)
REPL_W	0.122	0.050***	0.030
	(0.315)	(0.003)	(0.787)
lPENSION_MILLION	0.275	−0.028	−0.150
	(0.395)	(0.559)	(0.307)
PENSION_SPEND	0.918***	1.251***	1.118***
	(0.001)	(0.000)	(0.001)
SOC_CONTR	0.079	−0.065	0.017
	(0.650)	(0.703)	(0.933)
SOC_SPEND	–	–	–
	–	–	–
UNEMP	0.070	0.067*	0.021
	(0.422)	(0.078)	(0.793)
Constant	−16.183	−17.009	–
	(0.430)	(0.419)	–
Observations	530	530	506
R-squared	0.751	0.980	
Country Cluster SE	Yes	Yes	Yes
Number of CountryCode			32

Robust pval in parentheses
*** $p < 0.01$, ** $p < 0.05$, * $p < 0.1$
Source Authors' calculations

Table 5.3d Regression summary

	(10)	*(11)*	*(12)*
VARIABLES	*pooled_cl* *PENS_SPEND*	*fixed* *PENS_SPEND*	*GMM* *PENS_SPEND*
lAGE_DEP	5.319**	3.521***	3.636***
	(2.333)	(0.882)	(0.527)
FERT	−2.125***	−0.159	−0.941***
	(0.688)	(0.277)	(0.244)
INFL	−0.005	−0.013	0.003
	(0.071)	(0.023)	(0.013)
lPOP	0.268	−0.970	1.228***
	(0.285)	(0.820)	(0.106)
HEALTH	0.107	−0.161***	−0.475***
	(0.098)	(0.043)	(0.037)
PENSION_SHARE	−0.012	0.005*	−0.015***
	(0.009)	(0.003)	(0.002)
lMIG	0.139	0.124*	−0.095**
	(0.162)	(0.066)	(0.042)
REPL_M	0.061	0.059***	0.019
	(0.052)	(0.012)	(0.015)
REPL_W	−0.048	−0.059***	−0.022
	(0.049)	(0.012)	(0.015)
lPENSION_MILLION	−0.126	0.089***	0.250***
	(0.170)	(0.024)	(0.051)
PENSION_SPEND	–	–	–
	–	–	–
SOC_CONTR	0.146***	−0.012	0.079***
	(0.042)	(0.016)	(0.014)
SOC_SPEND	0.260***	0.408***	0.449***
	(0.054)	(0.019)	(0.009)
UNEMP	0.146*	0.083***	0.085***
	(0.080)	(0.018)	(0.015)
Constant	−23.523***	−0.179	−32.451***
	(8.260)	(15.540)	(2.891)
Observations	530	530	530
R-squared	0.815	0.983	
Country Cluster SE	YES	YES	YES
Number of CountryCode			32

Robust pval in parentheses
***$p < 0.01$, **$p < 0.05$, *$p < 0.1$
Source Authors' calculations

Holding out a fraction of the dataset for testing helps ensure the generalizability of any supervised machine learning model to data not seen during training (ibid.). In accordance with these recommended practices, we split our data into training and test subsets containing 75 and 25%, respectively, of the entire dataset and will report training and test results separately.

To ensure reproducible results, we set a seed of 1 for SciKit-Learn's pseudo-random number generator. This random seed governed not only the splitting of data into training and test subsets, but also the inherently stochastic processes underlying the random forest and extra trees algorithms.

Many machine learning algorithms perform more accurately when data is scaled (Müller & Guido, 2017, pp. 134–142). We applied standard scaling to training data. In other words, our machine learning methods evaluated all and reported all results in terms of Gaussian *z*-scores, or multiples of a dependent or independent variable's standard deviation from its mean. Care must be taken to withhold the test data while scaling the training data and then applying the scale of the training data to the test data, lest data leakage contaminates all predictive tests (ibid., pp. 138–140).

Standard scaling also harmonizes variables whose nominal measurements would otherwise straddle several orders of magnitude. In this respect, standard scaling performs one of the tasks typically asked of logarithmic transformation of data. Logarithmic transformation, however, is mathematically undefined for zero and negative values. Standard scaling can overcome this limitation. Having applied standard scaling to all variables for purposes of machine learning, we elected to forgo logarithmic transformation.

Two of the variables in our dataset, migration (MIG) and autonomous pension assets in millions of dollars (PENSION_MILLION), contained negative value. After logarithmic transformation, our traditional econometric tests omitted observations with negative migration or autonomous pension asset values. The standard-scaled training and test datasets for machine learning retained all of these observations. As a result, machine learning proceeded with 572 total observations (429 training, 143 test), more than the 530 or 506 observations in any of our traditional econometric models.

Insofar as we use machine learning as a complement to conventional econometrics rather than a substitute, we do not regard these differences in the treatment of the data to be materially consequential. Indeed, both attributes of the machine learning dataset—the retention of nominal values before standard scaling and the retention of observations containing negative migration or pension asset values—should enhance the value of machine learning as a tool for checking robustness and validating other aspects of traditional econometric analysis.

Bias, Variance and Hyperparameter Tuning

Proper use of machine learning requires careful management of the *bias-variance* tradeoff. This dilemma arises from an intrinsic property of all supervised machine learning models: Greater inaccuracy, or bias, in the estimates of a model's parameters can reduce the variance among parameter estimates across samples (Kohavi & Wolpert, 1996). While excessive bias reduces a model's accuracy during training, excessive variance hampers efforts to apply supervised machine learning more generally beyond the data on which a machine learning algorithm has been trained (Geman et al., 1992).

Roughly speaking, *bias* refers to a method's overall accuracy, particularly in training. Excessive bias results in a model that *underfits* its data. Accurate as certain models may be during training, such as high-degree polynomial models, models overfit to training data do not provide reliable results unless they generalize well to new, unseen data. High-variance models tend to *overfit* training data. *Variance* therefore affects the generalizability and consistency of results with new data.

This image illustrates the bias-variance tradeoff as a quest to minimize prediction error (Kubben et al., 2019, p. 107, Fig. 8.3). At the optimal level of complexity, a model strikes the best attainable balance between under- and overfitting (Fig. 5.3).

In practice, the problem is that most machine learning models offer a wide, sometimes daunting, list of adjustable hyperparameters (Géron, 2019, pp. 31–32). If these settings are not properly tuned, a machine learning model may fall far short of its predictive potential. We obtained all of our machine learning results through a grid search of each algorithm's hyperparameter space and *k*-folds cross-validation (Müller & Guido, 2017, pp. 258–282).

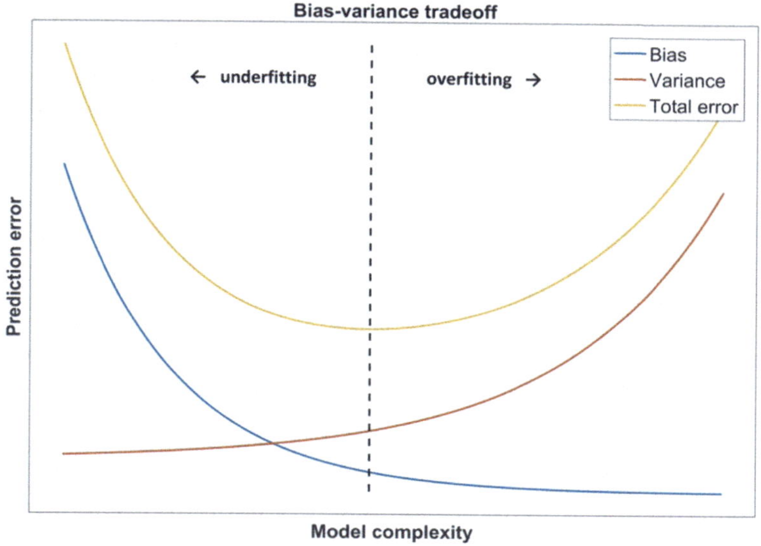

Fig. 5.3 Bias-variance tradeoff illustration (*Source* Kubben et al., 2019, p. 107, Fig. 8.3)

Trees, Forests and Support Vector Machines

The classification and regression tree (CART) algorithm is the basis for a dazzling constellation of machine learning methods (Breiman et al., 1984; Loh, 2008). Decision trees and ensembles of decision trees often outperform linear regression. They are not limited to linear relationships. All decision tree-based algorithms are robust in the presence of outliers. These algorithms are also quite forgiving of misspecified models. The inclusion of weakly predictive or even wholly non-predictive variables generally does not weaken a decision tree or tree-based ensemble.

The simplest way to diversify the results of a decision tree algorithm is to sample random subsets (either with or without replacement) of the training set. Bagging, short for *bootstrap aggregating*, samples with replacement (Breiman, 1996). Pasting samples without replacement (Breiman, 1999). Because $1/e$ of any dataset (approximately 0.367879) will escape sampling even in an infinite bagging process (Géron, 2019, p. 195, n. 6), the "out-of-bag" subset of training instances *not* chosen in bagging provides an additional validation set by which to evaluate the effectiveness and generalizability of the decision tree on previously unseen data.

Other methods aggregate decision trees rather than slices of the dataset. Among ensemble and boosting methods based on aggregations of decision trees, random forests are perhaps the simplest (Ho, 1995). Random forests require the tuning of only two hyperparameters: the maximum number of features that a randomized tree may contain, plus the maximum depth of each tree (or the number of splits we will allow within each tree). Randomizing the threshold for each predictor yields an even more diversified algorithm called *extremely random trees*, or extra trees (Geurts et al., 2006).

The tuning of hyperparameters for these ensemble models can be visualized vividly in three dimensions (Figs. 5.4 and 5.5).

One weakness of decision trees and tree-based ensemble methods is that they are not amenable to evaluation according to *p*-values and conventional tests of statistical significance. But the contribution of each predictive variable can be quantified. All tree-based methods in SciKit-Learn report "feature importances," a vector of values whose sum is 1 and whose individual values correspond to each regressor's contribution to the model's predictions (Géron, 2019, pp. 198–199). Specifically, feature importances in SciKit-Learn "is a weighted average, where each node's weight" in a decision tree or across all trees in a forest "is equal to the number of training samples that are associated with it" (ibid., p. 198).

We will also report results from support vector machine regression (Géron, 2019, pp. 153–174). This powerful and versatile class of machine learning algorithms has been applied to a wide range of regression tasks, including time series prediction of stock returns (Yang et al., 2002). Support vector machine regression performs especially well with complicated, "highly nonlinear objects" (Balabin & Lomakina, 2011, pp. 1710–1711). Although support vector machines do not report feature importances, they provide additional validation of results obtained through traditional econometric methods and through decision tree-based ensemble methods such as random forests and extra trees.

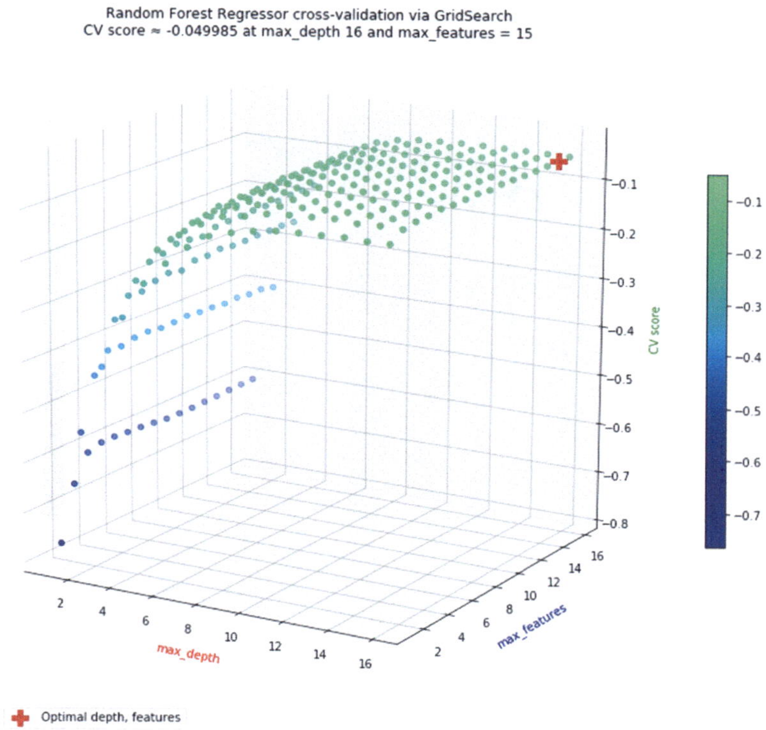

Fig. 5.4 Random forest regressor hyperparameters visualization in three dimensions (*Source* Authors' calculations)

5.4 Results and Result Interpretation

5.4.1 Econometric Models

The regressions show that some of the variables align as we had anticipated. Other relationships, however, warrant further investigation. We first comment on the purely demographic variables: population, the age dependency ratio, the fertility rate, migration and unemployment. We then present findings on variables related to social security: health spending (as a share of GDP), pension assets (as a share of GDP), the replacement rate (for males and females), pension assets (in monetary

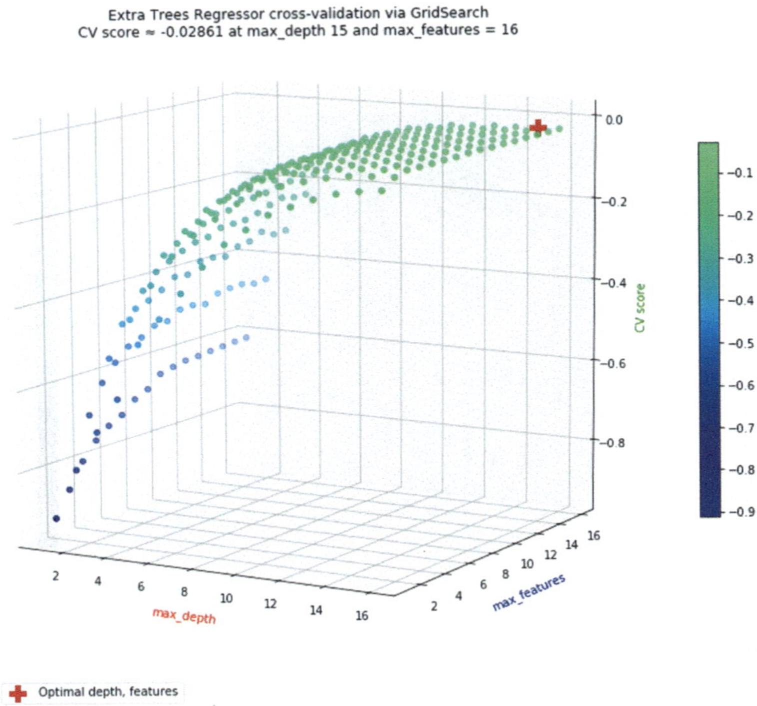

Fig. 5.5 Extra trees regressor hyperparameters visualization in three dimensions (*Source* Authors' calculations)

terms), pension spending (as a share of GDP), social security contributions (as a share of GDP) and social spending (as a share of GDP). Finally, we highlight our only macroeconomic variable, which is inflation.

5.4.1.1 Demographic Variables

Results

Pension assets as a share of GDP are positively correlated with the (logarithm of the) age dependency ratio at all significance levels when the GMM is used. It is positively correlated at all significance levels with the logarithm of the population when the fixed effects model is used, but negatively correlated at the 5% level with the population when the pooled

OLS or GMM are employed. It is positively related with unemployment according to GMM at the 10% significance level.

Health spending is positively related at all significance levels with the age dependency ratio, the fertility rate and the population and at the 5% level with the logarithm of immigration as a percent of the population under the fixed effects model.

Social spending as a percent of GDP is positively correlated with age dependency at the 10% significance level when the pooled OLS is used but is negatively correlated to age dependency at all significance levels in the fixed effects model. It is positively correlated to population at the 5% significance level in the fixed effects model, but negatively correlated when pooled OLS is employed. It is positively correlated with unemployment at the 10% significance level under the fixed effects approach.

Finally, pension spending as a percent of GDP is positively correlated to the age dependency ratio at all significance levels when the fixed effects and GMM methods are followed and at the 5% level under pooled OLS. It is negatively correlated at all levels with the fertility rate under pooled OLS and GMM. It is positively correlated with the population at all levels under GMM. It is positively correlated at the 10% level with immigration under the fixed effects approach, but negatively correlated at the 5% level under GMM. It is positively correlated with unemployment at all levels when the fixed effects method is applied, and at 10% under pooled OLS.

Interpretation

The positive correlation of the age dependency ratio with pension, health and social spending (or assets) is probably anticipated. In all likelihood, growth in the rate of age dependency arises from an increase in the number of citizens who are 65 or older. As a result, higher amounts need to be spent to support them. Higher spending may also increase pension assets.

The negative correlation with social spending in the fixed effects model may need further investigation. One possible explanation: In countries exhibiting a low age dependency ratio, the denominator—that is, the working age portion of the population—is bigger and needs more social support.

The positive correlation of fertility with health spending may be explained this way: When more infants are born, the need for health benefits also grows. Compared to young- and middle-aged adults, children tend to need more health services. By contrast, negative correlation with pension spending suggests that increased fertility may indicate that the aged population entitled to pension benefits is proportionally lower. As a result, pension spending becomes proportionally lower.

The positive correlation of population with all dependent variables when present is probably expected. The larger the population, the larger its needs in pension, health and social spending (or assets), even as a percent of GDP. Larger populations, especially when combined with larger dependency ratios, probably demand even more resources.

The negative correlation of population with pension assets within the pooled OLS and GMM approaches needs further investigation. Perhaps larger populations attract a bigger share of governmental budget, leaving a smaller portion for pension savings.

The negative correlation of population with social spending under pooled OLS may also need a closer look. Smaller populations may command a bigger portion of the GDP through social expenditures, as there are resources to cover it. This relationship may also be a methodological artifact of the pooled OLS approach: as OLS does not look at the countries in a distinctive way, it could be that as the overall population increases the social spending (as a percent of GDP) does not increase proportionally.

The positive relation of immigration with health spending implies that a higher influx of immigrants, who probably arrive at younger ages and whose ranks often include children, generates higher demand for health benefit needs. These impacts are likely to be especially acute at the beginning of the immigration process, when new arrivals do not support the GDP of the host countries. As such, immigration tends to absorb more resources, at least in the short run.

The mixed sign observed in pension spending needs to be investigated further. The positive sign within the fixed effects model may reflect immigration-driven increases in the population and a consequential increase in demand for pension expenditures. This inference, however, contradicts suppositions about the relative youth of the immigrant population.

The negative sign in the GMM model probably arises from the confluence of two facts: First, immigrants increase the population. Second, their economic contributions exceed their subsequent needs for social support.

As a group, immigrants are younger than other inhabitants of the host country. This reduces the pension spending as a percentage of GDP.

Finally, the positive correlation of unemployment with social spending and pension spending may be explained by the fact that higher unemployment increases the expenditures required to fund pensions and other social benefits. By their very nature, social expenditures are directed toward unemployed and young persons. Indeed, many people fit both categories; it is quite common for young people to be unemployed, and unemployed people to be young.

Increased pension spending may be an artifact of a high unemployment rate. Fewer workers mean lower contributions as well as increased pension spending. The positive correlation of unemployment with pension assets under GMM may need additional investigation. However, this correlation could also indicate that countries with low unemployment also have low pension assets as a share of GDP, if only because fuller employment also raises the GDP.

5.4.1.2 Social Security Variables

Results

Turning now to our remaining control variables, we see that the replacement rate for men and women always exhibits the opposite sign. Specifically, the male replacement rate is negatively correlated with pension assets, health spending and social spending and positively correlated with pension spending within the fixed effects model. These correlations are exactly the opposite for the female replacement rate: positive with respect to pension assets, health spending and social spending, but negative with respect to pension spending. These correlations occur at all significance levels, except with respect to pension assets for men and for women and with respect to health spending for men.

The social security contribution (as a percent of GDP) is positively related with pension spending (as a percent of GDP) at all significance levels in pooled OLS and GMM.

Pension assets as a percent of GDP are positively related with health spending as a percent of GDP at the 5% significance level in the pooled OLS and GMM models. They are positively related with pension assets in monetary terms at all significance levels in the pooled OLS approach and at the 5% level under fixed effects. They are positively correlated at the 10% level with pension spending under the fixed effects model. They are negatively correlated at the 5% level with social security spending under the fixed effects and GMM approaches.

Health spending as a percent of GDP is positively correlated with pension assets as a percent of GDP at all significance levels under pooled OLS and GMM and at the 10% level in the fixed effects model. Health spending is positively correlated with pension assets in monetary terms at the 5% level in the fixed effects model and at 10% under GMM. Health spending is positively correlated with social security spending at all significance levels under the pooled OLS and fixed effects models. It is negatively correlated with pension spending at all significance levels in the fixed effects model.

Social security spending is positively related with health spending at the 5% level in pooled OLS, at 1% in fixed effects and at 10% under GMM. It is negatively related at all significance levels to pension assets as a percent of GDP under the fixed effects model. It is positively related with pension spending as a percent of GDP.

Pension spending is negatively correlated with health spending at all significance levels under the fixed effects and the GMM approaches. It is positively related with pension assets in millions of USD at all significance levels under the fixed effects and GMM models. It is positively related with social security spending at all significance levels and with all models. It is positively related with pension assets as a percent of GDP with the pension assets as a percent of GDP at the 10% level in the fixed effects model, but negatively correlated at 1% significance in GMM.

Interpretation

The negative correlation of the replacement rate for men with health spending and social spending may suggest that a high replacement rate consumes resources that could be directed to health and social expenditures. The same applies to pension assets. A high male replacement rate increases pension spending, which may be needed to secure the high replacement rate.

The opposite signs on correlations with the female replacement rate, however, demand closer attention. Perhaps the income of women is much lower globally, so that a high replacement rate emerges in countries with higher health and social consciousness and thus spending. The same holds true with regard to pension assets. These countries may already have superior pension consciousness.

The negative sign with respect to pension spending may be attributed to the fact that more and more women are working. In some countries, however, women tend to retire at younger ages compared to men, which may lower replacement rates. At the same time, pension expenditures may rise in order to support the increased number of retirees, male or female. Alternatively, pension spending may rise to meet the greater needs of men.

The positive relation of social security contributions with pension spending probably arises from the fact that social security contributions by citizens are directed toward covering pensions. Higher pension spending follows directly from this relationship.

We may be able to explain the positive relation of pension assets with health expenditures by positing that countries with higher health spending can help their populations age successfully. As a result, such countries need more assets to support pensions. The positive relation of pension assets as a percent of GDP with pension assets in monetary terms and pension spending is justified by the fact that these variables imply an increase in assets, either available or needed. The negative correlation with social security spending may arise from the fact that increased social securing spending absorbs resources and leaves fewer resources to support pension assets.

A potential interpretation of the positive relation of health expenditures with pension assets as a percent of GDP as well as in dollars may be given if we consider the opposite direction. Namely, residents of countries with increased health spending tend to age successfully. Thanks to increased productivity from longer and healthier lives, these countries have more assets to fund pensions when their citizens retire.

The positive relation of health expenditures with social security spending may reflect a country's overall propensity to foster practices that support the well being of its population by delivering social benefits and health services to those in need. The negative correlation with pension spending may be due to the fact that increased pension spending diverts resources from health spending (and vice versa).

The positive relation of the social security spending with health spending, as well as its negative relation with pension assets, may be explained with arguments similar to those used to explain the reverse relation. Positive correlation with pension spending suggests that countries with high pension spending are also likely to have high social security spending. These policies reflect a broad attitude of generosity toward citizens.

The correlation of pension spending as a percent of GDP with health spending, pension assets (as a percent of GDP and in monetary terms) and social security spending may be explained with the arguments used to justify these relationships in reverse. The negative sign with pension assets under GMM needs further investigation. Countries with ample pension assets could afford to lower their pension spending, since these assets suffice to cover the pensions.

5.4.1.3 *Macroeconomic Variable*

Results

Finally, the only pure macroeconomic variable that we have introduced in our models is inflation. It is positively correlated at the 5% significance level with the pension assets under the pooled OLS approach and negatively correlated with social spending at the 10% significance level in the GMM.

Interpretation

The positive correlation of inflation with the pension assets suggests that inflation may affect contributions as well as return on invested assets. Both of these effects would increase the pension asset pool. On the other hand, the negative correlation of inflation with social spending implies that high inflation erodes the value of all financial resources and leaves a smaller share of GDP for social spending on needy citizens.

Other combinations of variables and models generated no statistical significance. However, we have retained these variables because they improve the explanatory power of the models.

5.4.2 *Machine Learning Techniques*

We administered decision trees, random forests, extra trees and support vector machines to standard-scaled training and test datasets for each of our four target variables representing a distinct proxy for social security support:

- Autonomous pension funds as a share of GDP.
- Health spending as a percentage of GDP.
- Social spending as a percentage of GDP.
- (Public) pension spending as a share of GDP.

We now report each set of machine learning results in turn.

5.4.2.1 Autonomous Pension Funds as a Share of GDP

Our baseline machine learning model for each target variable is a naked CART decision tree. The optimal decision tree for autonomous pension funds reached a depth of 13 levels.

During training, this decision tree almost perfectly learned the relationships between autonomous pension assets and their predictor variables. It attained an r^2 value of 0.999701 on training data and an adjusted r^2 of 0.999690. The application of this optimal decision tree to test data modestly reduced accuracy as measured by r^2 and adjusted r^2, to 0.963140 and 0.958460 respectively.

Training data outcomes for all machine learning methods remained close to 1.00. The true test of supervised machine learning, however, lies in the application of a trained model to test data not revealed to the algorithm during training. As it turned out, test set accuracy was higher across the board for autonomous pension assets than any other proxy for social security spending.

Two basic tree-based ensemble methods, random forests and extra trees, yielded similar performances on the test subset of the autonomous pension assets data. The random forest and extra trees algorithms, respectively, raised r^2 to 0.981949 and a truly outstanding 0.987448. Adjusted r^2 was 0.979657 for random forests and 0.985854 for extra trees.

These test set scores are more representative of these ensemble methods' generalizability to unseen data. Both random forests and extra trees delivered accuracy as measured by unadjusted r^2 exceeding 0.98. Even at such high levels of accuracy, extra trees held an edge over random forests. In highly sensitive machine learning applications, extra trees would be able to boast a 30.5% improvement in accounting for the final 1.8% of variance not captured by random forests. In all events, these tree-based ensembles successfully accounted for nearly all of the variance in autonomous pension assets as a share of GDP.

Of arguably greater importance to the interpretation of the predictive model are the vectors of feature importances for all three tree- or forest-based methods (Figs. 5.6, 5.7, and 5.8).

The progression from a naked decision tree to random forests and extra trees shows a continuous decline in the dominance of the weightiest variable: the level of social benefits. This decline is unsurprising; it is an artifact of the increasingly Delphic, or diversified, nature of machine

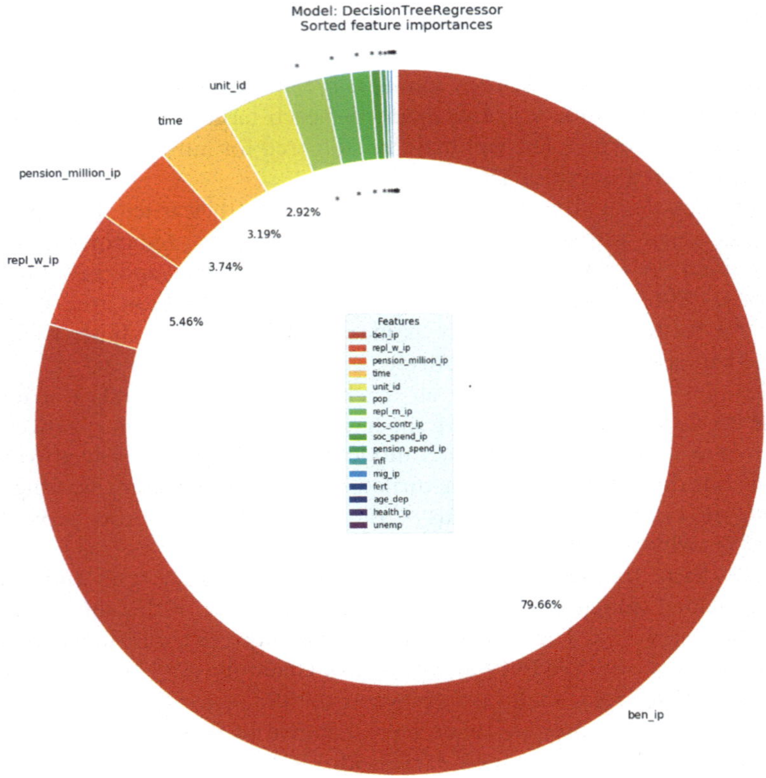

Fig. 5.6 Feature importances for decision tree regressor model when autonomous pension funds as a share of GDP is the target variable (*Source* Authors' calculation)

learning along this methodological progression. A random forest contains trees of variable depth and a variable number of determinative factors. The extra trees method introduces additional stochasticity by randomly varying the point at which nodes in individual trees split into new branches and leaves.

A quick glance at the Herfindahl-Hirschman index (HHI) of dominance (Liston-Heyes & Pilkington, 2004) for the three feature importance vectors quantifies the precipitous rate at which the leading features

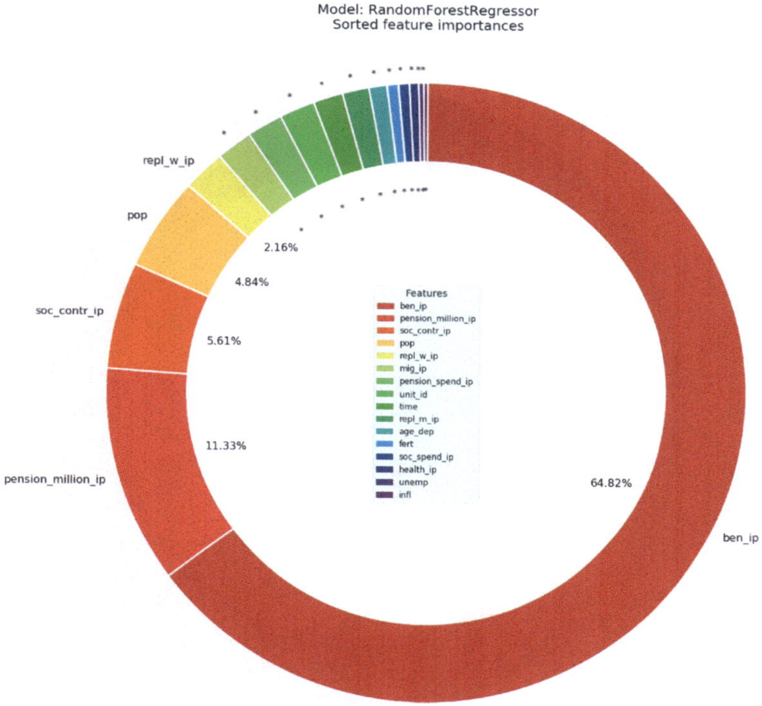

Fig. 5.7 Feature importances for random forest regressor model when autonomous pension funds as a share of GDP is the target variable (*Source* Authors' calculation)

in the decision tree, random forest and extra trees models lose their dominance. The HHI is merely the sum of the squares of each feature's share, often scaled by a multiple of 10,000 to ease interpretability, such that:

$$H = \sum_{i=1}^{N} s_i^2$$

The HHI of feature importances for these three models is as follows:

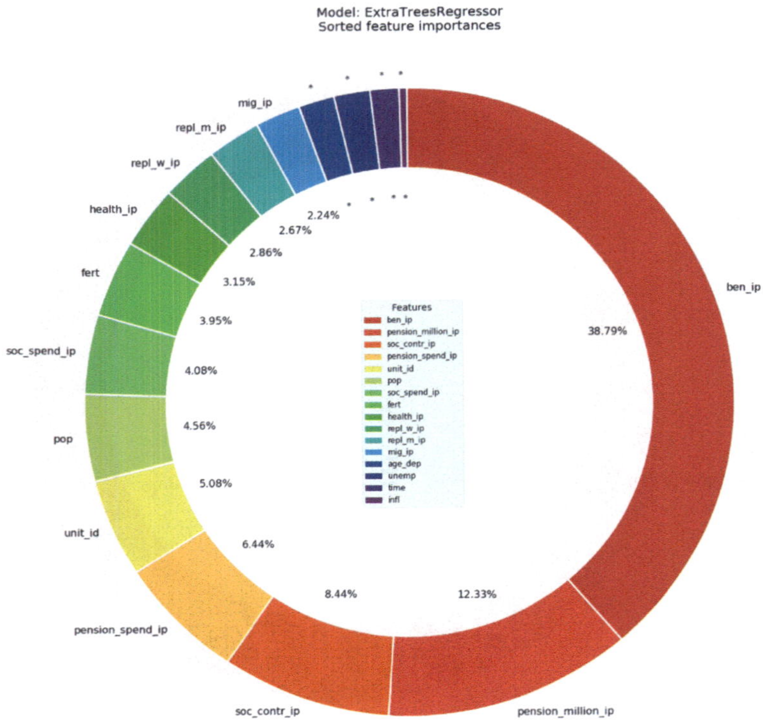

Fig. 5.8 Feature importances for extra tree regressor model when autonomous pension funds as a share of GDP is the target variable (*Source* Authors' calculation)

- Decision tree: 6413.76
- Random forests: 4404.68
- Extra trees: 1887.38.

Where complete dominance by a single factor would result in an index of 10,000 and perfectly even distribution of importances among 16 factors would be 10,000/16, or 625.

Support vector regression results confirm the outcomes of the tree- and forest-based methods. Support vector regression reported an r^2 value of 0.998159 during training and an adjusted r^2 of 0.998088. Although all margins are small, the support vector machine proved slightly more resistant to overfitting. It yielded a test set r^2 of 0.980217 and adjusted r^2 of 0.977705. By a very thin margin, those results outperformed those of extra trees.

Although the eponymous support vectors of this model do not bolster the interpretability of its results, their dual coefficients and vector means can be computed and visualized as a three-dimensional plot where the x-axis assigns a unique integer value to each of the observations in the subset of training data (Fig. 5.9).

Tables 5.4a–5.4d provide a summary of machine learning results. Table 5.4a reports training and test set results for machine learning predictions involving autonomous pension assets as a share of GDP.

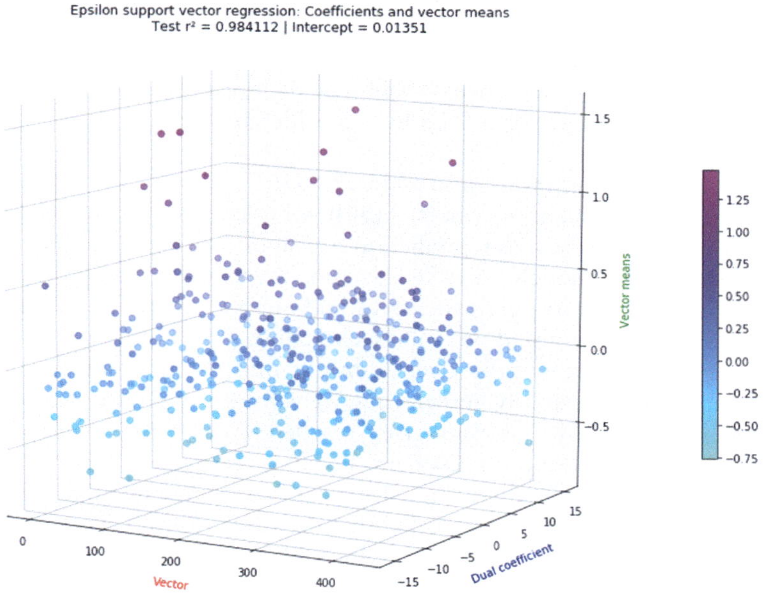

Fig. 5.9 Graphical representation of the coefficients and the vector means of the epsilon support vector model when autonomous pension funds as a share of GDP is the target variable (*Source* Authors' calculation)

Table 5.4a Target variable: autonomous pension assets as a share of GDP

Model	*r^2, training set*	*Adjusted r^2, training set*	*r^2, test set*	*Adjusted r^2, test set*
Linear	0.724265	0.713557	0.721339	0.685954
Decision tree	0.999877	0.999872	0.975308	0.972172
Bagged trees	0.997131	0.997020	0.979178	0.976534
Random forest	0.997290	0.997185	0.981949	0.979657
Extra trees	0.999910	0.999907	0.987448	0.985854
Support vector	0.998070	0.997996	0.984112	0.982094

Source Authors' calculations

This plot summarizes observed and fitted values for training and test sets for autonomous pension assets. In addition to the four machine algorithms described in detail, this chart includes the results of a basic OLS regression and bootstrap aggregation of CART decision trees based on random samples of predictive variables with replacement. All machine learning models outperform OLS by a considerable margin (Fig. 5.10).

5.4.2.2 *Health Spending (as a Share of GDP)*

Like autonomous pension assets, health spending as a share of GDP proved quite amenable to prediction through machine learning. All machine learning models—a naked decision tree, bootstrap aggregation (bagging), random forests, extra trees and support vector regression—delivered r^2 and adjusted r^2 values exceeding 0.994 during training. Because test set results offer deeper insight into the generalizability of these models for previously unseen data, we will focus on those outcomes.

The baseline CART decision tree reached r^2 of 0.963140 and an adjusted r^2 of 0.958460 on test data. Bagging reported r^2 of 0.966013 and adjusted r^2 of 0.961697. The out-of-bag score generated naturally by bootstrap aggregation placed r^2 slightly lower at 0.959570. These values suggest that tree-based machine learning did not overfit data predicting health expenditures.

Random forests and extra trees also excelled in predicting health expenditures. The random forest algorithms maximized r^2 at 0.965809 and adjusted r^2 at 0.961467. The corresponding values for extra trees were r^2 of 0.978795 and adjusted r^2 of 0.976102. As with autonomous pension assets, extra trees performed better at the margin than random forests.

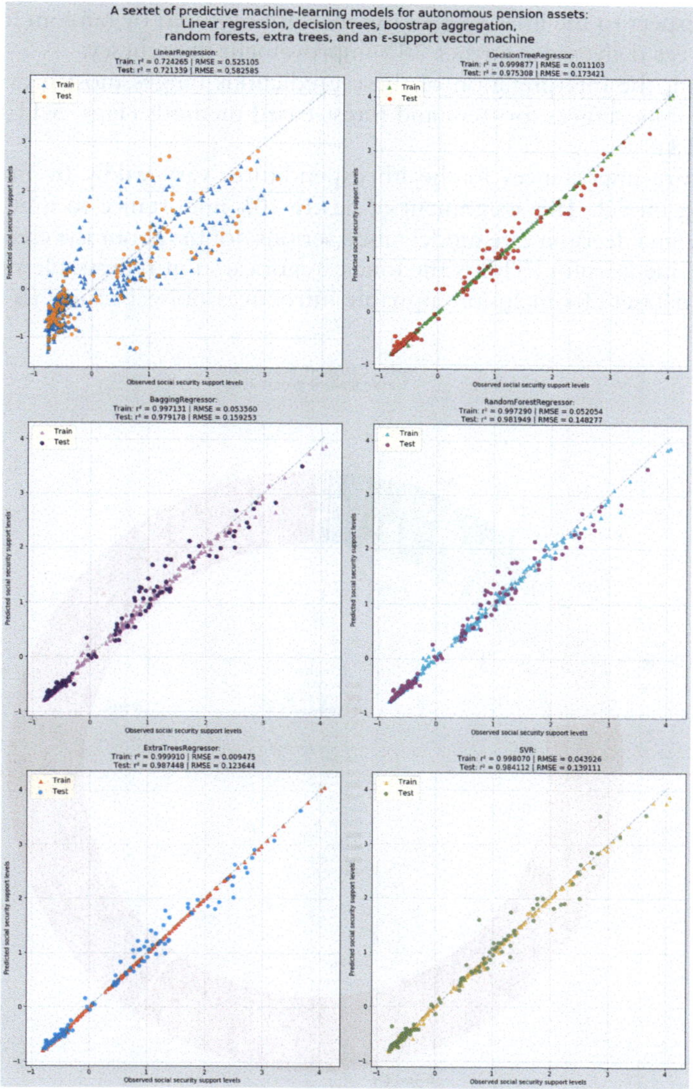

Fig. 5.10 Visualization of the training and the test sets for decision tree regressor, random forest regressor, extra trees regressor and support vector regressor model when autonomous pension funds as a share of GDP is the target variable (*Source* Authors' calculation)

With respect to the final 3.4% of variance not captured by random forests, extra trees delivered a further 38% improvement in accuracy.

Again, the interpretation of these predictions hinges most heavily on feature importances for tree- and forest-based methods (Figs. 5.11, 5.12, and 5.13).

Feature importances for health expenditures vary wildly by machine learning model. The assignment of nearly 40% importance to unit ID in the baseline decision tree model raised serious doubts about the credibility of machine learning. This is the lone categorical, non-regressable variable in the dataset. Its inclusion arguably introduces noise because its value,

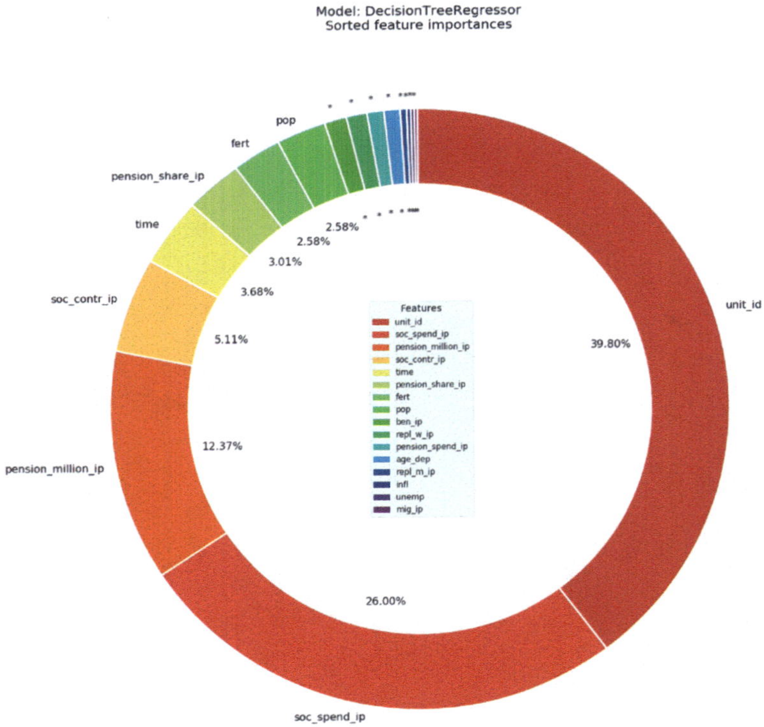

Fig. 5.11 Feature importances for decision tree regressor model when health spending is the target variable (*Source* Authors' calculation)

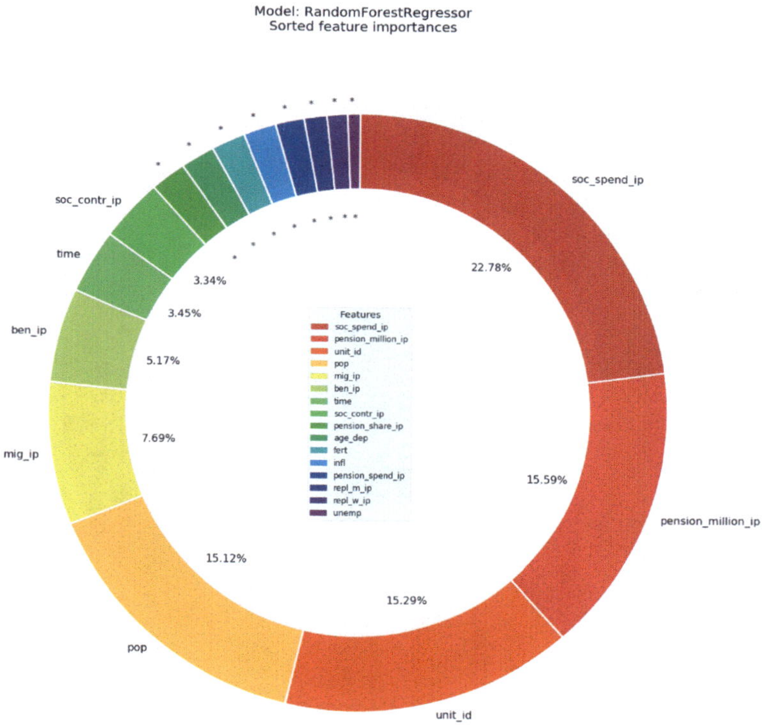

Fig. 5.12 Feature importances for random forest regressor model when health spending is the target variable (*Source* Authors' calculation)

fixed for all observations from the same country, is arbitrary and reflects neither demographic nor political differences along any measurable scale.

The ensemble methods, however, progressively weaken the hold of unit ID. That categorical variable declines to 15.29% importance in random forests and even more precipitously to 4.26% in extra trees. The same intuition underlying the reduction in dominance explains why ensemble methods progressively diminish the prominence of a non-regressable categorical variable. Each iteration of the random forest model may exclude unit ID (or, for that matter, any other variable). The extra trees algorithm adds further stochasticity by randomizing the threshold at

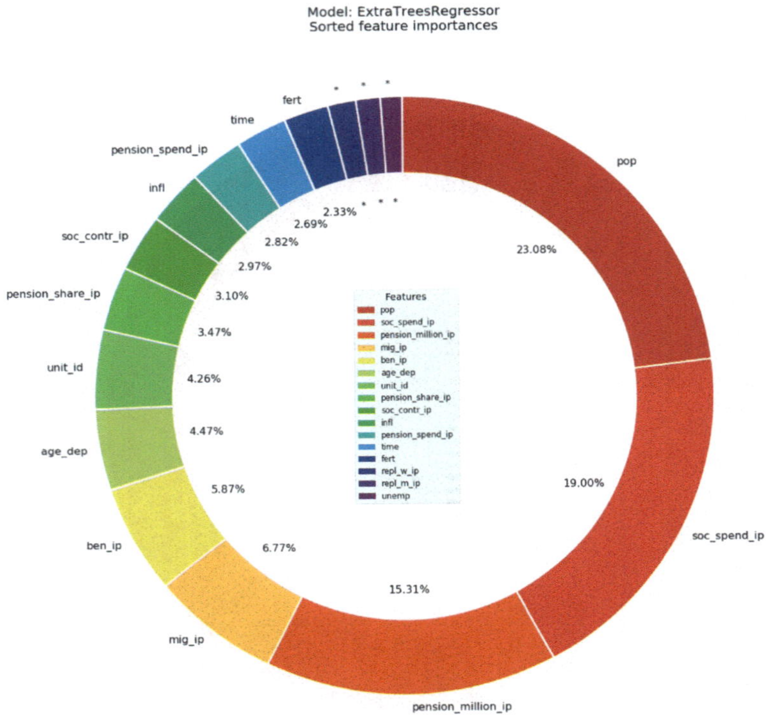

Fig. 5.13 Feature importances for extra tree regressor model when health spending is the target variable (*Source* Authors' calculation)

which each node is split. Insofar as the overall population of most countries in the dataset remains stable or grows only modestly, population may serve as a proxy for the categorical identification of each country. Unsurprisingly, this variable eventually rises to a modestly dominant position in the feature importances of the extra trees model.

Support vector regression also proved effective in predicting health expenditures. Its test accuracy—r^2 of 0.984112 and adjusted r^2 of 0.982094—came between that of random forests and extra trees. The support vectors for the health expenditures model look like this (Fig. 5.14).

Table 5.4b reports training and test set results for machine learning predictions involving health spending as a share of GDP.

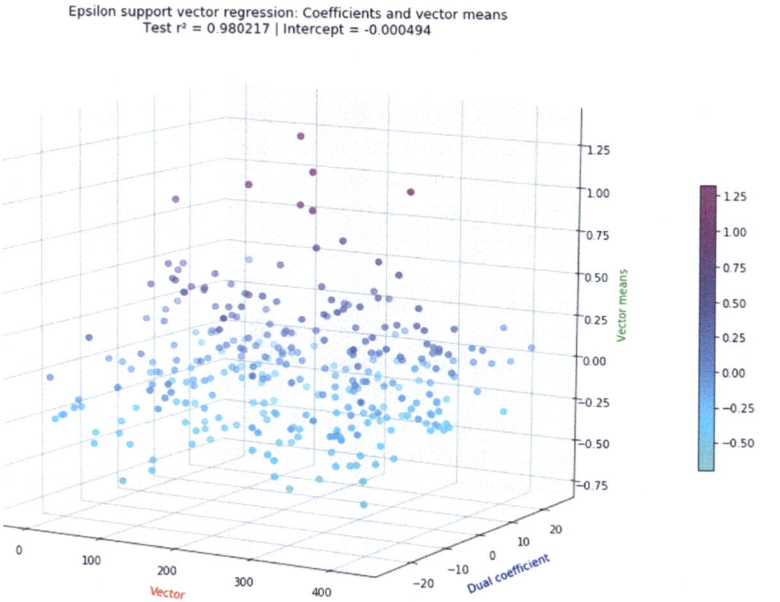

Fig. 5.14 Graphical representation of the coefficients and the vector means of the epsilon support vector model when health spending is the target variable (*Source* Authors' calculation)

Table 5.4b Target variable: health expenditures as a share of GDP

Model	*r^2, training set*	*Adjusted r^2, training set*	*r^2, test set*	*Adjusted r^2, test set*
Linear	0.764744	0.755608	0.724876	0.689939
Decision tree	0.999701	0.999690	0.963140	0.958460
Bagged trees	0.994357	0.994138	0.966013	0.961697
Random forest	0.994678	0.994471	0.965809	0.961467
Extra trees	0.999882	0.999877	0.978795	0.976102
Support vector	0.998159	0.998088	0.980217	0.977705

Source Authors' calculations

As before, this plot summarizes six models: linear regression, a naked decision tree, bagging, random forests, extra trees, and support vector regression. Once again, all machine learning models outperform OLS by a considerable margin. In particular, machine learning outperformed linear regression not only in the heart of the distribution, where observed and fitted values fall between $\pm 2z$, but also at the high end of the distribution, where our standard-scaled data for machine learning contains outliers exceeding $+2z$ (Fig. 5.15).

5.4.2.3 *Social Spending (as a Share of GDP)*

The third of our proxies, social spending as a share of GDP, also performed admirably in machine learning. All machine learning models delivered r^2 and adjusted r^2 values exceeding 0.994 during training. Indeed, the baseline decision tree attained a flawless r^2 of 1.000000 during training. Because test set results offer deeper insight into generalizability, we will spend most of our effort evaluating the performance of supervised machine learning on test data.

As applied to test data, the baseline CART decision tree reported r^2 of 0.972089 and adjusted r^2 of 0.968545. Bagging reported r^2 of 0.976136 and adjusted r^2 of 0.973106. The bagging algorithm's out-of-bag score reported a slightly lower value of r^2 at 0.963035. The closeness of these values implies that tree-based machine learning was properly fit to the social spending dataset.

As predictors of social spending, random forests and extra trees also performed very well. Random forests reached an r^2 of 0.971307 and an adjusted r^2 of 0.967663. Extra trees reported an r^2 of 0.984917 and adjusted r^2 of 0.983002. Extra trees thus added 58% in further accuracy with respect to the final 2.9% of variance not explained by random forests.

Feature importances for these tree- and forest-based models revealed intriguing relationships among variables hypothesized to predict social spending as a portion of GDP (Figs. 5.16, 5.17, and 5.18).

The naked decision tree assigned nearly half of its feature importance on a single factor, pension spending. Somewhat surprisingly, however, the decision tree attributed half of its predictive weight to migration. By contrast, the two ensemble methods assigned nearly half of their feature importance weights to three social security variables: pension spending, health spending and social contributions. Migration fades in

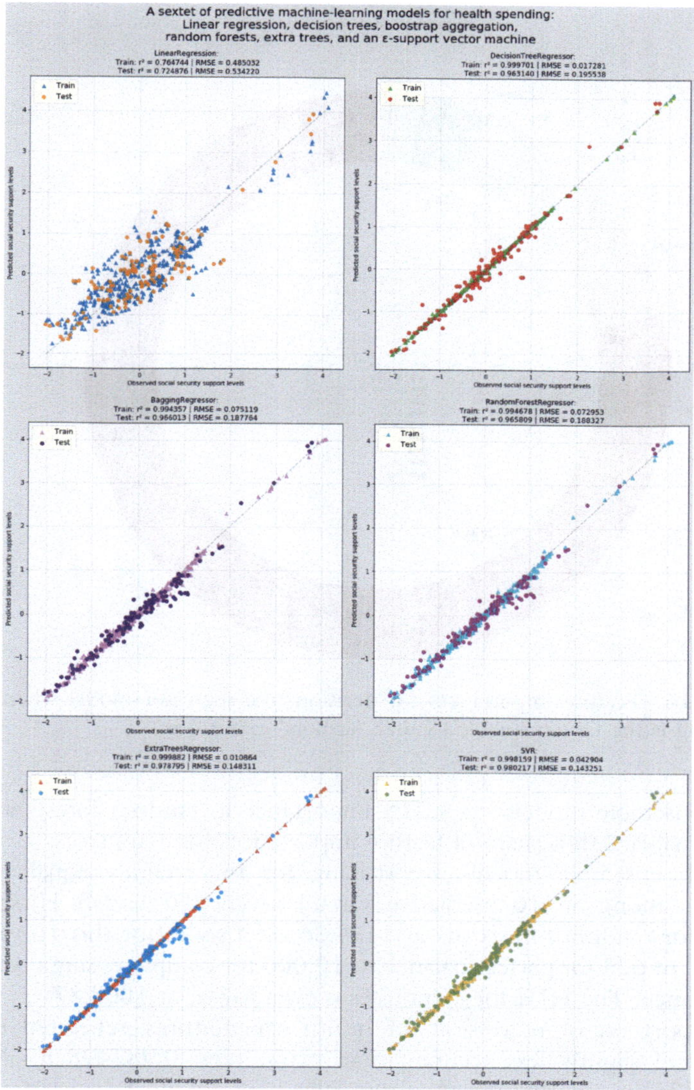

Fig. 5.15 Visualization of the training and the test sets for decision tree regressor, random forest regressor, extra trees regressor and support vector regressor model when health spending is the target variable (*Source* Authors' calculation)

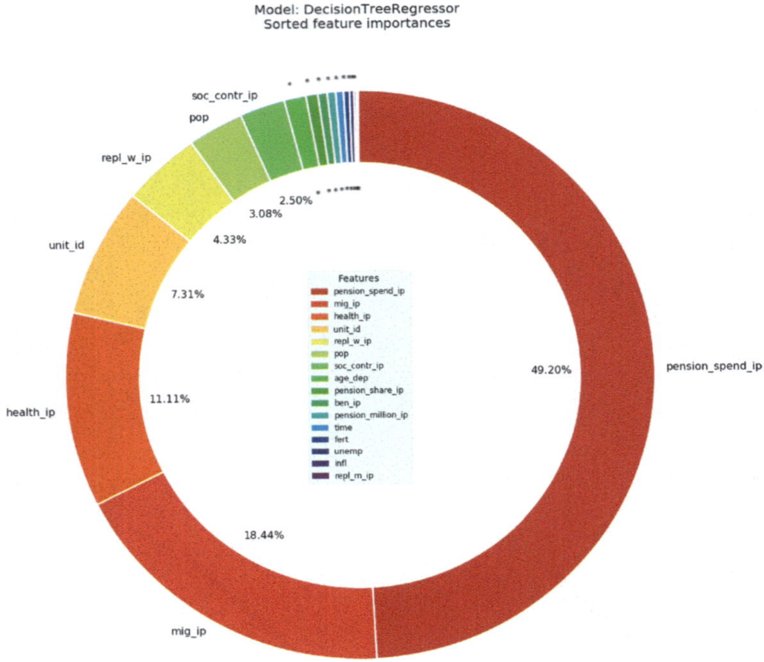

Fig. 5.16 Feature importances for decision tree regressor model when social spending is the target variable (*Source* Authors' calculation)

both ensemble models: to 4.21% importance in random forests and an even smaller 2.09% share of feature importances for extra trees.

Both ensemble models are striking for the roughly equal contribution among all 16 predictive variables. The Herfindahl-Hirschman index for random forests sits at 1134.36 on a scale (for this 16-variable model) of 625 for perfect balance to 10,000 for complete, single-variable dominance. The HHI for extra trees is even lower, at 1008.87.

Support vector regression for health expenditures generated results that were slightly less accurate than extra trees: 0.982498 in r^2 and 0.980275 in adjusted r^2. An unusually high value of hyperparameter C (158.4) generates a visibly more compact pattern of support vectors. Although higher values of C are typically associated with overfitting

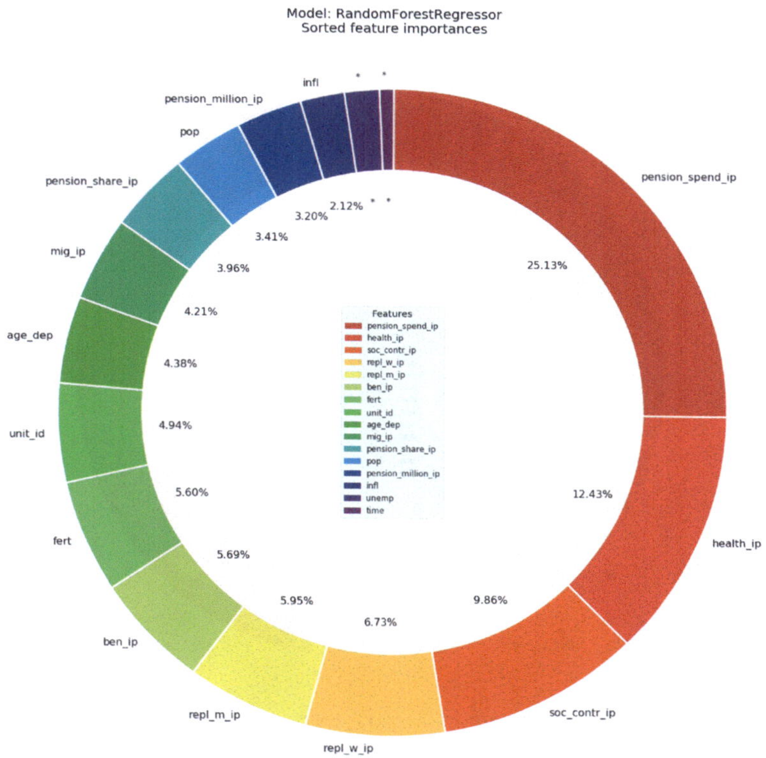

Fig. 5.17 Feature importances for random forest regressor model when social spending is the target variable (*Source* Authors' calculation)

(Géron, 2019, p. 155), this support vector machine exhibited no unusual vulnerability to overfitting (Fig. 5.19).

Table 5.4c reports training and test set results for machine learning predictions involving social spending as a share of GDP.

This visual summary of linear regression, a naked decision tree, bagging, random forests, extra trees and support vector regression shows how machine learning models dominate OLS. As well behaved as the baseline linear model is for the social spending proxy, all machine learning models deliver far more accurate predictions across the entire breadth of both the training and the test datasets (Fig. 5.20).

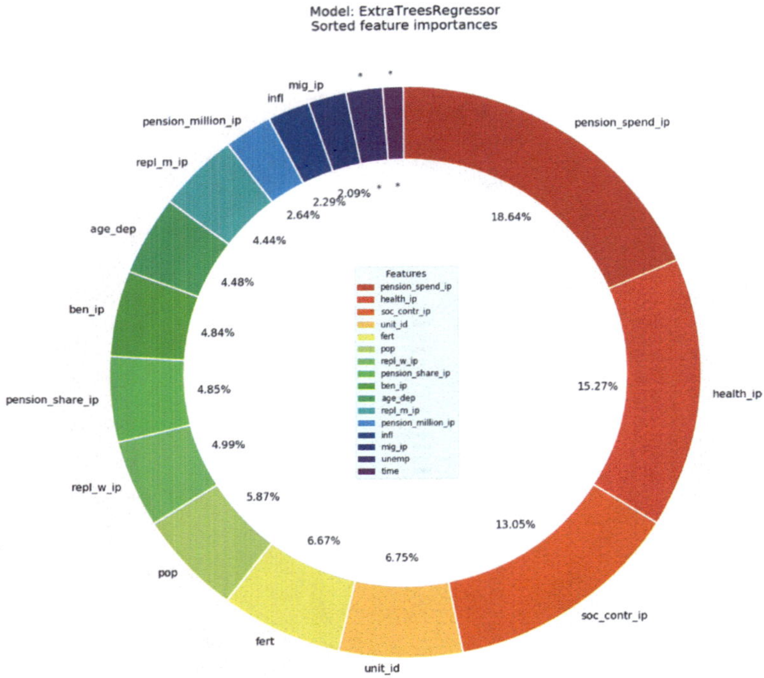

Fig. 5.18 Feature importances for extra trees regressor model when social spending is the target variable (*Source* Authors' calculation)

5.4.2.4 *Pension Spending (as a Share of GDP)*

Our final social security proxy, pension spending as a share of GDP, posed the greatest challenges to machine learning. Although extra trees exceeded 0.94 in r^2, several models struggled to predict pension spending as a function of social security and demographic factors. Of the proxies we have enlisted to model different countries' commitment to social security, the discernibly greater struggle to predict pension spending suggests that this variable requires more data along either or both of two dimensions. Better prediction of pension spending may require a greater number of predictive variables, a deeper set of observations (from the same set of countries or, ideally, a broader pool of countries), or in all likelihood, data enhancement in every respect.

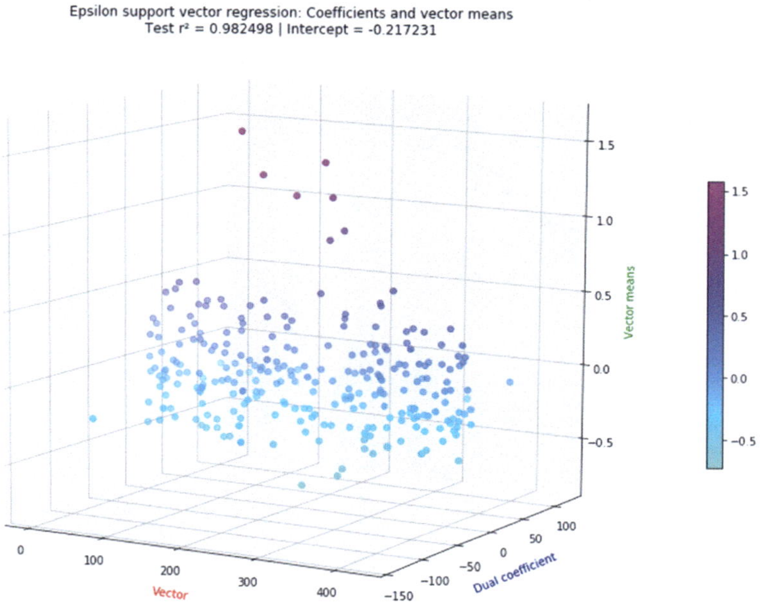

Fig. 5.19 Graphical representation of the coefficients and the vector means of the epsilon support vector model when social spending is the target variable (*Source* Authors' calculation)

Table 5.4c Target variable: social spending as a share of GDP

Model	r^2*, training set*	*Adjusted* r^2*, training set*	r^2*, test set*	*Adjusted* r^2*, test set*
Linear	0.761814	0.752564	0.771094	0.742026
Decision tree	1.000000	1.000000	0.972089	0.968545
Bagged trees	0.994988	0.994793	0.976136	0.973106
Random forest	0.995387	0.995207	0.971307	0.967663
Extra trees	0.999950	0.999948	0.984917	0.983002
Support vector	0.999054	0.999017	0.982498	0.980275

Source Authors' calculations

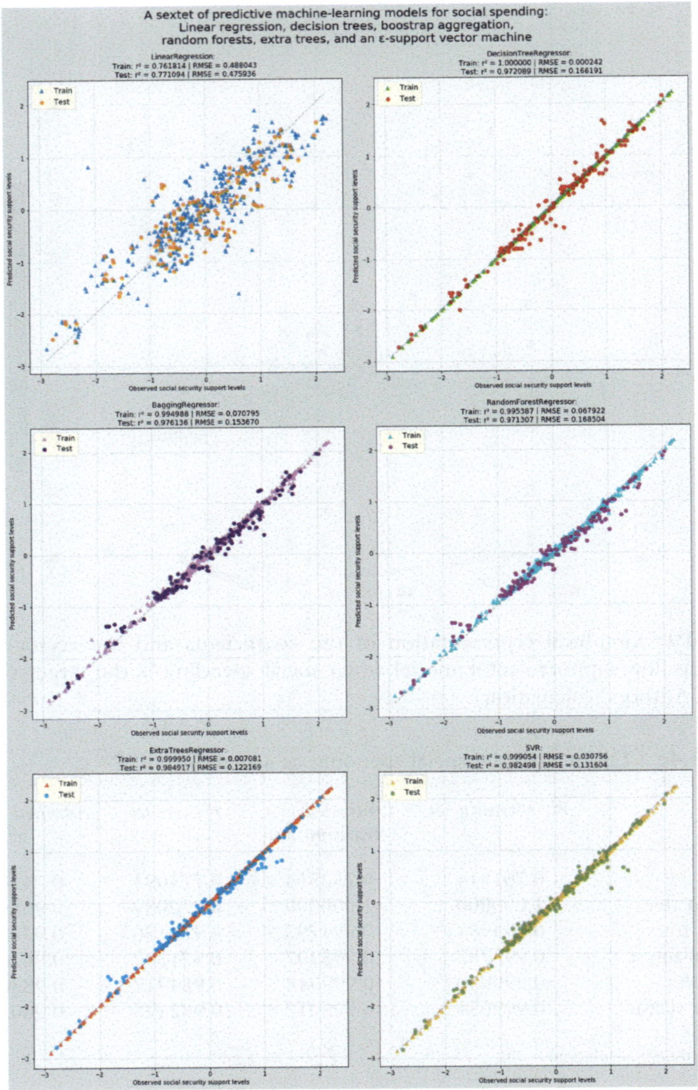

Fig. 5.20 Visualization of the training and the test sets for decision tree regressor, random forest regressor, extra trees regressor and support vector regressor model when social spending is the target variable (*Source* Authors' calculation)

Machine learning struggles with the pension spending proxy emerged during training. Although tree- and forest-based models delivered r^2 and adjusted r^2 values exceeding 0.96 during training, support vector regression reported r^2 of 0.764276 and adjusted r^2 of 0.755122, respectively. Although test set results are much more indicative of any machine learning model's predictive success, a discrepancy of that size in training accuracy foresages wide differences in success between classes of methods. If nothing else, these differences vindicate the "no free lunch" theorem of machine learning and the wisdom of applying a wider variety of methods to every problem (Wolpert, 1996).

The CART decision tree for pension spending proved to be the only machine learning result in this study that failed to beat a baseline linear regression. The decision tree generated r^2 of 0.613453 and adjusted r^2 of 0.564368. The respective values for a simple OLS regression were 0.708667 and 0.671672.

The simplest method for improving a naked decision tree, bootstrap aggregation, did elevate this elementary machine learning method over the linear benchmark. Bagging improved r^2 to 0.810854 and adjusted r^2 to 0.786835. The discernibly lower out-of-bag score of 0.728536 in r^2 suggests, however, that decision tree-based methods for predicting social spending might struggle to duplicate their success, both in absolute terms and in terms of avoidance of overfitting, relative to machine learning predictions for other proxy variables.

Despite lagging their performance in predicting autonomous pension assets and health and social spending, random forests and extra trees dramatically improved upon the accuracy of a naked decision tree and bootstrap aggregation in predicting pension spending. Random forests attained r^2 of 0.878616 and an adjusted r^2 of 0.863202. Alone among methods applied to pension spending, extra trees crossed the 0.90 threshold for r^2 and adjusted r^2. Extra tree results for those benchmarks, respectively, were 0.941217 and 0.933753.

Feature importances for tree- and forest-based models affirmed the primacy of social security factors in predictions of pension spending—as well as the surprising prominence of certain demographic factors (Figs. 5.21, 5.22, and 5.23).

Feature importances for random forests and extra trees highlight the same five predictive variables: social spending, social contributions, the fertility rate, autonomous pension assets as a share of GDP and unemployment. Fertility and the pension asset share switch places—third and

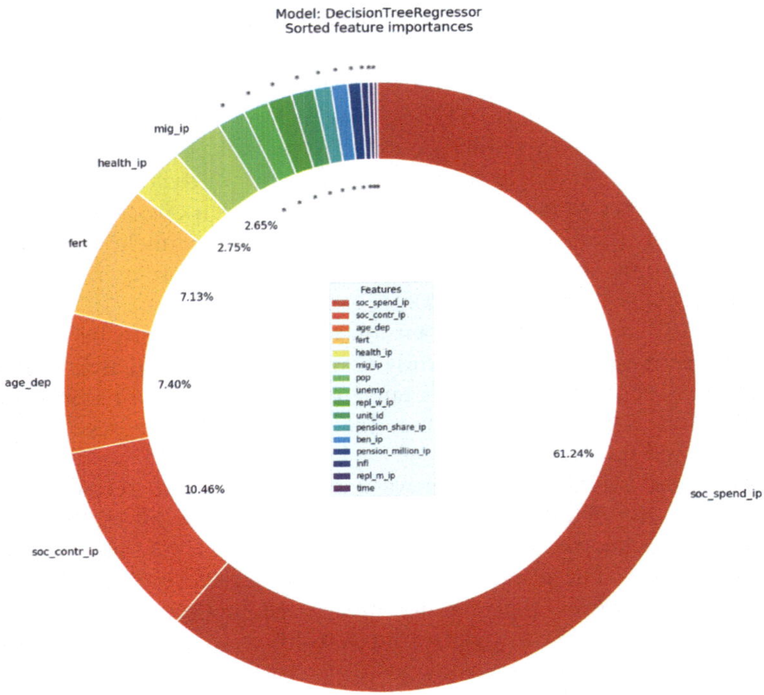

Fig. 5.21 Feature importances for decision tree regressor model when pension spending is the target variable (*Source* Authors' calculation)

fourth in extra trees, but fourth and third in random forests—in a very tight ranking.

The relative prominence of these features confirms many of the intuitions inferred from conventional econometric analysis. Growth (or decline) in population and employment profoundly affect the health and sustainability of pensions. Unlike coefficients in linear models, machine learning feature importances are invariably cast as positive values in a vector of probabilities whose sum is 1. Although feature importances, on their own, cannot reveal the direction of the relationship between a predictor and target variable, we may infer that fertility and employment carry greater weight in influencing public-sector spending on pensions.

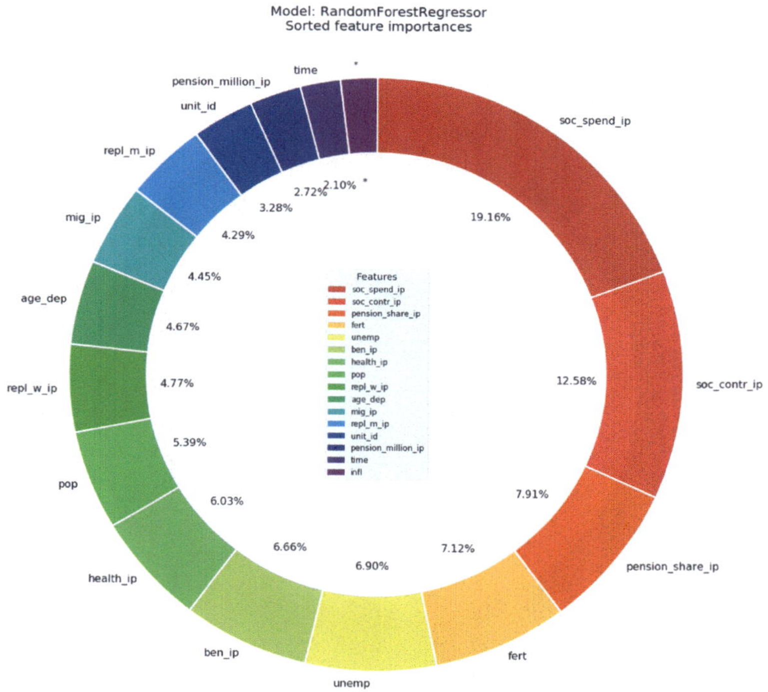

Fig. 5.22 Feature importances for random forest regressor model when pension spending is the target variable (*Source* Authors' calculation)

In all events, we should refrain from drawing excessively strong conclusions from this analysis of feature importances. The Herfindahl-Hirschman indexes for the random forest and extra trees method are quite low: 905.44 and 839.85 respectively, far closer to the minimum HHI value of 625 for 16 features than the maximum value of 10,000.

Among our four proxies for social security spending, pension spending proved most resistant to prediction through support vector regression. Test r^2 of 0.833713 and adjusted r^2 of 0.812598 were by far the lowest levels of accuracy achieved by a support vector machine in this study. Those accuracy measures lagged far behind the scores posted by random forests and extra trees, which were 0.878515 and 0.941217, respectively, for unadjusted r^2.

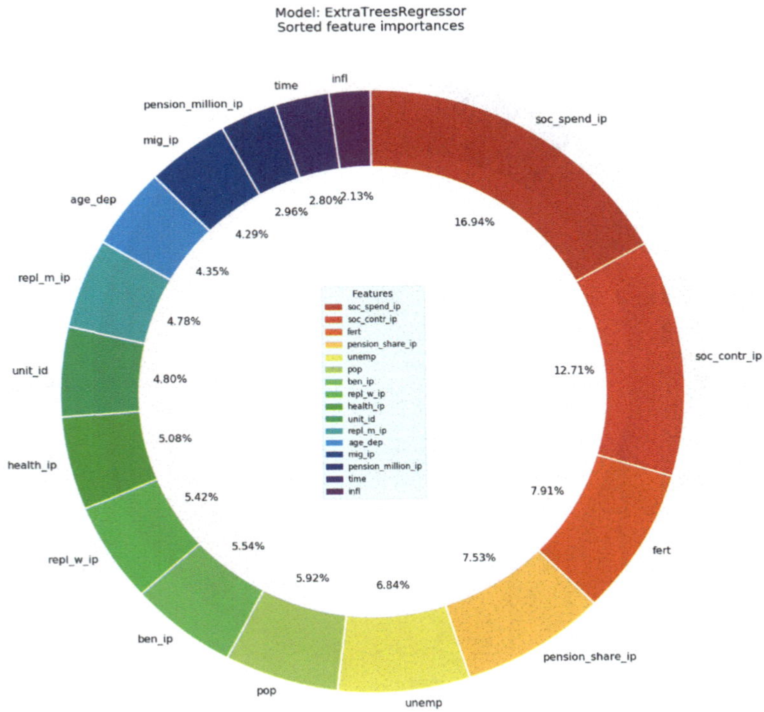

Fig. 5.23 Feature importances for extra trees regressor model when pension spending is the target variable (*Source* Authors' calculation)

The *C* hyperparameter for pension spending was an unusually low 3.2, by stark contrast with a value of 158.4 for *C* in the support vector machine for social spending. The resulting plot of support vectors for *C* = 3.2 more closely resembles random, Brownian motion than the same three-dimensional plot for any other proxy (Fig. 5.24).

Table 5.4d reports training and test set results for machine learning predictions involving pension spending as a share of GDP.

Unlike other visual summaries of linear regression, a naked decision tree, bagging, random forests, extra trees and support vector regression, the accuracy scatterplot for social spending had to be clipped so that values between $\pm 3z$ on a standardized scale could be highlighted.

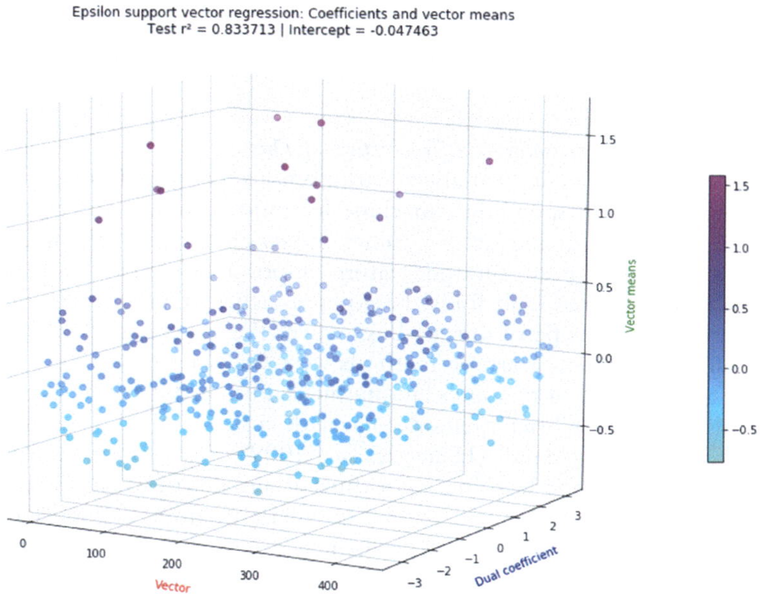

Fig. 5.24 Graphical representation of the coefficients and the vector means of the epsilon support vector model when pension spending is the target variable (*Source* Authors' calculation)

Table 5.4d Target variable: pension spending as a share of GDP

Model	r^2, *training set*	*Adjusted* r^2, *training set*	r^2, *test set*	*Adjusted* r^2, *test set*
Linear	0.604976	0.589635	0.708667	0.671672
Decision tree	0.999540	0.999523	0.613453	0.564368
Bagged trees	0.963522	0.962105	0.810854	0.786835
Random forest	0.972256	0.971178	0.878616	0.863202
Extra trees	0.998189	0.998118	0.941217	0.933753
Support vector	0.764276	0.755122	0.833713	0.812598

Source Authors' calculations

Lower test set accuracy suggests more trouble with the possible overfitting of machine learning models than with other proxies for social security spending (Fig. 5.25).

5.4.2.5 *The "Unreasonable Effectiveness of Data"*

For three of four proxy variables (autonomous pension funds, health spending and social spending), machine learning accuracy converged at very high levels. Unadjusted r^2 values approached 1 for all machine learning methods, even though feature importances might not have aligned across all tree- and forest-based approaches. The lone exception to this tendency was pension spending, where the lowest and highest r^2 scores among machine learning methods were 0.33 apart.

The convergence of r^2 values among more advanced machine learning methods warrants a brief methodological discussion of "the unreasonable effectiveness of data" (Halevy et al., 2009). Given sufficient data, very different machine learning algorithms attain almost identical results on complex problems such as natural language disambiguation (Banko & Brill, 2001). Convergence in performance in spite of differences in these algorithms' complexity or effectiveness on smaller datasets suggests the primacy of data over theoretical elaboration, experimental design and algorithmic sophistication. "[I]nvariably, simple models and a lot of data trump more elaborate models based on less data" (Halevy et al., 2009, p. 9).

At least for three of four proxies for social security spending, this chapter reached very similar conclusions through machine learning methods based on radically different algorithmic foundations. Whether those methods used decision trees or support vectors, they all approached perfect predictive accuracy. Any gap in the accuracy of machine learning results and those attained through conventional econometrics may reflect something besides intrinsic differences in the efficacy of these methods. Rather, given the admittedly constrained amount of data available, superior performance in machine learning suggests that these methods attain optimal predictive power at a lower threshold relative to traditional methods such as OLS regression.

The same insight holds with respect to disparities between machine learning outcomes for pension spending. All machine learning datasets used in this chapter share the same basic structure and underwent the same standard scaling and train/test splitting steps in preprocessing. Differences in performance are likely to have arisen from the adequacy of

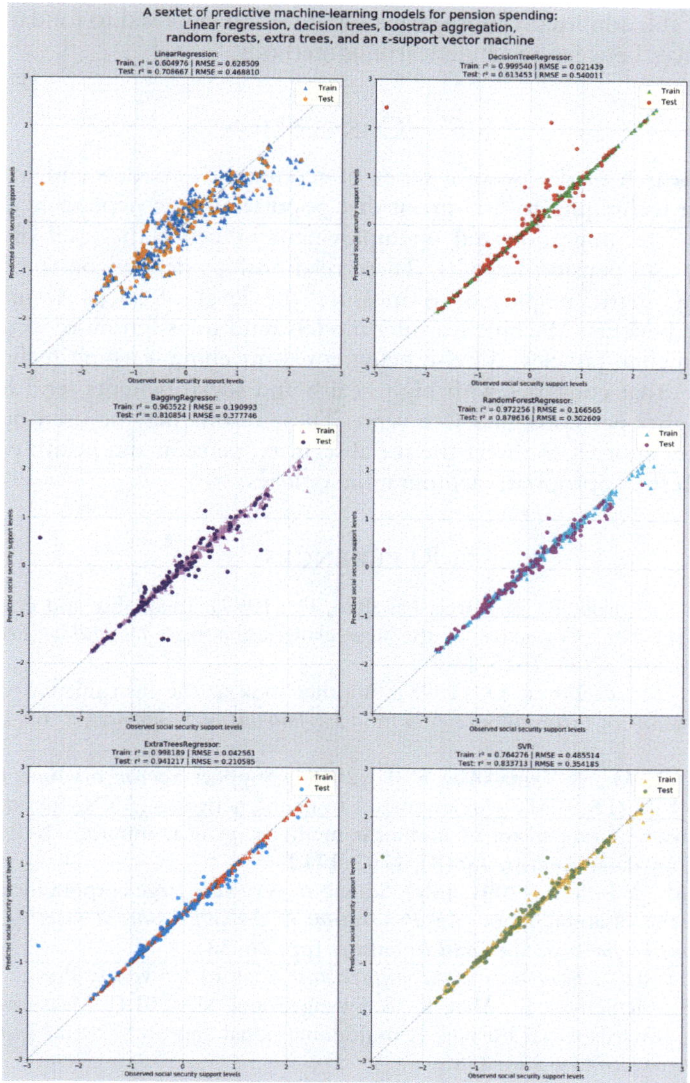

Fig. 5.25 Visualization of the training and the test sets for decision tree regressor, random forest regressor, extra trees regressor and support vector regressor model when pension spending is the target variable (*Source* Authors' calculation)

data for this admittedly more challenging task, as opposed to fundamental differences between machine learning methods.

5.5 Conclusion

This research made use of a series of econometric models and machine learning techniques to find proof that population, age dependency ratio, fertility rate, migration and unemployment influence the level of social security and pension benefits. These relationships depend on the model and the metric employed to measure the level of social security or pension benefits. Machine learning models tend to assign more weight to governmental policies. All else being equal, machine learning techniques indicate, that countries with high health and social benefits tend to also have higher pensions, and vice versa. These results may be used by policymakers in order to direct the social security, pension and health policies through the appropriate demographic policies.

References

Aghion, P., Caroli, E., & Garcia-Penalosa, C. (1999). Inequality and economic growth: The perspective of the new growth theories. *Journal of Economic Literature, 37*(4), 1615–1660.

Arellano, M., & Bover, O. (1995). Another look at the instrumental variable estimation of error-components models. *Journal of Econometrics, 68*(1), 29–51.

Balabin, R. M., & Lomakina, E. I. (2011). Support vector machine regression (SVR/LS-SVM)—An alternative to neural networks (ANN) for analytical chemistry? Comparison of nonlinear methods on near infrared (NIR) spectroscopy data. *Analyst, 136*(8), 1703–1712.

Banko, M., & Brill, E. (2001, July). Scaling to very very large corpora for natural language disambiguation. In *Proceedings of the 39th annual meeting of the association for computational linguistics* (pp. 26–33).

Barr, N. (2020). *Economics of the welfare state*. Oxford University Press.

Baute, S., Meuleman, B., Abts, K., & Swyngedouw, M. (2018). Measuring attitudes towards social Europe: A multidimensional approach. *Social Indicators Research, 137*(1), 353–378.

Blundell, R., & Bond, S. (1998). Initial conditions and moment restrictions in dynamic panel data models. *Journal of Econometrics, 87*(1), 115–143.

Börsch-Supan, A., & Schnabel, R. (1997). Social security and declining labor-force participation in Germany. *The American Economic Review, 88*(2), 173–178.

Borstlap, H. (1996). Labour market, social protection and economic performance. In P. A. G. van Bergeijk et al. (Eds.), *Economic science: Art or asset? The case of the Netherlands* (85–94). OCFEB, Rotterdam.

Breiman, L. (1996). Bagging predictors. *Machine Learning, 24*(2), 123–140.

Breiman, L. (1999). Pasting small votes for classification in large databases and on-line. *Machine Learning, 36*(1–2), 85–103.

Breiman, L. (2001). Statistical modeling: The two cultures (with comments and a rejoinder by the author). *Statistical Science, 16*(3), 199–231.

Breiman, L., Friedman, J., Stone, C. J., & Olshen, R. A. (1984). *Classification and regression trees*. CRC Press.

British White Paper on Social Security Reform. (1969). H.M. Stationery Office.

Connolly, S., & Munro, A. (1999). *The economics of the public sector*. Prentice Hall.

European Parliament. (2015). European Union pension systems: Adequate and sustainable? Briefing November 2015. https://www.europarl.europa.eu/RegData/etudes/BRIE/2015/571327/EPRS_BRI(2015)571327_EN.pdf. Accessed Nov 2020.

Geman, S., Bienenstock, E., & Doursat, R. (1992). Neural networks and the bias/variance dilemma. *Neural Computation, 4*(1), 1–58.

Géron, A. (2019). *Hands-on machine learning with Scikit-Learn, Keras, and TensorFlow: Concepts, tools, and techniques to build intelligent systems*. O'Reilly Media.

Goodhart, C., & Pradhan, M. (2017). *Demographics will reverse three multi-decade global trends*. Available https://www.bis.org/publ/work656.pdf. Last Accessed 29 Sept 2020.

Geurts, P., Ernst, D., & Wehenkel, L. (2006). Extremely randomized trees. *Machine Learning, 63*(1), 3–42.

Hagist, C., Moog, S., Raffelhüschen, B., & Vatter, J. (2009). Public debt and demography—An international comparison using generational accounting. *CESifo DICE Report, 7*(4), 29–36.

Halevy, A., Norvig, P., & Pereira, F. (2009). The unreasonable effectiveness of data. *IEEE Intelligent Systems, 24*(2), 8–12.

Ho, T. K. (1995, August). Random decision forests. In *Proceedings of 3rd international conference on document analysis and recognition* (Vol. 1, pp. 278–282). IEEE.

Kohavi, R., & Wolpert, D. H. (1996, July). Bias plus variance decomposition for zero-one loss functions. *ICML, 96*, 275–283.

Kotlikoff, L. J. (1998). Simulating the privatization of social security in general equilibrium. In *Privatizing social security* (pp. 265–311). University of Chicago Press.

Kubben, P., Dumontier, M., & Dekker, A. (2019). *Fundamentals of clinical data science* (p. 219). Springer Nature.

Lesthaeghe, R. (2010). The unfolding story of the second demographic transition. *Population and Development Review, 36*(2), 211–251.

Lesthaeghe, R. (2014). The second demographic transition: A concise overview of its development. *Proceedings of the National Academy of Sciences, 111*(51), 18112–18115.

Lesthaeghe, R. J., & Neidert, L. (2006). The second demographic transition in the United States: Exception or textbook example? *Population and Development Review, 32*(4), 669–698.

Lesthaeghe, R., & Neidert, L. (2009). US presidential elections and the spatial pattern of the American second demographic transition. *Population and Development Review, 35*(2), 391–400.

Liston-Heyes, C., & Pilkington, A. (2004). Inventive concentration in the production of green technology: A comparative analysis of fuel cell patents. *Science and Public Policy, 31*(1), 15–25.

Loh, Wei-Yin. (2008). Classification and regression tree methods. In F. Ruggeri, R. S. Kennet & F. W. Faltin (Eds.), *Encyclopedia of statistics in quality and reliability* (pp. 315–323). Wiley.

Lu, C., & Liu, J. (2017). Does social security promote regional economic growth? A dynamic spatial panel model analysis based on time and space effect and decomposition. *Journal of Huazhong University of Science and Technology* (Soc. Sci. Ed.).

Marimon, R., & Zilibotti, F. (1999). Unemployment vs. mismatch of talents: Reconsidering unemployment benefits. *The Economic Journal, 109*(455), 266–291.

Mimoun, M. B., & Raies, A. (2009). Education and economic growth: The role of public expenditures allocation. *Economics Bulletin, 29*(3), 2404–2416.

Miron, J. A., & Weil, D. N. (1997). *The genesis and evolution of social security* (No. w5949). National Bureau of Economic Research.

Müller, A. C., & Guido, S. (2017). *Introduction to machine learning with Python: A guide for data scientists*. O'Reilly Media, Inc.

Okun, A. M. (1975). *Equality and efficiency: The big tradeoff*. Brookings Institution. See also the discussion of unidimensionality below.

Persson, T., & Tabellini, G. (1994). Is inequality harmful for growth? *American Economic Review, 84*(3), 600–621.

Pieters, D. (1998). *Social protection of the next generation in Europe: EISS yearbook 1997* (Vol. 2). Kluwer Law Intl.

Pietro, G. D. (2003). Equality of opportunity in Italian university education: Is there any role for social welfare spending? *International Journal of Educational Development, 23*(1), 5–15.

Scicchitano, S. (2010). Complementarity between heterogeneous human capital and R&D: Can job-training avoid low development traps? *Empirica, 37*(4), 361–380.

United Nations. (1948). Universal declaration of human rights. https://www.un.org/en/about-us/universal-declaration-of-human-rights. Accessed Nov 20 2020.

Wolpert, D. H. (1996). The lack of a priori distinctions between learning algorithms. *Neural Computation, 8*(7), 1341–1390.

World Social Protection Report 2017–2019. (2017). Universal social protection to achieve the Sustainable Development Goals.

Yang, H., Chan, L., & King, I. (2002, August). Support vector machine regression for volatile stock market prediction. In *International conference on intelligent data engineering and automated learning* (pp. 391–396). Springer.

CHAPTER 6

Debt and Social Security

Thomas Poufinas, George Galanos, and Charalampos Agiropoulos

6.1 Introduction

The fiscal deficit of several countries around the world reached its highest point in early 2007 when the global financial crisis began to approach one country after another. The result of this economic volatility is the excessive debt growth of the countries that have entered this crisis in recent years. Several countries are still suffering from the effects of the crisis today, searching the right formula to exit this unpleasant situation.

In the aftermath of the most recent (2008) financial crisis and its subsequent debt crisis, several countries have realized the effect that social security had in their sovereign debt and have tried to find measures to contain it. Of course the contribution of social security to the country debt very much depends on the system each country operates and the

T. Poufinas (✉)
Department of Economics, Democritus University of Thrace, Komotini, Greece
e-mail: tpoufina@econ.duth.gr

G. Galanos · C. Agiropoulos
Department of International and European Studies, University of Piraeus, Piraeus, Greece

T. Poufinas (ed.), *Debt in Times of Crisis*,
https://doi.org/10.1007/978-3-030-74162-4_6

(in)dependence of social security from the government budget. The mix in some countries became even more explosive due to the increase in unemployment, the decrease in social security contribution and the drop in the fertility and replacement rate. The debate is vivid both in the United States and in the European countries, as the authorities and the practitioners argue whether Social Security adds to the country debt. At the same time, one needs to recall that social security (almost independently from the system in force) is one of the top investors—lenders of the country as it puts the majority of its accumulated funds into government bonds. In this chapter we seek evidence of the contribution of social security to the debt of the countries, especially the ones that faced serious debt burden over the last decade with the use of a series of econometric models (pooled OLS, fixed effects and random effects). We realize that the relationship between debt and social security appears to be quite robust and may be one of the most important issues that certain countries still may have to face. Although several researchers have investigated the variables that affect government debt, few of them have examined the determinants of private debt and its impact on the global economy, especially in the context of social security and pensions. This chapter attempts to capture the link between public debt or private debt and a series of pension and social security proxies, and there lies its contribution to the field. The novelties of the study are the consideration of a series of countries (and not a single one), the breadth of the pension and social security variables introduced, the simultaneous investigation of public and private debt, as well as the employment of a series of econometric models.

6.2 Literature Review

The available literature is separated in three main strands; the research that deals with public debt; the studies that treat private debt; and finally the papers that tackle social security along with public and private debt.

6.2.1 Public Debt

Three main features have been noted in the literature considering public debt management. Giavazzi and Pagano (1990) and Calvo and Guidotti (1990) have identified and modelized efficiently the problem of variation of fiscal policies. A different approach has been proposed by Barro (2003) who tried to structure the public debt in a way where the tax revenue could be appropriately decreased given that public expending works exogenously in an applicable environment. Furthermore, Missale et al. (2002), as well as Giavazzi and Missale (2004), attempt to tackle the stability of the public debt over Gross Domestic Product (GDP). All three approaches end up in similar conclusions: the optimized strategy for public debt management should be followed by an increase in the average maturity and the partial indexation of public debt.

On the other hand, Georges (2006) contradicts with many authors and suggests that a short maturity of the public debt is on average cheaper and can imply less risk to the public budget. Through an analysis that considers the effect of several maturity frameworks on interest rate and on primary surplus for Canada, Georges (2006) observed that when both effects are considered, the trade-off between cost and risk can decrease.

As Wolswijk and de Haan (2006) have noted, following the creation of the Eurozone, a combination of a decrease in the foreign exchange risk, increases in the maturity of the public debt, use of derivatives (swaps) and inflation-linked government bonds, was observed. Although this strategy has not been enough to prevent the harmful effect of the crisis of 2007 in the European countries, Anderson et al. (2010) based on a sample of 24 emerging economies, pointed out that the improvement in the public debt management (particularly the increase in the maturity of the public debt) moderated the impact of the crisis in those countries.

6.2.2 *Private Debt*

According to Myers (1984), firms facing high costs of asymmetric information will use external funds only when internally generated funds are not adequate. If external funds are required, the firm will issue the "safest" security first—the one whose value changes least when inside information is revealed to the market—first debt and then, only as a last resort, equity. Because private debt lenders are better informed through monitoring and screening, and are usually senior (Welch, 1997) and collateralized (Rajan & Winton, 1995), it is hypothesized that private debt will be a safer instrument than arm's length debt, holding constant the degree of information asymmetry between the firm and the outside market. Thus, firms with higher levels of asymmetric information, and a higher probability of default, will issue private debt before public debt. As the degree of asymmetric information decreases, the scale of safety becomes less important, and the debt choice for firms with lower asymmetry will be determined by other factors—e.g. transactions costs, the flexibility of covenants (Gilson & Warner, 1997), credit quality (Diamond, 1991) and the possibility of rent extraction by banks (Rajan, 1992).

Bank debt and non-bank private debt differ in terms of regulatory requirements, maturity, placement structure and the concentration and identity of debtholders. This regulation allows companies to market debt directly to private institutional investors rather than going through the more time-consuming public securities issuance process. Carleton and Kwan (1995) describe non-bank private loans as tightly held and relatively illiquid. In addition, non-bank private loans tend to have lower flotation costs than public issues and have custom-designed covenants.

6.2.3 *Social Security*

Several studies have analyzed public pension and population aging in economic growth models (e.g. Futagami & Nakajima, 2001; Meijdam & Verbon, 1997; Pecchenino & Pollard, 1997; Pecchenino & Utendorf, 1999). However, these studies do not consider a social security policy together with public debt. Gertler (1999), who modified the Blanchard (1985) and Weil (1989) framework in order to allow life-cycle behavior, analyzed social security as financed by public debt. However, his study assumed a perfect annuity market, and the analysis was therefore unable to capture the economic impact of a pension reform toward an actuarially fair scheme.

Ono (2003) develops an overlapping generations model of growth and aging according to the model suggested by Pecchenino and Pollard (1997), and then uses this framework to analyze the economic impact of social security financed by public debt. Ono (2003) argues that when an economy with an aging population is heavily burdened with social security payments and the government issues public debt to finance payments, the economy experiences a dynamically inefficient equilibrium characterized by excessive savings, i.e. overaccumulation of capital.

Werding (2006) shows that implicit pension debt related with pay-as-you-go public pension schemes, is an important driver of the long-term sustainability of general government finances. At the same time he realizes that unfunded pension schemes potentially have a negative effect on human capital accumulation and thus on future contributions.

Bovenberg and van Ewijk (2011) argue that more private retirement saving is necessary to maintain old-age incomes under a debt crisis that dictate the cut of public pensions; and that private saving in pension funds may prove to be a stabilizer of sovereign debt markets.

Mendonça and Tiberto (2014) confirmed that the social security deficit significantly contributes to an increase in the public debt in the case of Brazil only. Regarding the effects on social security, it was observed that an increase in the level of formality in the economy reduces the deficit. In contrast, Mendonça and Tiberto (2014) show that a reduction in income inequality, a real increase in the minimum wage, and an increase in health benefits imply an increase in the social security deficit. Therefore, these variables play a crucial role in the search for an efficient social security management system and cannot be overlooked in ensuring fiscal sustainability.

Poufinas and Kouskouna (2016) discuss a potential way to rearrange social security contributions so that they alleviate the burden of the state and at the same time create value for the state and the society. They employ an actuarial model to split the contributions to defined benefit and defined contribution schemes. This facilitates the transition from defined benefit to defined contribution pension schemes in a way that optimizes the output for the beneficiaries. The same authors show, with the use of econometric models, that such a split may be beneficial for the growth of the country (Poufinas & Kouskouna, 2017).

The evolution and determinants of China's social security debt, its spread in the different provinces and its projection in the future is discussed in Li and Lin (2019). The authors recommend an increase in social security revenue through the reduction of contribution evasion; an increase in the (investment) return to the social security fund; a decrease in the social security expenditure via a reduction of the replacement rate, an increase of the retirement age and unification of the social security system within the country; and a shift to a defined contribution social security system.

The topic has been discussed also by governments and policymakers; Huston and Driessen (2020) realize that an increase in social security deficits will lead to an increase of the federal deficits. In addition, if social security begins to run deficits (as the Board of Trustees projects as of 2021), one way the government can finance it is by increasing publicly held debt, next to increasing revenues or reduce its spending elsewhere.

Going now to private debt, Hurst and Willen (2007) use a calibrated life-cycle model to show that when households are allowed to use (part of) their social security wealth to repay their debt or are fully excluded from social security contributions (when young), then life-cycle planning becomes more effective.

Lin et al. (2019) examine the role of pensions in corporate debt to find a significant and robust relationship between corporate short-term debt ratio and pension liabilities. At the same time they realize that an increase in pension obligations results in an increase in the cost of debt. This effect can be mitigated by short-term debt.

6.3 Problem Description and Theoretical Background

The intuition behind the investigation of the influence of social security on debt stems from the effort of countries to contain their government debt at levels that can be sustained by their economic activities in total and in particular by their GDPs. High public debt to GDP can lead to distressed economies and can create problems to other aspects of the economic (and not only) lives of the countries. However, the same holds true with the private debt; high private debt to GDP may result in distressed households and enterprises, which can also lead to further problems for the interested parties, including the country as a whole.

The question that the countries try to answer is what measures to take so as to maintain primarily their public and secondarily their private debt (as a portion of their GDP) at amounts that they can serve. The contribution of social security benefits and in particular pension benefits and spending to debt has long been debated. It came once and again at the forefront during the latest economic crisis, during which in certain countries pension cuts were enforced as a means to sustain debt.

In our research, we try to find evidence of the link between public and private debt (as a percent of GDP) and social security metrics for the countries of interest. We do that with the use of certain econometric models that will be presented in the following sections. At the same time we incorporate in our models other macroeconomic variables that are known or believed to also influence the public and private debt.

Revealing this relationship can be beneficial to the respective authorities and policymakers, as they can decide on the social security and more specifically on the pension benefits they may want to maintain or alter or which other country figures they may want to improve so as to maintain the public and private debt at the desired levels. Countries that have suffered the most during the latest economic crisis may have experienced higher debt levels compared to countries that have managed to weather the crisis more successfully. As a matter of fact high public and private debt compared to GDP could have been among the causes of heavier suffering. Consequently, tackling or avoiding a potential (new) crisis is in their interest; knowing in advance what to do is of key importance and it requires a global approach rather than the management of one or a few determinants—variables.

6.4 Data, Variables and Methodology

6.4.1 Data

Our dataset consists of Australia, Austria, Belgium, Canada, Chile, Czech Republic, Denmark, Estonia, Finland, France, Germany, Greece, Hungary, Iceland, Ireland, Israel, Italy, Japan, Korea, Latvia, Lithuania, Luxembourg, Mexico, Netherlands, New Zealand, Norway, Poland, Portugal, Slovak Republic, Slovenia, Spain, Sweden, Switzerland, Turkey, United Kingdom and the United States. These are essentially the OECD countries.

Our data source is the Organization for Economic Cooperation and Development—OECD (2019) for the public debt (general government gross debt as a % of GDP), the private debt (as a percent of GDP), the pension fund assets (autonomous—in million USD and as a share of GDP), the pension spending (public as a % of GDP), the social expenditure (as a % of GDP), the expenditure in health (current—as a share of GDP), as well as pension benefits (as a share of GDP) and contributions (as a share of GDP) for all countries except for the United States; for the latter the data comes from the Federal Reserve Bank of St. Louis (2019). It is the World Bank (2019) for the unemployment (rate—% of labor force), the inflation (rate—%), the GDP per capita (current USD) and the foreign direct investment—FDI (net inflows, current USD).

Our time series extends from 2001 to 2017, which is deemed a sufficient period for allowing us to draw reliable results.

6.4.2 *Descriptive Statistics*

The descriptive statistics of our dataset, i.e. the mean, the 50th percentile, the standard deviation, the variance, the number of observations, the range, the minimum value and the maximum value of the relevant metric are summarized in Table 6.1.

We observe that the inflation exhibits the biggest standard deviation compared with its mean (1.39 times), the benefits the second bigger (1.37 times), whereas the logarithm of the GDP the smallest (0.07 times).

The biggest correlation is that of the contributions with the benefits with a correlation coefficient of 0.891, whereas the smallest is the one of the pension spending with the pension fund assets with a correlation coefficient of −0.442 (Table 6.2).

6.4.3 *Variables*

As the purpose of our work is to find potential evidence of the link between debt and social security financials, the variables that are used as measures of debt are the public debt (general government gross debt as a % of GDP) and the private debt (as a % of GDP). These are our dependent variables. The social security metrics are measured by the pension fund assets (autonomous—in million USD and as a share of GDP), the pension spending (public as a % of GDP), the pension benefits (as a share of GDP) and contributions (as a share of GDP), as well as the social expenditure (as a % of GDP) and the expenditure in health (current – as a share of GDP). These are our independent variables. However, as the level of both public and private debt depends on other variables we use as control variables the unemployment (rate—% of labor force), the inflation (rate—%), the GDP per capita (current USD), and the foreign direct investment—FDI (net inflows, current USD), which all go on the independent variable side.

In our models we use the notation in Table 6.3.

Table 6.1 Descriptive statistics

Descriptive statistics	*BEN*	*CON*	*EXP*	*LEXP*	*LGDP*	*INF*	*PENS*	*PENA*	*PPS*	*PRD*	*SOC*	*UNEMP*	*PUD*
Mean	1.461	2.118	8.337	23.03	10.21	2.576	30.60	10.50	7.217	199.8	19.56	7.799	58.91
p50	0.367	0.927	8.254	23.16	10.37	2.116	9.299	10.57	6.807	193.1	19.49	6.953	48.51
SD	2.004	2.599	2.143	1.780	0.718	3.573	38.59	2.743	3.383	70.93	5.773	4.222	40.04
Variance	4.016	6.756	4.593	3.168	0.515	12.76	1489	7.525	11.45	5031	33.32	17.83	1603
N	484	502	612	570	612	612	578	577	552	558	607	537	612
Range	10.05	15.38	12.98	12.81	3.640	58.88	184.2	22.82	16.24	427.5	27.42	25.66	232.7
Min	0	0	4.139	14.51	8.045	−4.478	0	−6.215	0.844	61.62	4.793	1.805	3.664
Max	10.05	15.38	17.12	27.32	11.69	54.40	184.2	16.61	17.09	489.2	32.21	27.47	236.3

Note BEN: Benefits as a share of GDP, CON: Contributions as a share of GDP, EXP: Current expenditure in health (all functions), LEXP: Foreign direct investment, net inflows (BoP, current US$), LGDP: GDP per capita (current US$), INF: Inflation, consumer prices (annual %), PENS: Pension funds (autonomous) Assets as a Share of GDP, PENA: Pension funds (autonomous) US Dollar, Millions, PPS: Pension spending Public, % of GD, PRD: Private Sector Debt, SOC: Social Expenditure as % GDP, UNEMP: Unemployment, total (% of total labor force) (national estimate), PUD: General government gross debt as %GDP (OECD, 2019)

Source Authors' calculations

Table 6.2 Correlation matrix

Correlation matrix	*PUD*	*PRD*	*BEN*	*CON*	*EXP*	*LEXP*	*LGDP*	*INF*	*PENA*	*PENS*	*PPS*	*SOC*	*UNEMP*
PUD	1												
PRD	0.0507	1											
BEN	−0.0677	0.0988	1										
CON	−0.198	0.0410	0.891	1									
EXP	0.408	0.269	0.440	0.290	1								
LEXP	0.133	0.367	0.283	0.176	0.401	1							
LGDP	0.192	0.673	0.396	0.304	0.612	0.396	1						
INF	−0.170	−0.231	−0.0762	−0.0143	−0.299	−0.144	−0.367	1					
PENA	−0.0544	0.235	0.803	0.803	0.373	0.319	0.391	−0.0782	1				
PENS	0.203	0.235	0.569	0.468	0.533	0.628	0.443	−0.243	0.593	1			
PPS	0.493	−0.183	−0.327	−0.400	0.238	−0.0552	0.0601	−0.178	−0.442	−0.220	1		
SOC	0.385	0.202	−0.154	−0.262	0.480	0.0829	0.460	−0.309	−0.219	−0.0339	0.757	1	
UNEMP	0.226	−0.254	−0.224	−0.259	−0.116	−0.217	−0.360	−0.0325	−0.281	−0.325	0.443	0.224	1

Note BEN: Benefits as a share of GDP, CON: Contributions as a share of GDP, EXP: Current expenditure in health (all functions), LEXP: Foreign direct investment, net inflows (BoP, current US$), LGDP: GDP per capita (current US$), INF: Inflation, consumer prices (annual %), PENS: Pension funds (autonomous) Assets as a Share of GDP, PENA: Pension funds (autonomous) US Dollar, Millions, PPS: Pension spending Public, % of GD, PRD: Private Sector Debt, SOC: Social Expenditure as % GDP, UNEMP: Unemployment, total (% of total labor force) (national estimate), PUD: General government gross debt as %GDP (OECD, 2019)

Source Authors' calculations

Table 6.3 Notation

Indicator	*Variable*	*Indicator*	*Variable*
BENEFITS	benefits	FDI	foreign direct investment
CONTRI~S	contributions	GDP	GDP per capita
PENSI~TS	assets (% of GDP)	INF	inflation
PENSI~S	assets (million USD)	UNEMP	unemployment
PENSIO~D	spending	PDEBT	public debt
EXP SO~L	social expenditure	PRDEBT	private debt
EXP HE~H	expenditure in health		

Source Created by the Authors

6.4.4 Methodology

We regressed the public debt and private debt with the aforementioned social security metrics and macroeconomic variables to identify the potential impact of social security on debt and find potential evidence of whether the decrease of the social security spending or benefits can contribute to the reduction of debt.

For that we employed three models. The first one is the ordinary least squares (OLS) regression, whereas the remaining two are panel data models, namely the fixed effects and the random effects regressions.

Before proceeding to unit root and cointegration tests we test for cross-section dependence. We use the cross-section dependence test (CD test) proposed by Pesaran (2004). CD test strongly rejects the null hypothesis of cross-section independence for all the sample variables. In face of this evidence, we proceed to test for unit roots using the so-called "second generation" tests for unit roots in panel data that are robust to cross-section dependence (see Pesaran, 2015). To examine the stationarity properties of the variables in our models we use the second generation panel unit root tests developed by Maddala and Wu (1999) and Pesaran (2003) both suitable for unbalanced panel data set and cross-section dependence. The null hypothesis of a unit root (non-stationarity) cannot be rejected for all the sample variables. This means that the variables contain a unit root (e.g. integrated of order one) as expected by the visual inspection of their time series. In order to investigate whether a long-run equilibrium relationship exists among the sample variables we implement Pedroni's (1999) ADF-based and PP-based cointegration tests as well as Kao's (1999) ADF-based tests. Both tests suggest the rejection of the null hypothesis of no cointegration null at any significance level.

6.4.4.1 *OLS*

We used a multivariate OLS regression on our data using Stata to calculate the coefficients and error terms for public debt and private debt.

$$\begin{aligned}\text{PDEBT} = {} & a + \beta_1 \cdot \text{BENEFITS} + \beta_2 \cdot \text{CONTRI}{\sim}\text{S} + \beta_3 \cdot \text{EXP HE}{\sim}\text{H} \\ & + \beta_4 \cdot \text{LogFDI} + \beta_5 \cdot \text{LogGDP} + \beta_{6\cdot} \cdot \text{INF} \\ & + \beta_7 \cdot \text{PENSI}{\sim}\text{TS} + \beta_8 \cdot \text{LogPENSI}{\sim}\text{S} + \beta_9 \cdot \text{PENSIO}{\sim}\text{D} \\ & + \beta_{10} \cdot \text{EXP SO}{\sim}\text{L} + \beta_{11} \cdot \text{UNEMP} + \varepsilon\end{aligned}$$

and

$$\begin{aligned}\text{PRDEBT} = {} & a + \beta_1 \cdot \text{BENEFITS} + \beta_2 \cdot \text{CONTRI}{\sim}\text{S} + \beta_3 \cdot \text{EXP HE}{\sim}\text{H} \\ & + \beta_4 \cdot \text{LogFDI} + \beta_5 \cdot \text{LogGDP} + \beta_{6\cdot} \cdot \text{INF} \\ & + \beta_7 \cdot \text{PENSI}{\sim}\text{TS} + \beta_8 \cdot \text{LogPENSI}{\sim}\text{S} + \beta_9 \cdot \text{PENSIO}{\sim}\text{D} \\ & + \beta_{10} \cdot \text{EXP SO}{\sim}\text{L} + \beta_{11} \cdot \text{UNEMP} + \varepsilon\end{aligned}$$

6.4.4.2 *Fixed Effects*

The fixed effects model is simply a linear regression model in which the intercept terms vary over the individual units *i*, i.e.

$$y_{it} = a_i + x'_{it}\beta + \varepsilon_{it}, \quad \varepsilon_{it} \sim IID\left(0, \sigma_\varepsilon^2\right)$$

where it is usually assumed that all x_{it} are independent of all ε_{it}. We can write this in the usual regression framework by including a dummy variable for each unit *i* in the model (Verbeek, 2008). That is,

$$y_{it} = \sum_{j=1}^{N} a_j d_{ij} x'_{it}\beta + \varepsilon_{it}$$

where $d_{ij} = 0$ when $i = j$ and 0 elsewhere. We have also assumed the strictly exogenous regressors case in the conditional moments (see Wooldridge, 1995). We have not assumed equal-sized groups in the panel.

The vector β is a set of parameters of primary interest, α_i is the group-specific heterogeneity. We have included time-specific effects but, they are only tangential in what follows. Since the number of periods is usually fairly small, these can usually be accommodated simply by adding a set of time-specific dummy variables to the model. Our interest here is in the case in which N is too large to do likewise for the group effects.

6.4.4.3 Random Effects

It is commonly assumed in regression analysis (Verbeek, 2008) that all factors that affect the dependent variable, but that have not been included as regressors, can be appropriately summarized by a random error term. In our case, this leads to the assumption that the α_i are random factors, independently and identically distributed over individuals. Thus we write the random effects model as

$$y_{it} = \mu + a_i + x_{it}^{'}\beta + \varepsilon_{it}, \varepsilon_{it} \sim IID\left(0, \sigma_{\varepsilon}^2\right); \alpha_i \sim IID\left(0, \sigma_{\alpha}^2\right)$$

where $a_i + \varepsilon_{it}$ is treated as an error term consisting of two components: an individual specific component, which does not vary over time, and a remainder component, which is assumed to be uncorrelated over time. It is also assumed that a_i and ε_{it} are mutually independent and independent of x_{js} (for all j and s).

6.5 Regression Summary

The particulars of the regressions we ran appear in the following Tables 6.4 and 6.5 for the public and private debt respectively. The output of all three models, i.e. OLS, fixed and random effects is shown per dependent variable for comparison purposes also.

In Tables 6.4 and 6.5 for each of the independent variables, the first row indicates the coefficients, whereas the second row, where the numbers are put in the parentheses, indicates the standard deviation.

Their explanation is given in the next section and their implications are drafted in the section that follows it.

Table 6.4 Public debt regression results

Public debt	*OLS*	*Fixed effects*	*Random effects*
Benefits as a shar~P	3.431**	6.523**	6.281**
	(1.61)	(2.83)	(2.71)
Contributions asa~P	−7.466***	−4.341*	−4.540**
	(1.38)	(2.18)	(2.13)
Currentexpenditur~a	3.305***	3.992	4.387
	(0.83)	(3.02)	(2.67)
Log of Foreign dir~t	−3.006**	−0.518	−0.504
	(1.32)	(0.83)	(0.81)
Log GDP per capita	8.894**	2.558	2.276
	(3.59)	(4.55)	(4.24)
Inflation, consume~u	1.230	0.388	0.322
	(0.89)	(0.58)	(0.57)
Pensionfunds (aut~t	0.224***	0.141	0.144
	(0.06)	(0.15)	(0.14)
lPENSION FUNDS	3.562***	0.296	0.680
	(1.33)	(0.66)	(0.77)
Pensionspending P~D	7.388***	9.967***	9.161***
	(0.95)	(3.06)	(2.56)
Social Expenditure~P	−2.468***	−1.243	−1.476
	(0.60)	(1.48)	(1.27)
Unemployment, tota~	1.334***	1.505**	1.661***
	(0.46)	(0.66)	(0.61)
Constant	−42.45	−55.64	−53.24
	(33.59)	(33.46)	(33.00)
R-sqr	0.506	0.613	
dfres	330	33	
BIC	3245	2486	

$^{*}p < 0.10$, $^{**}p < 0.05$, $^{***}p < 0.01$
Source Authors' calculations

6.6 Results

6.6.1 Public Debt

The OLS regression indicates that the public debt is positively correlated at all levels with the pension assets (as a % of GDP as well as logarithm of the amount), the pension spending, the health expenditure as well as the unemployment. It is positively correlated at the 5% significance level with the logarithm of GDP per capita and the pension benefits as a share of GDP. It is negatively correlated at all levels with the contributions

Table 6.5 Private debt regression results

Private debt	*OLS*	*Fixed effects*	*Random effects*
Benefits as a shar~P	−4.329*	−1.518	−2.390
	(2.24)	(2.16)	(2.16)
Contributions asa~P	−5.148**	−0.403	−0.949
	(2.00)	(2.08)	(1.98)
Currentexpenditur~a	−2.682	−14.24	−11.80
	(1.88)	(11.04)	(9.32)
Log of Foreign dir~t	4.082*	0.580	0.372
	(2.34)	(1.39)	(1.39)
Log GDP per capita	69.620***	59.874***	61.666***
	(9.14)	(12.30)	(12.07)
Inflation, consume~u	−0.456	0.551	0.254
	(1.85)	(0.72)	(0.74)
Pensionfunds (aut~t	0.462***	0.532**	0.552***
	(0.15)	(0.21)	(0.20)
lPENSION FUNDS	−3.780*	−0.323	0.119
	(2.04)	(2.21)	(2.06)
Pensionspending P~D	−4.619***	−1.716	−4.898
	(1.49)	(4.34)	(3.02)
Social Expenditure~P	1.799**	8.890*	7.788**
	(0.89)	(4.66)	(3.29)
Unemployment, tota~	0.559	1.803*	2.574***
	(0.81)	(1.02)	(0.84)
Constant	−547.920***	−497.613***	−495.094***
	(99.40)	(137.70)	(129.34)
R-sqr	0.470	0.433	
dfres	287	32	
BIC	3255	2622	

**p* < 0.10, ***p* < 0.05, ****p* < 0.01
Source Authors' calculations

as a share of GDP and the social expenditure as a share of GDP. It is negatively correlated at the 5% level with the logarithm of the FDI. The remaining of the variables shows no statistical significance.

The fixed effects and random effects models show that the public debt is positively correlated with the pensions spending as a share of GDP at all levels and with the unemployment and the benefits as a share of GDP at the 5% level. As a matter of fact the random effects model indicates that the unemployment is statistically significant at all levels. The public debt is negatively correlated with the contributions as a share of GDP at the 10% (fixed effects) or at the 5% (random effects) level. The rest of the variables have no statistical significance. Following the evaluation of the consistency of the fixed effects estimators, Hausman test privileges the selection of the fixed effects model against the random effects approach for the particular dataset.

6.6.2 Private Debt

The OLS regression indicates that the private debt is positively correlated at all levels with the pension assets as a percent of GDP and the logarithm of the GDP per capita. It is positively correlated at the 5% level with the social expenditure and at the 10% level with the logarithm of FDI. It is negatively correlated at all levels with the pensions spending (as a share of GDP), at the 5% level with the contributions as a share of GDP and at the 10% level with the benefits (as a share of GDP), as well as the logarithm of the pension assets. The remaining of the variables exhibits no statistical significance.

The fixed effects and random effects models show that the private debt is positively correlated at all levels with the logarithm of the GDP per capita, at all levels (random effects) or at the 5% level (fixed effects) with the pension assets as a % of GDP, at the 5% level (random effects) or at the 10% level (fixed effects) with the social expenditure and at all levels (random effects) or at the 10% level (fixed effects) with the unemployment rate. The other variables seem to have no statistical significance. Similarly with the public debt fixed effects model has been preferred using the Hausman test for this particular dataset.

6.7 Result Interpretation and Implications

6.7.1 Public Debt

Looking at public debt it seems that all OLS fixed and random effects subscribe to the point of view that the reduction of pension spending can contribute to the decrease of debt (as a percent of GDP), as the higher the spending the higher the public debt (as a percent to GDP). Thus, assuming a constant GDP, the debt is reduced in absolute figures with the decrease of pension spending.

Furthermore, both models consent to the impact of pension benefits; the higher the pension benefits, the higher the debt (as a percent of GDP). Therefore, for a flat GDP, the decrease of benefits may have beneficial results to the level of public debt.

In addition, they are aligned also in the case of contributions; the higher the contributions, the lower the public debt (as a percent of GDP). Consequently, for a stable GDP, the increase of contributions (by the employers and the employees) assists in reducing the public debt.

All models yield the same output also with regard to unemployment; the higher the unemployment, the higher the public debt (as a percent of GDP). One potential interpretation is that during periods of higher unemployment the GDP drops, hence the public debt increases as a percent of GDP—even if it remains stable in absolute amounts.

The OLS model indicates that the higher the health expenditure the higher the public debt (as a percent of GDP). This is most likely due to the fact that increased health spending is supported by increased borrowing by the state.

The OLS model implies that higher pension assets (both as a percent of GDP and amount) result in higher public debt. This can be possibly interpreted by the fact that increased pension assets are backed by increased government debt.

The OLS model shows that the higher the social expenditure, the lower the debt as a percent of GDP. This is probably due to the fact that such provisions help sustain the GDP level at circumstances that adversely affect the welfare of the targeted households and individuals.

According to the OLS model, the higher the FDI, the lower the public debt to GDP ratio becomes, which is the expected direction. In addition, again as per the OLS model, the higher the GDP per capita, the higher the public debt to GDP ratio is. An interpretation we could offer for this result is that in times of higher GDP per capita countries live in euphoric environments and thus attempt increased borrowing, which potentially fosters the increased GDP per capita. Consequently the latter is somehow leveraged.

6.7.2 *Private Debt*

Going now to private debt, we realize that it becomes higher (as a percent of GDP) as the pension funds assets grow higher as a percent of GDP, as verified by all models. This probably means that individuals feel more confident to seek lending, as they have secured a higher income (as implied by the higher pension fund assets) at their retirement years.

The same holds true with the increase of social expenditure. Consequently, for a level GDP, the increase of social expenditure leads to an increase of private debt. This is probably due to the fact that individuals and households feel once and again confident borrowing, as they know that social provisions may kick in when their welfare is at risk.

All models indicate that the higher the GDP per capita the higher the private debt as a percent of GDP. This is probably attributed to the fact that the increased GDP per capita of a country makes the lending of its households and enterprises easier and thus private debt increases.

The OLS posts that the higher the pension spending, the lower the private debt to GDP ratio is, which is probably interpreted by the fact as retirees receive higher amounts they need to rely less on loans. The same is observed for the benefits. A similar rationale holds true; knowing that at the age of retirement the individuals will receive higher flows they need to rely less on debt.

The OLS shows that the increase of contributions reduces private debt as a percent of GDP; this is probably due to the fact that as individuals and enterprises contribute more they can withstand less borrowed funds. This is in line with the findings of Hurst and Willen (2007). The same is observed for the pension assets. A similar reasoning can be applied; increased pension assets are possibly partially due to increased money put in the fund by the individuals and the enterprises. Consequently they abstain from borrowing.

Based on OLS the increase of FDI increases the private debt (as a percent of GDP), which is probably due to the fact that increased investments allow individuals and enterprises to borrow more.

Finally, the fixed effects and the random effects models yield that the higher the unemployment the higher the private debt to GDP ratio. This is probably explained by the fact that in periods of increased unemployment the GDP drops, hence the ratio increases.

Our findings can be of value to the competent authorities and policymakers that are looking for ways to control public or private debt. First of all, social security seems to have a more straightforward impact on the public debt as a portion of GDP. Consequently, containing the pension benefits, the pension spending and the health expenditure or increasing the contributions of the employees and the employers may help in better controlling the public debt. However, we have to admit that our study does not investigate the impact of such measures in other aspects of the lives of the affected individuals. As a result, countries may want to consider the level of pension benefits and health expenditures made by the state in better controlling the public debt, weighing at the same time the consequences of reduced spending or increased contributions in their economy as a whole. Poufinas and Kouskouna (2016, 2017) offer solutions that can help alleviate the state from the burden without sacrificing the benefits and at the same time achieve a contribution to growth.

Private debt seems to be moving in a different path and the aforementioned actions will not necessarily steer private debt to the same direction. It is primarily the increase of contributions that leads to the reduction of public and private debt at the same time. It could also be the reduction of the pension fund assets as a % of GDP, but this is not desired as it would reduce the income of the retirees.

Furthermore, the decrease of unemployment seems to have beneficial impact to both private and public debt as a percent of GDP. In addition, a drop in the GDP per capita would have a similar result; however this is not recommended as it would most likely result in a reduced income for the individuals. These observations, next to the evidence found on the impact of social security on public and private debt, are probably not new; they are nevertheless confirmed by our work as well.

6.8 Conclusions

This chapter investigates the contribution of social security and in particular pensions as measured by pension assets, pension spending, pension benefits, contributions, health expenditure and social expenditure to public and private debt in the OECD countries with a series of econometric models. At the same time a series of macroeconomic variables is considered. The empirical evidence initially verifies standard conclusions at the relevant literature. The fact that debt, either government or private is related to the social security of each country is significantly testified by this study. More specifically though, we conclude that (at a significance level that depends on the model) public debt is positively correlated with pension assets, pension spending, pension benefits, health expenditure; it is negatively correlated with contributions and social expenditure. When it comes to macro-socioeconomic factors, public debt is positively correlated with unemployment, and (the logarithm of) GDP per capita; it is negatively correlated with the (logarithm of the) FDI. Inflation seems to have no statistical significance under any model. Turning to private debt, we find that (at a significance level that depends on the model) it is positively correlated with the pension assets, the social expenditure; it is negatively correlated with pension spending, the contributions, the benefits and the (logarithm of the) pension assets. The health expenditure posts no statistical significance. With regard to the macroeconomic variables, we see that it is positively correlated with the (logarithm of the) GDP per capita, the (logarithm of the) FDI and unemployment. For all models, inflation is not statistically significant. Policymakers can put these findings at use in order to direct the pension and social security factors in such a way the public debt is contained. More specifically, the share of the state in pension benefits, pension spending and health expenditure needs to be reduced and the share of the employees and employers in contributions has to be increased in order to better control the public debt. The latter seems to also be beneficial for the containment of private debt—if desired. A reduction in unemployment seems to be helping both sovereign and private debt. Consequently, actions that will increase employment may have to be enforced for this reason as well. Some of them may come from demography, as the previous chapter indicates. As to future research, the debt-social security nexus can be further tested using principal component analysis by combining proxies for financial development and other social policy variables that affect the private and public debt respectively.

References

Anderson, J. L., Markides, C., & Kupp, C. (2010). The last frontier: Market creation in conflict zones, deep rural areas, and urban slums. *California Management Review, 52*(4), 6–28.

Barro, R. J. (2003). Determinants of economic growth in a panel of countries. *Annals of Economics and Finance, 4*, 231–274.

Blanchard, O. J. (1985). Debt, deficits, and finite horizons. *Journal of Political Economy, 93*(April), 223–247.

Bovenberg, L., & van Ewijk, C. (2011). *Private pensions for Europe*. VOX, CERP Policy Portal. https://voxeu.org/article/private-pensions-europe. Accessed 23 Nov 2020.

Calvo, G., & Guidotti, P. (1990). Indexation and maturity of government bonds: An exploratory model. In *Public debt management: Theory and history* (pp. 52–93).

Carleton, W. T., & Kwan, S. H. (1995). *The role of private placement debt issues in corporate finance* (pp. 95–13) Federal Reserve Bank of San Francisco (Working Papers in Applied Economic Theory).

Diamond, D. W. (1991). Monitoring and reputation: The choice between bank loans and directly placed debt. *Journal of Political Economy, 99*(4), 689–721.

Federal Reserve Bank of St. Louis. (2019). *Federal reserve economic data*. https://fred.stlouisfed.org. Accessed 21 Sept 2019.

Futagami, K., & Nakajima, T. (2001). Population aging and economic growth. *Journal of Macroeconomics, 1*(23), 31–44.

Georges, P. (2006). Borrowing short- or long-term: Does the government really face a trade-off? *Public Finance and Management, 6*(2), 206–243.

Gertler, M. (1999), Government debt and social security in a life-cycle economy. In *Carnegie-Rochester Conference Series on Public Policy*, North Holland (Vol. 50, pp. 61–110).

Giavazzi, F., & Missale, A. (2004). *Public debt management in Brazil*. National Bureau of Economic Research (Working Paper 10394). https://www.nber.org/papers/w10394. Accessed 21 Sept 2019.

Giavazzi, F., & Pagano, M. (1990). Can severe fiscal contractions be expansionary? Tales of two small European countries. *NBER Macroeconomics Annual, 5*, 75–111.

Gilson, S. C., & Warner, J. B. (1997). Junk bonds, bank debt, and financing corporate growth. *SSRN*. https://ssrn.com/abstract=47269. Accessed 21 Sept 2019.

Hurst, E., & Willen, P. (2007). Social security and unsecured debt. *Journal of Public Economics, 91*, 1273–1297.

Huston, B. F., & Driessen, G. A. (2020). Social security, deficits, and debt. In Focus. *Congressional Research Service, IF11560, VERSION 1, NEW*. https://crsreports.congress.gov. Accessed 23 Nov 2020.

Kao, C. (1999). Spurious regression and residual-based tests for cointegration in panel data. *Journal of Econometrics, 90*, 1–44.

Li, C., & Lin, S. (2019). China's explicit social security debt: How large? *China Economic Review, 53*, 128–139.

Lin, Y., Liu, S., & Yu, J. (2019). Corporate pensions and the maturity structure of debt. *The Journal of Risk and Insurance, 86*(2), 315–350.

Maddala, G. S., & Wu, S. (1999). A comparative study of unit root tests with panel data and a new simple test. *Oxford Bulletin of Economics and Statistics, 61*, 631–652.

Meijdam, L., & Verbon, H. A. (1997). Aging and public pensions in an overlapping generations model. *Oxford Economic Papers, 49*(1), 29–42.

Mendonça, H. F., & Tiberto, B. P. (2014). Public debt and social security: Level of formality matters. *Economic Modelling, 42*, 490–507.

Missale, A., Giavazzi, F., & Benigno, P. (2002). How is the debt managed? Learning from fiscal stabilizations. *Scandinavian Journal of Economics, 104*(3), 443–469.

Myers, S. C. (1984). The capital structure puzzle. *The Journal of Finance, 39*(3), 574–592.

OECD. (2019). OECD. Stats. https://stats.oecd.org/. Accessed 21 Sept 2019.

Ono, T. (2003). Social security policy with public debt in an aging economy. *Journal of Population Economics, 16*(2), 363–387.

Pecchenino, R. A., & Pollard, P. S. (1997). The effects of annuities, bequests, and aging in an overlapping generations model of endogenous growth. *The Economic Journal, 107*(440), 26–46.

Pecchenino, R. A., & Utendorf, K. R. (1999). Social security, social welfare and the aging population. *Journal of Population Economics, 12*(4), 607–623.

Pedroni, P. (1999). Critical values for cointegration tests in heterogeneous panels with multiple regressors. *Oxford Bulletin of Economics and Statistics, 61*, 653–670.

Pesaran, M. H. (2003). *A simple panel unit root test in the presence of cross section dependence* (Cambridge Working Papers in Economics 346), Faculty of Economics, University of Cambridge.

Pesaran, M. H. (2004). *General diagnostic tests for cross section dependence in panels* (IZA Discussion Paper, No. 1240). Bonn.

Pesaran, M. H. (2015). *Time series and panel data econometrics* (1104 pp.). Oxford University Press. https://doi.org/10.1007/s00362-016-0816-1. Accessed 23 Nov 2020.

Poufinas, T., & Kouskouna, E. (2016). Rearranging social security contributions: Alleviating the burden of the state and returning value to the state and the society. In *A new growth model for the Greek economy: Requirements for long-term sustainability* (pp. 201–224). Palgrave Macmillan.

Poufinas, T., & Kouskouna, E. (2017). On the split of social security contributions between funded and pay-as-you-go pension schemes; contribution to growth. In *The Greek debt crisis—In quest of growth in times of austerity* (pp. 129–152). Palgrave Macmillan.

Rajan, R. G. (1992). Insiders and outsiders: The choice between informed and arm's-length debt. *The Journal of Finance, 47*(4), 1367–1400.

Rajan, R., & Winton, A. (1995). Covenants and collateral as incentives to monitor. *The Journal of Finance, 50*(4), 1113–1146.

The World Bank. (2019). *Data*. https://data.worldbank.org/. Accessed 21 Sept 2019.

Verbeek, M. (2008). *A guide to modern econometrics*. Wiley.

Welch, I. (1997). Why is bank debt senior: A theory of asymmetry and claim priority based on influence costs. *The Review of Financial Studies, 10*(4), 1203–1236.

Weil, P. (1989). The equity premium puzzle and the risk-free rate puzzle. *Journal of Monetary Economics, 24*(3), 401–421.

Werding, M. (2006). Implicit pension debt and the role of public pensions for human capital accumulation: An assessment for Germany. Ifo Institute for Economic Research & CESifo. http://hermes-ir.lib.hit-u.ac.jp/hermes/ir/re/14172/pie_dp283.pdf. Accessed 23 Nov 2020.

Wolswijk, G., & De Haan, J. (2006). Government debt management in Europe: Recent changes in debt managers' strategies. *Public Finance and Management, 6*(2), 244.

Wooldridge, J. M. (1995). Selection corrections for panel data models under conditional mean independence assumptions. *Journal of Econometrics, 68,* 115–132.

CHAPTER 7

Debt Versus Non-Performing Loans: An Investigation on the Causality Direction Within the Countries of Eurozone

Charalampos Agiropoulos, George Galanos, and Thomas Poufinas

7.1 Introduction

It has been already more than twelve years, during the summer of 2007, when we realized that a big portion of the sub-prime mortgage loans in the United States could not be paid; big enough to trigger—according to some—a global financial and economic crisis. Several companies in and out of the banking—financial sector and even some countries have not made it. Many academic and non-academic articles, books and posts have been written, several opinions have been expressed by experts and non-experts, millions of hours of broadcasting have been aired and

C. Agiropoulos (✉) · G. Galanos
Department of International and European Studies,
University of Piraeus, Piraeus, Greece

T. Poufinas
Department of Economics, Democritus University of Thrace, Komotini, Greece

T. Poufinas (ed.), *Debt in Times of Crisis*,
https://doi.org/10.1007/978-3-030-74162-4_7

even some cinema movies have been shot in an effort to explain what happened. However, no matter what the explanations offered or the different root causes identified were, they all had one common factor; the over-lending of all the players of the financial system, i.e. the households, the enterprises—businesses and the governments—countries.

The first two, i.e. the households and the enterprises, have limited capacity to maneuver when their lending comes from the banking sector, as the bank claims its asset. When they cannot pay their loan installments for a certain period of time the loan is characterized as non-performing, a.k.a. NPL (Non-Performing Loan). The latter, i.e. the governments—countries, were also in a difficult situation, with some of them barely making it, or even selectively defaulting. The provision of liquidity to the system by the central banks, the FED and the ECB, which became known as quantitative easing (QE), assisted the governments, the banks and to a great extent the enterprises all these years. The infamous phrase "whatever it takes" spelled out by the President of the ECB Mario Draghi at the Global Investment Conference in London, on 26 July 2012 (ECB, 2012) pretty much summarizes the ammunition that the central banks were willing to dispose so as to implement an unconventional monetary policy in order to influence the supply and demand of credit. In the case of the ECB the objective was even clearer; to preserve the Euro.

Consequently, Draghi's "whatever it takes" speech and the stance of the ECB that followed affected the lending conditions. Banks could then have increased liquidity to keep financing the entrepreneurial and household activity. According to some this did not necessarily take place to the extent it could, in particular to countries that had a harder time weathering the crisis, such as the countries of South Europe.

The NPLs in some countries increased significantly, exceeding even one-third of the disbursed loans, further limiting the capacity of banks to offer new loans. In some cases the governments tried to support the banks of their respective countries with a varying level of success. At the same time though banks were in some countries among the biggest borrowers of the respective governments through the purchase of government bonds. In both cases we had governments and banks that had to face distressed conditions. In the former case the banks were considered responsible for the indebtedness of the government (such as in Ireland for example); in the latter the government was considered responsible for the indebtedness of the banks (such as in Greece for example).

No matter who was the first to find itself in distressed conditions, the banks or the governments, the outcome was not pleasant, as rescue programs had to be enforced. The economies of the Eurozone heavily depend on the banking sector. As a result neither the governments, nor the banks could fail. It sounds a bit like the chicken and the egg causality dilemma. Several opinions have been offered; however, the issue is still discussed, as NPLs and public debt are still tantalizing banks and countries.

In our study we try to address this issue of NPLs by performing a panel VAR analysis and Granger causality to identify the impact of any two variables among NPLs, Public Debt and Unemployment (interchangeably CPI or Income Tax) on the third variable. This covers the full spectrum of potential relationship of the variables under investigation.

The novelties of our research lie precisely on the aforementioned approach. Namely, (i) the use of additional variables such as Income Tax and CPI; (ii) a panel VAR analysis and Granger causality so that the impact of any pair of variables is examined on the third. The available literature has not covered any of the two to the best of our knowledge.

7.2 Literature Review

The available literature focuses on the examination of the relation of NPLs with bank-specific or macroeconomic factors either on a set of countries on a country only. We split it in two, with the cross-national literature coming first and the country-specific literature following. What we have not included is literature pertaining to the NPLs or any other variable only, as this has been done already by some of the articles that follow. We start from the oldest and reach to the most recent papers.

Kauko (2012) analyzed the deterioration of the bank credit quality during the recent financial crisis in a cross-national sample of 34 countries to find that the rapid credit growth in 2000–2005 predicted the relative non-performing loans only if it was combined with a current account deficit.

Makri et al. (2014) investigate which factors determine NPLs on aggregate level for the period 2000–2008, just before the latest global financial crisis, to find that there are strong correlations between NPLs and various macroeconomic and bank-specific factors. The former are public debt, unemployment, annual percentage growth rate of gross domestic product, whereas the latter are capital adequacy ratio, rate of non-performing loans of the previous year and return on equity.

Roman and Bilan (2015) evaluate the effects of certain macroeconomic factors on non-performing bank loans in EU countries for the period 2000–2013 to find evidence that the GDP growth, the unemployment, the domestic bank credit are the main determinants of non-performing loans. At the same time they find that the quality of public finances affects the financial soundness of banks.

Anastasiou et al. (2016) consider income tax and output gap on top of the bank-specific and country-specific variables that have been proposed up to that point for the period Q1 1990–Q2 2015 to find that these variables are significant. The same authors (Anastasiou et al., 2019) examine the causes of the NPLs in the Euro area for the period Q1 2003–Q1 2016 and whether there is a fragmentation between core and periphery banking markets by estimating the long-run effects of bank-specific and macroeconomic factors on NPLs. They find that NPLs have experienced an increase, which was much higher in the periphery, after 2008, which is primarily attributed to the worsening of macroeconomic factors.

Ari et al. (2019) present a new dataset on the dynamics of NPLs during 88 banking crises since 1990 to find that (i) there are similarities across crises during NPL build-ups but less during NPL resolutions; (ii) there is a close relationship between NPL problems and the severity of post-crisis recessions; (iii) there is a set of pre-crisis predictors of NPL problems related to weak macroeconomic, institutional, corporate and banking sector conditions. Their findings can be used to reduce pre-crisis weakness and to properly address potential NPL problems during a crisis so as to achieve a post-crisis recovery.

At a country-specific level, Ghosh (2015) examines state-level banking industry-specific and region economic determinants of non-performing loans for all commercial banks and savings institutions across 50 US states and the district of Columbia for 1984–2013 to find that (i) greater capitalization, liquidity risks, poor credit quality, greater cost inefficiency and banking industry size to significantly increase NPLs, while greater bank profitability lowers NPLs; (ii) higher state real GDP and real personal income growth rates, and changes in state housing price index reduce NPLs, while inflation, state unemployment rates, and US public debt significantly increase NPLs. His findings suggest that the stress tests that the banks have to undergo should consider the e impact of "micro" or state-level economic conditions on NPLs, on top of banks' capital and credit quality, and effective cost management while evaluating the solvency of the banks.

Konstantakis et al. (2016) attempt to shed light on the determining factors of the Greek banking sector NPLs to find that in line with the international evidence both macroeconomic (GDP cycle, public debt, unemployment) and financial factors (FDI, domestic credit provided by the banking sector) have a significant impact on the NPLs of the country.

Bahruddin and Masih (2018) find that lending interest rates and NPLs have an asymmetric relationship in the short-term and symmetric relationship in the long term in the case of Malaysia. This suggests that banks can improve their quality credit management through the streamlining of their collection process and the quality of the chosen customers so as to reduce the number of NPLs in the short term. At the same time they can diversify their loan portfolios so as to suppress their total risk.

Our study introduces additional variables, as mentioned in the intuition section. We trust that the addition of Income Tax and CPI adds value to the available knowledge, as since 2008 CPI has entered a negative territory and seems to affect the development of NPLs. The same holds true for Income Tax; several countries have increased taxes in order to weather the latest financial crisis. This also influenced the evolution of NPLs.

Furthermore, not only do we study the impact of Public Debt on NPLs, but we address the reverse relationship as well. We do the same for all the other variables, i.e. Public Debt and Unemployment; the latter is replaced by Income Tax and CPI, which are variables that have not been studied in the past. This mutual exchange of variables so as to identify all potential relationships is a significant progress to the research in the field.

7.3 Data Sources and Descriptive Statistics

The empirical analysis uses data for 19 countries of Eurozone that cover a time span from 2000 until 2018. All data are taken from the World Bank Dataset which combines information from archived databases as well. The main variables we use are Bank Non-Performing Loans (NPL) as a percentage of the total gross loans, General Government Gross Debt (DEBT), Consumer Price Index (CPI), Tax on income, profits and capital gains (TAX) as a percentage of total taxes and Unemployment (UNEMP).

Following Anastasiou et al. (2016, 2019), Ozili (2019) among others, we use the income tax as a proxy of someone's capacity to pay back the overdue debt to the bank. In addition, Anastasiou et al. (2016) consider as one of the most important determinant of the NPLs the level of unemployment for a country. Anastasiou et al. (2016) reveal that an increase in unemployment makes more borrowers unable to meet their debt obligations. Although there is a proven relationship between NPLs and unemployment, this study tries to investigate the direction of this particular link.In order to investigate further the ambiguous relation between the government's fiscal position and the NPLs ratio we use the general government gross debt, which is taken from the World Bank database and measured as a percentage of GDP. Finally, we use CPI, which is derived also from the World Bank database as a proxy variable of the economic expansion. The reference value (100) for the Consumer Price Index has been set to 2015 for all countries. Table 7.1 provides the definitions and summary statistics of the corresponding variables:

A first review of the data indicates the key variables included in the model. The variable through which we approximate the notion of overdue

Table 7.1 Summary statistics

Variables	*Definitions*	*Units*	*Mean*	*Standard deviation*	*Minimum*	*Maximum*
NPL	Bank Non-Performing Loans to total gross loans	Ratio (%)	5.652	7.578	0.146	47.75
DEBT	General Government Gross Debt over GDP	Ratio (%)	64.181	36.808	3.800	184.900
CPI	Consumer Price Index	Index (Ref. 2015 = 100)	97.441	23.870	55.022	208.950
UNEMP	Unemployment Rate	% of active population	8.973	43.672	1.900	27.491
TAX	Taxes on Income, profits and capital gains to total taxes	Ratio (%)	42.608	8.997	15.880	60.122

Source Authors' calculations based on World Bank databases (current and archived)

private debt is the percentage of the non-performing loans over the total gross loans. The mean value in our panel is nearly 5.6%, with Greece exhibiting the highest average value throughout the relevant years with more than 17.8% of the total gross loans issued. The lowest number comes from Finland, which averages 0.7% during the nineteen years of our sample. Cyprus and Italy stand out from the countries as they present the second higher NPL ratio across Eurozone countries (15 and 10.2%, respectively).

It is interesting to compare the findings for the government gross debt. While Greece and Italy lead in this list, we see that smaller countries like Belgium and Portugal have a substantial share of public debt as it can be seen in Fig. 7.1. The Baltic countries (Finland, Estonia, Latvia and Germany) all exhibit a mean value of less than the overall average in the gross government debt for all countries.

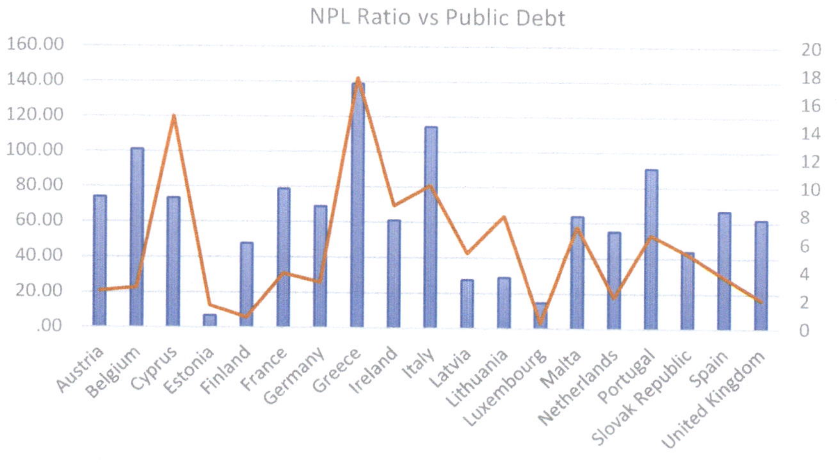

Fig. 7.1 Non-performing loans versus government gross debt across EU19 (*Source* Authors' calculations)

7.4 Empirical Analysis

The data construct an unbalanced panel with 19 cross-section units (countries) and 19 time observations. Given the dynamic nature of the relationship among the variables in question we estimate a three-equation Vector Autoregressive Model (VAR) with two lags. Individual tests for each panel based on the information criteria point to the use of two lags in the VAR process. The presence of feedback effects among NPLs, public debt, consumer price index, income tax and employment constitutes the VAR methodology necessary in the lines of inter alia: Anastasiou et al. (2016), Benigno and Ricci (2011), Holtz-Eakin and Kao (2003), Plehn-Dujowich (2009) and Koellinger and Thurik (2012). Thurik et al. (2008) who elaborate on the relationship between similar variables. The main questions addressed through this approach is to determine whether the effect of public debt and unemployment creation co-exists with the effect of past unemployment toward NPLs and whether similar results can be found when we consider consumer price index and income tax as control variables.

The presence of a lagged dependent variable in the right-hand side of each equation renders First Difference (FD) and Fixed Effects (FE) estimators biased. Verbeek (2012) demonstrates how the Fixed Effects Estimator is biased and inconsistent while Nickell (1981) illustrates the magnitude of this bias as the cross-sections of the panel reach infinity. Taking first differences does not solve the problem since lagged values of the dependent variable are obviously correlated with lagged values of the idiosyncratic error term. Thus, some form of instrumenting is required to estimate each regression. Anderson and Hsiao (1981) proposed the two-period lagged value of the dependent variable ($y_{i,t-2}$) as an instrument for the first difference ($y_{i,t} - y_{i,t-1}$) since it is uncorrelated with $u_{i,t} - u_{i,t-1}$. Nevertheless, Verbeek (2012) underlines that this instrumental variables estimator imposes only one moment condition in the estimation process. In order to increase the efficiency of the estimators we follow the methodology suggested by Arellano and Bond (1991) who use a list of instruments to exploit additional moment conditions in the first-differenced model.

Arellano and Bover (1995) and Blundell and Bond (1998) move one step further from the Dynamic GMM Estimator and impose more moment conditions to improve the efficiency of the estimators. The authors keep the set of exogenous instruments for the differenced equation and add lagged differences of the endogenous variable as instrument for the level equation. The estimation of this system of two equations yields the System GMM Estimator which we also report in our set of results. Bond and Hoeffler (2001) underline that in models with finite time dimension the Difference GMM estimator is substantially downward-biased. This caveat is more pronounced in the presence of high persistence in the data as is often the case with data on output. Given the fundamental difficulties of providing valid outside instruments for the lagged dependent variables, the authors strongly favor the implementation of the System GMM Estimator for macroeconomic panels with a limited time span.

7.5 Results

Our results from the estimation of the three-equation Panel VAR(1) follow the lines of Plehn-Dujowich (2009). It is well known that the magnitude of the coefficients in the VAR has no significant interpretation. Nevertheless, the sign of these coefficients gives us the indication of Granger causality of one endogenous variable to another (Greene, 2003). The results are summarized in Tables 7.2, 7.3 and 7.4 using different control variables at a time, i.e. (Unemployment, Consumer Price Index and Income Tax). The odd columns represent Difference GMM (Arellano & Bond, 1991) while the even columns represent system GMM estimation (Arellano & Bover, 1995; Blundell & Bond, 1998).

Keeping in mind that the VAR structure contains one lag of each variable, the p-values from the individual t-tests can be relied upon to infer Granger causality. Tables 7.2, 7.3 and 7.4 provide strong evidence that public debt Granger causes future NPLs. The feedback effect seems to hold as lagged values of Government Gross Debt are estimated to have a positive and significant effect on Non-Performing Loans as in Beck et al. (2013) and Siakoulis (2017). The estimation from Table 7.2 reveals that the most robust effect is from lagged unemployment to public debt thus validating the theory of Vogiazas and Nikolaidou (2011) and Nkusu (2011). Although past unemployment does not Granger cause the Non-Performing Loans as can be seen in Column 2 of Table 7.2, Columns 3 and 4 of the same table show that past unemployment Granger causes the sovereign debt of a country which causes Non-Performing Loans (Columns 1 and 2). This particular result is totally in line with the empirical findings of Nkusu (2011), Beck et al. (2013) and Reinhart and Rogoff (2010).

Table 7.2 Panel VAR using unemployment

	Non-performing loans		*Government gross debt*		*Unemployment*	
Model	*(1)*	*(2)*	*(3)*	*(4)*	*(5)*	*(6)*
Variables	*Difference GMM*	*System GMM*	*Difference GMM*	*System GMM*	*Difference GMM*	*System GMM*
Non-performing loans (−1)	0.731***	0.820***	−0.246***	−0.318***	−0.030	−0.080***
	(0.000)	(0.000)	(0.004)	(0.000)	(0.153)	(0.000)
Government gross debt (−1)	0.038***	0.062***	0.913***	0.986***	−0.011*	0.006
	(0.001)	(0.000)	(0.000)	(0.000)	(0.085)	(0.115)
Unemployment (−1)	0.133**	0.063	0.417***	0.528***	0.869***	0.956***
	(0.022)	(0.192)	(0.007)	(0.000)	(0.000)	(0.000)
Constant	−2.005***	−3.413***	4.428***	−0.833	1.985***	0.385
	(0.002)	(0.000)	(0.002)	(0.474)	(0.000)	(0.165)
Observations	315	334	315	334	315	334
Number of country code	19	19	19	19	19	19
Sargan-Hansen Statistic	563.29	846.42	412.34	590.87	525.31	819.04

Source Authors' calculations
p-value in parentheses
***$p < 0.01$, **$p < 0.05$, *$p < 0.1$

Results from Columns 5 and 6 of Table 7.2 provide mixed evidence in favor of the positive effect of the past increase of NPLs on unemployment. The System GMM estimator reveals a negative significant coefficient for lagged NPLs, however, this effect is insignificant at all levels once we use the Difference GMM approach. Similar results are presented in Table 7.2 for the past sovereign debt on the unemployment rate. It is interesting that using the Difference GMM approach at 10% level of significance the past government debt has negative effect on the unemployment rate.

In Table 7.3 is presented the VAR(1) panel model using the Consumer Price Index as the control variable. Similar results with Table 7.2 concerning the gross government debt are presented in Columns 1 and 2 of Table 7.3. Past sovereign debt positively affects the NPLs since the coefficients are statistically significant using both System and Difference GMM approaches. As it can be seen in Columns 3 and 4 past

Table 7.3 Panel VAR using consumer price index

	Non-performing loans		*Government gross debt*		*Consumer price index*	
Model	*(1)*	*(2)*	*(3)*	*(4)*	*(5)*	*(6)*
Variables	*Difference GMM*	*System GMM*	*Difference GMM*	*System GMM*	*Difference GMM*	*System GMM*
Non-performing loans (−1)	0.801***	0.844***	−0.021	−0.162**	−0.092***	−0.014
	(0.000)	(0.000)	(0.766)	(0.017)	(0.000)	(0.463)
Government gross debt (−1)	0.025*	0.062***	0.813***	1.001***	0.006	−0.053***
	(0.067)	(0.000)	(0.000)	(0.000)	(0.549)	(0.000)
Consumer price index (−1)	0.033**	0.005	0.247***	0.062**	0.955***	1.006***
	(0.014)	(0.667)	(0.000)	(0.044)	(0.000)	(0.000)
Constant	−3.541***	−3.444***	−10.531***	−3.799	6.458***	4.786***
	(0.000)	(0.000)	(0.000)	(0.145)	(0.000)	(0.000)
Observations	315	334	315	334	315	334
Number of country code	19	19	19	19	19	19
Sargan-Hansen Statistic	557.33	840.50	421.53	615.97	375.01	616.91

Source Authors' calculations
p-value in parentheses
$^{***}p < 0.01$, $^{**}p < 0.05$, $^{*}p < 0.1$

inflation positively affects the government debt which is totally in line with Greenidge and Grosvenor (2010), Vogiazas and Nikolaidou (2011), Louzis et al. (2011), Prasanna (2014) and Rinaldi and Arellano (2006). Looking in Columns 5 and 6 it can be seen the negative effect of NPLs on Consumer Price Index. This also provides evidence to the case of Greenidge and Grosvenor (2010) who supported their empirical results that inflation rate has a strongly negative impact on the levels of NPLs.

During the sovereign debt crisis, peripheral Eurozone countries were forced to follow a strict fiscal policy through austerity measures expressed in the form of tax increases and a reduction in government expenditures. This increased the fiscal burden of households and businesses, affecting at the same time their bank debt servicing capacity. In Columns 1 and 2 of Table 7.4, it is empirically supported the positive effect of the income tax

Table 7.4 Panel VAR using income tax

	Non-performing loans		*Government gross debt*		*Income Tax*	
Model	*(1)*	*(2)*	*(3)*	*(4)*	*(5)*	*(6)*
Variables	*Difference GMM*	*System GMM*	*Difference GMM*	*System GMM*	*Difference GMM*	*System GMM*
Non-performing loans (−1)	0.819***	0.942***	−0.126*	−0.177**	−0.069**	−0.092***
	(0.000)	(0.000)	(0.088)	(0.010)	(0.020)	(0.003)
Government gross debt (−1)	0.050***	0.041***	0.947***	1.015***	−0.000	0.025***
	(0.000)	(0.000)	(0.000)	(0.000)	(0.972)	(0.004)
Income tax (−1)	0.318***	0.373***	0.094	−0.151	0.673***	0.947***
	(0.000)	(0.000)	(0.457)	(0.100)	(0.000)	(0.000)
Constant	−15.689***	−18.107***	1.390	7.817*	14.302***	1.143
	(0.000)	(0.000)	(0.815)	(0.067)	(0.000)	(0.492)
Observations	315	334	315	334	298	317
Number of country code	19	19	19	19	19	19
Sargan-Hansen Statistic	540.61	753.75	418.14	595.02	179.74	200.79

Source Authors' calculations
p-value in parentheses
***$p < 0.01$, **$p < 0.05$, *$p < 0.1$

on the levels of Non-Performing Loans. On the other side, past income taxation does not seem to affect significantly the Government Gross Debt. Policymakers should take into deep consideration this result, especially in times of crisis, when, trying to decrease the sovereign debt, many countries have proceeded to an increase of the taxation.

The trajectory of these effects is depicted in the Impulse Response Functions (IRF) where we monitor the effect of a one standard deviation shock in the impulse variable to the path of the response variable,[1] taking into consideration the interrelationships underpinning the system of the three equations. An exogenous shock to Debt has a direct impact

[1] See Abrigo and Love (2016) for the computation of Panel VARs and Impulse Response Functions using the Stata 15 software.

on NPLs which peaks after 1 period but does not die out in the near-term horizon (Fig. 7.1). On the other hand, the reaction of the NPLs variable to one standard deviation positive improvement in unemployment is greater in magnitude and peaks after two years as shown in the corresponding graph (Fig. 7.2).

Figure 7.3 shows the effect of a positive effect of Consumer Price Index to Non-Performing Loans. The cumulative effect on non-performing loans ratio reaches 0.1 after ten years. As it can be seen in Fig. 7.4, a one standard deviation shock to CPI, which lies approximately to 24 units increases NPL ratio. This positive response gradually declines but it never reaches its steady value remaining in the positive region. One could possibly suggest that shocks to CPI will have a positive impact on government gross debt both in the short run and long run.

Finally, Figs. 7.5 and 7.6 present the impact of income tax to Non-Performing Loans ratio and government debt. In both cases the Impact-Response-Function seems to follow a steady-state line on the x-axis. These results reveal the weak effect of the income tax on NPLs and CPI which

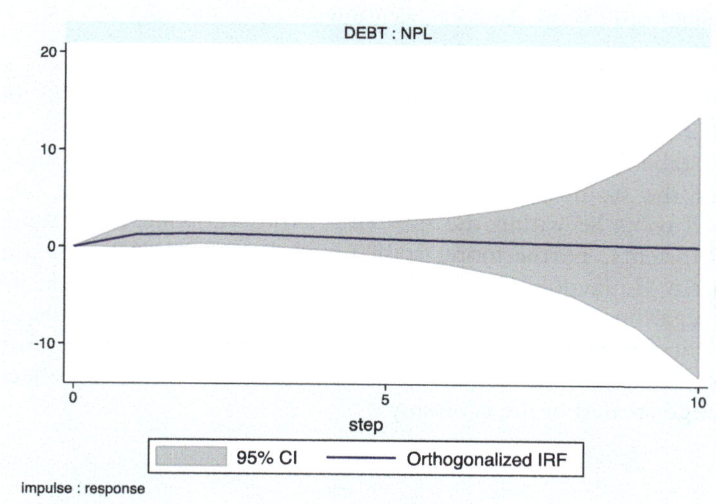

Fig. 7.2 Orthogonalized impulse response function debt to non-performing loans (*Source* Authors' calculations)

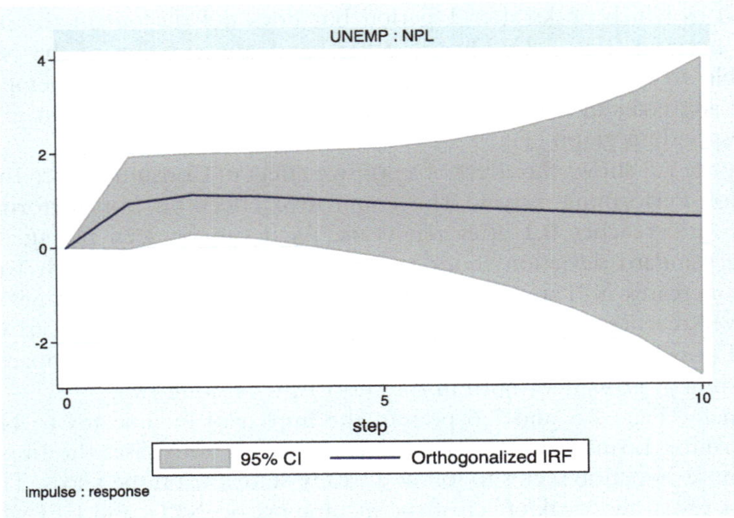

Fig. 7.3 Orthogonalized impulse response function unemployment to non-performing loans (*Source* Authors' calculations)

is totally in line with the previous results taken from the VAR(1) model using Difference and System GMM.

The stability of the Panel VAR estimation is examined through the roots of the Companion Matrix as shown in Figs. 7.7, 7.8, 7.9 and 7.10. All roots lie within the unit circle, thus verifying the stability of the coefficients. Furthermore, stability in the panel VAR also implies stationarity (Lutkepohl, 2005). Overall, the empirical results yield mixed effects regarding the hypothesis of the debt effect predicted by the European Central Bank where decreasing the Non-Performing Loans ratio can spur economic growth by helping disseminate the productivity effects of knowledge created in the economy.

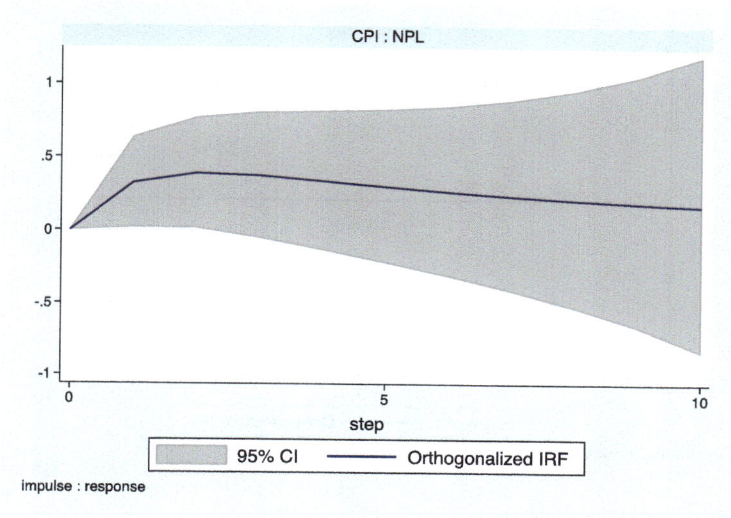

Fig. 7.4 Orthogonalized impulse response function consumer price index to non-performing loans (*Source* Authors' calculations)

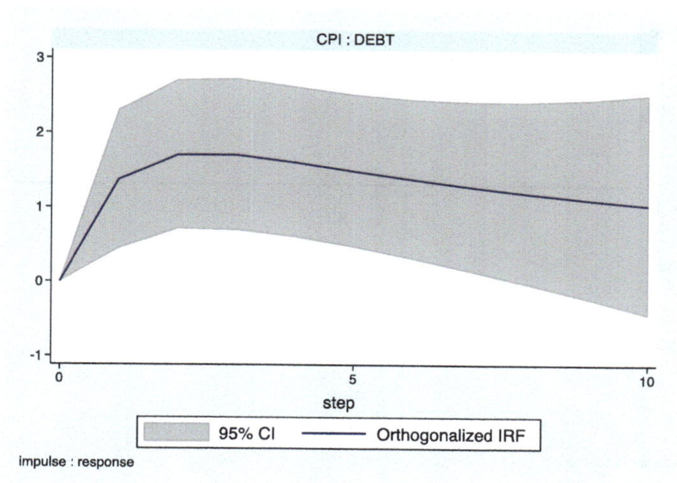

Fig. 7.5 Orthogonalized impulse response function consumer price index to debt (*Source* Authors' calculations)

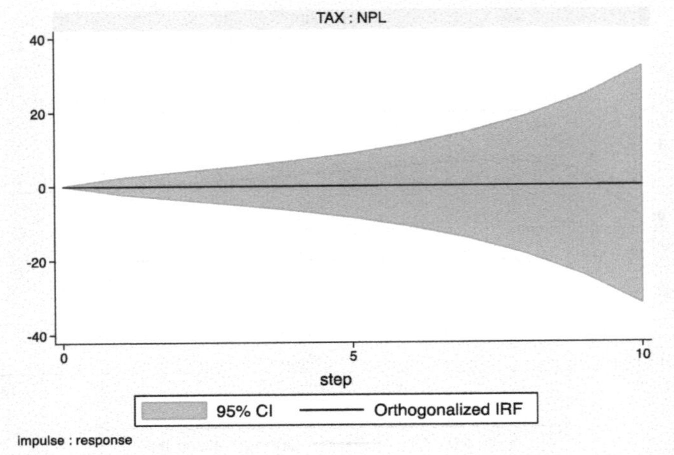

Fig. 7.6 Orthogonalized impulse response function income tax to non-performing loans (*Source* Authors' calculations)

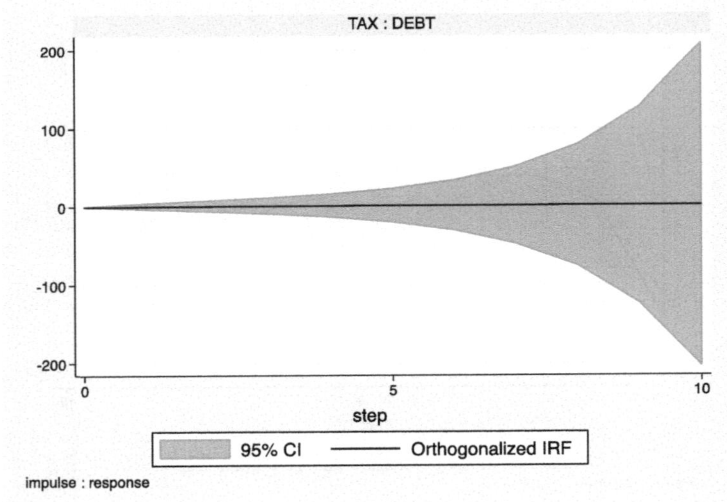

Fig. 7.7 Orthogonalized impulse response function income tax to debt (*Source* Authors' calculations)

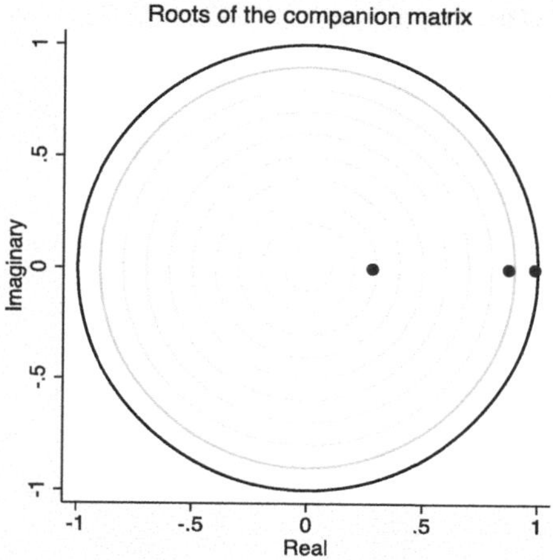

Fig. 7.8 Stability of panel VAR estimations (non-performing loans—government debt—unemployment) (*Source* Authors' calculations)

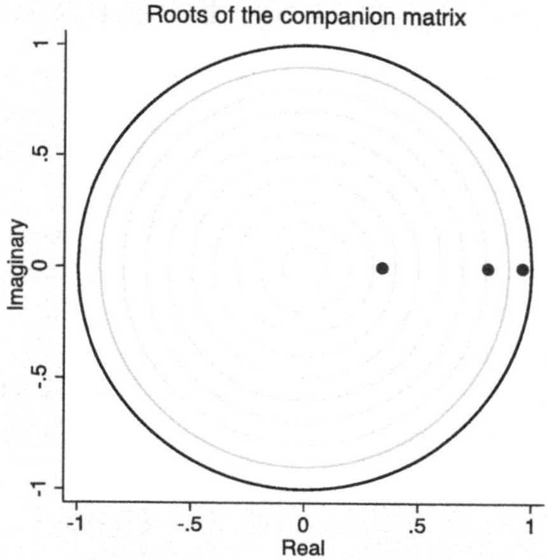

Fig. 7.9 Stability of panel VAR estimations (non-performing loans—government debt—consumer price index) (*Source* Authors' calculations)

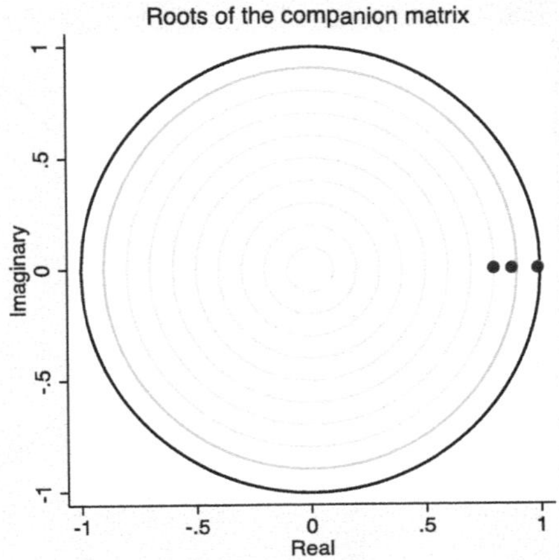

Fig. 7.10 Stability of panel VAR estimations (non-performing loans—government debt—consumer price index) (*Source* Authors' calculations)

7.6 Further Research

Given the limited time span of our macroeconomic dataset we will like to employ in the future the Least Squares Dummy Variable Corrected (LSDVC) estimation method (Bun & Kiviet, 2003; Kiviet, 1995) as further robustness. Bruno (2005) has extended this methodology to unbalanced panel datasets.[2] This approach incorporates a correction for the bias associated with the standard fixed effects methodology for panel data and is more suitable for panels with a small number of time periods, which is usually the case in the analysis of country-level data. In addition, the results from the forecast error variance decompositions (FEVD) will help us further elaborate on the underlying interrelationships.

7.7 Conclusion

We used a panel VAR Analysis and Granger causality to find evidence that Public Debt and Unemployment have an impact on the level of NPLs of a country. The same holds true when Public Debt and Unemployment take the place of NPLs, i.e. any two of the variables affect the third. Similar

[2] The estimation is undertaken using the authors xtlsdvc command in Stata.

results hold true when Unemployment is replaced by CPI and Income Tax. The latter seems to exhibit the lowest significance level. These findings may be used by the competent authorities and policymakers so as to steer the level of NPLs, but also to steer any of the other variables, i.e. Public Debt, Unemployment, Income Tax and CPI through NPLs.

References

Abrigo, M. R., & Love, I. (2016). Estimation of panel vector autoregression in Stata. *The Stata Journal, 16*(3), 778–804.

Anastasiou, D., Louri, H., & Tsionas, M. (2016). Determinants of non-performing loans: Evidence from Euro-area countries. *Finance Research Letters, 18,* 116–119. https://doi.org/10.1016/j.frl.2016.04.008.

Anastasiou, D., Louri, H., & Tsionas, M. (2019). Nonperforming loans in the euro area: A re core–periphery banking markets fragmented? *International Journal of Finance & Economics, 24*(1), 97–112. https://doi.org/10.1002/ijfe.1651.

Anderson, T. W., & Hsiao, C. (1981). Estimation of dynamic models with error components. *Journal of the American Statistical Association, 76*(375), 598–606.

Arellano, M., & Bond, S. (1991). Some tests of specification for panel data: Monte Carlo evidence and an application to employment equations. *The Review of Economic Studies, 58*(2), 277–297.

Arellano, M., & Bover, O. (1995). Another look at the instrumental variable estimation of error-components models. *Journal of Econometrics, 68*(1), 29–51.

Ari, A., Chen, S., & Ratnovski, L. (2019). *The dynamics of non-performing loans during banking crises: A new database* (IMF Working Paper, WP/19/272). https://www.imf.org/en/Publications/WP/Issues/2019/12/06/The-Dynamics-of-Non-Performing-Loans-during-Banking-Crises-A-New-Database-48839. Accessed 15 Feb 2020.

Bahruddin, W. A., & Masih, M. (2018). *Is the relation between lending interest rate and non-performing loans symmetric or asymmetric? Evidence from ARDL and NARDL* (Working Paper—Munich Personal RePEc Archive, 1–29). https://mpra.ub.uni-muenchen.de/91565/. Accessed 15 Feb 2020.

Beck, R., Jakubik, P., & Piloiu, A. (2013). Non-performing loans: What matters in addition to the economic cycle? *European Central Bank, Working Paper Series, No 1515, February 2013.* https://www.ecb.europa.eu/pub/pdf/scpwps/ecbwp1515.pdf. Accessed Feb 15 2020.

Benigno, P., & Ricci, L. A. (2011). The inflation-output trade-off with downward wage rigidities. *American Economic Review, 101*(4), 1436–66.

Blundell, R., & Bond, S. (1998). Initial conditions and moment restrictions in dynamic panel data models. *Journal of Econometrics, 87*(1), 115–143.

Bruno, G. S. (2005). Estimation and inference in dynamic unbalanced panel-data models with a small number of individuals. *The Stata Journal, 5*(4), 473–500.

Bun, M. J., & Kiviet, J. F. (2003). On the diminishing returns of higher-order terms in asymptotic expansions of bias. *Economics Letters, 79*(2), 145–152.

ECB. (2012). *Verbatim of the remarks made by Mario Draghi, Speech by Mario Draghi, President of the European Central Bank at the Global Investment Conference in London, 26 July 2012.* https://www.ecb.europa.eu/press/key/date/2012/html/sp120726.en.html. Accessed 15 Feb 2020.

Ghosh, A. (2015). Banking-industry specific and regional economic determinants of non-performing loans: Evidence from US states. *Journal of Financial Stability, 20,* 93–104. https://doi.org/10.1016/j.jfs.2015.08.004.

Greene, W. H. (2003). *Econometric analysis*. Publisher Prentice Hall.

Greenidge, K., & Grosvenor, T. (2010). Forecasting non-performimg loans in barbados. *Journal of Business, Finance & Economics in Emerging Economies,* 5(1), 80–107.

Hoeffler, A., Bond, S. R., & Temple, J. R. (2001). GMM estimation of empirical growth models. *CEPR Discussion Papers/Centre for Economic Policy Research Discussion Papers*.

Holtz-Eakin, D., & Kao, C. (2003). Entrepreneurship and economic growth: The proof is in the productivity. *Syracuse University Center for Policy Research Working Paper,* (50).

Kauko, K. (2012). External deficits and non-performing loans in the recent financial crisis. *Economics Letters, 115*(2), 196–199.

Kiviet, J. F. (1995). On bias, inconsistency, and efficiency of various estimators in dynamic panel data models. *Journal of Econometrics, 68*(1), 53–78.

Koellinger, P. D., & Roy Thurik, A. (2012). Entrepreneurship and the business cycle. *Review of Economics and Statistics, 94*(4), 1143–1156.

Konstantakis, K. N., Michaelides, P. G., & Vouldis, A. T. (2016). *Non-Performing Loans (NPLs) in a crisis economy: Long-run equilibrium analysis with a real-time VEC model for Greece (2001–2015)* (Working Paper—Munich Personal RePEc Archive, 1–22). https://mpra.ub.uni-muenchen.de/90000/. Accessed 15 Feb 2020.

Louzis, D. P., Xanthopoulos-Sisinis, S., & Refenes, A. N. (2011). Are realized volatility models good candidates for alternative value at risk prediction strategies? Available at SSRN 1814171. https://ssrn.com/abstract=1814171. Accessed Feb 15 2020.

Lutkepohl, H. (2005). *New introduction to multiple time series analysis*. New York: Springer.

Makri, V., Tsagkanos, A., & Bellas, A. (2014). Determinants of non-performing loans: The case of Eurozone. *Panoeconomicus, 61*(2), 193–206. https://doi.org/10.2298/PAN1402193M.

Nickell, S. (1981). Biases in dynamic models with fixed effects. *Econometrica: Journal of the Econometric Society*, 1417–1426.

Nkusu, M. M. (2011). Nonperforming loans and macrofinancial vulnerabilities in advanced economies. *International Monetary Fund, Working Paper, WP/11/161.* https://www.elibrary.imf.org/view/journals/001/2011/161/001.2011.issue-161-en.xml. Accessed Feb 15 2020.

Ozili, P. K. (2019). Non-performing loans and financial development: New evidence. *The Journal of Risk Finance, 20*(1), 59–81.

Plehn-Dujowich, J. M. (2009). Firm size and types of innovation. *Economics of Innovation and New Technology, 18*(3), 205–223.

Prasanna, P. (2014). Firm-level governance quality and dividend decisions: Evidence from India. *International Journal of Corporate Governance, 5*(3/4), 197–222.

Reinhart, C. M., & Rogoff, K. S. (2010). Growth in a time of debt. *American Economic Review, 100*(2), 573–78.

Rinaldi, L., & Sanchis-Arellano, A. (2006). Household debt sustainability: What explains household non-performing loans? An empirical analysis. *European Central Bank, Working Paper Series 570, January 2006.* https://www.ecb.europa.eu/pub/pdf/scpwps/ecbwp570.pdf. Accessed February 15 2020.

Roman, A., & Bilan, I. (2015). An empirical analysis of the macroeconomic determinants of non-performing loans in EU28 banking sector. *Revista Economică, 67*(2), 108–127.

Siakoulis, V. (2017). Fiscal policy effects on non-performing loan formation. *Bank of Greece, Working Papers, 224, May 2017*. https://www.bankofgreece.gr/ekdoseis-ereyna/ereynitiki-drastiriotita/anazitisi/synopsh?publication=a0fa42ce-d294-4605-8ce5-a2aa1800ae94. Accessed Feb 15 2020.

Thurik, A. R., Carree, M. A., Van Stel, A., & Audretsch, D. B. (2008). Does self-employment reduce unemployment? *Journal of Business Venturing, 23*(6), 673–686.

Verbeek M. (2012). A guide to modern econometrics. Wiley.

Vogiazas, S. D., & Nikolaidou, E. (2011). Investigating the determinants of nonperforming loans in the Romanian banking system: An empirical study with reference to the Greek crisis. *Economics Research International, 2011*, 2090–2123. https://doi.org/10.1155/2011/214689. Accessed Feb 15 2020.

CHAPTER 8

What Drives Sovereign Bond Yields in the Eurozone?

Nicholas Apergis, Giuseppina Chesini, and Thomas Poufinas

8.1 Introduction

This chapter aims to provide answers to the question of what drives sovereign yields of Eurozone countries' government bonds. In particular, we aim to identify a small number of very relevant macroeconomic variables able to determine sovereign bond yields in different Eurozone countries. Sovereign yields are the result of many different determinants. Of course, country default risk is a very relevant determinant, but the yields are also influenced by the liquidity risk and other endogenous and exogenous variables and events. In particular, even if countries' fiscal

N. Apergis (✉)
University of Derby, Derby, UK
e-mail: n.apergis@derby.ac.uk

G. Chesini
University of Verona, Verona, Italy
e-mail: giusy.chesini@univr.it

T. Poufinas
Democritus University of Thrace, Komotini, Greece

T. Poufinas (ed.), *Debt in Times of Crisis*,
https://doi.org/10.1007/978-3-030-74162-4_8

discipline, the competitiveness of their economy and global financing conditions are very relevant in the prevailing literature, other drivers such as market sentiments, investors' risk appetite or international risk factors play a role. Moreover, the sensitivity of these determinants is not static over time since countries frequently tend to vary fiscal conditions and introduce structural reforms. Even if extensive literature exists on this subject, the results of these studies are rather heterogeneous, because different papers report different variables as the main drivers of yields. This is to be attributed mainly to differences in country samples, observation periods and econometric models.

This chapter analyzes the sovereign debt yields in twelve Eurozone countries (Austria, Belgium, Finland, France, Germany, Greece, Ireland, Italy, Luxembourg, Netherlands, Portugal and Spain) in the time period 1999–first half 2020. The rationale behind the choice of these countries lies in their association as the founding (or almost founding countries) of the common European currency, i.e. the Euro. All of them joined the Euro on January 1, 1999 except for Greece that joined two years later, i.e. January 1, 2001. The analysis of sovereign bond yields for more than twenty years, when several exogenous events occur, gives us the possibility to define the main determinants and trends of yields.

Identifying the determinants of sovereign yields is a relevant issue because it helps the understanding of which factors determine the borrowing costs in different countries. This is important in smooth as well as in distressed time periods; similar to the ones the economies have experienced the last decade or so, whose duration and magnitude varied a lot. In addition, it can be influenced by the stance of the central banks and in particular the European Central Bank (ECB) in this particular research. The support that the ECB has provided has been also unprecedented in terms of time span, the available envelop, as well as the intensity and asset selection. Furthermore, given the size of several government debts, even small variations in yields may imply high borrowing costs. Consequently, the topic is of interest also to policymakers and to practitioners alike.

The contribution of this study in the field is identified in the consideration of a wide range of macroeconomic variables, especially when it comes to competitiveness, compared with the existing research; the breadth of the dataset in terms of the countries as well as the number of bond issues selected; the investigation of the role of both the financial and debt crisis; the assessment of the impact of the quantitative easing (QE) programs launched by ECB; the evaluation of the importance of the currency of issuance; and finally the examination of the influence of the maturity of the economy by dividing the countries in Northern and Southern.

8.2 Literature Review

Sovereign bond yields are determined by the riskiness of the indebted country and the relative risk in the existing literature is attributed mainly to credit risk (or default risk) and to liquidity risk (Favero et al., 2010); the first one is issuer-specific while the second is usually bond specific (Ejsing et al., 2012). Among the most important macroeconomic determinants of the sovereign risk price we can find the public debt level of a country, its fiscal deficit and its current account. Even if these factors are surely important, their intensity varies in different time periods and in some cases they do not explain the whole story. In fact, beyond these variables, some scholars have also unveiled the relevance of market perception of risk, country sentiment (Gomez-Bengoechea & Arahuetes, 2019; Maltritz, 2012), investor's risk appetite and also herding contagion (Beirne & Fratzscher, 2013; Silvapulle et al., 2016). So, it is evident that when the price of sovereign risk cannot be well explained by fundamentals, the riskiness must be driven by other factors.

A large number of papers have analyzed the determinants of the pricing of sovereign risk. Early studies tend to focus on long-term government bond yield spreads as the reference measure for sovereign risk, but in the literature it is possible to find other different measures of sovereign risk, for example, CDS spreads and sovereign ratings (Afonso et al., 2012); in particular, they find significant responses of sovereign yield spreads to changes in rating notations and outlook from the main rating agencies, with stronger result in the case of negative announcements.

Focusing on Eurozone countries, in the literature it is possible to find diverse results to our research question by differentiating five distinct time periods which present various characteristics (Afonso et al., 2015):

1. before the start of the EMU (January 1999)
2. the time period after the EMU until the Lehman Brothers collapse (September 2008)
3. from the Lehman Brother collapse to the inception of the sovereign debt crisis (February 2009)
4. after the inception of the sovereign debt crisis to the first intervention of European Central Bank (ECB) (May 2010)

5. from the first intervention of the ECB to 2020.

We have to point out that, starting from May 2010, sovereign yields are biased by European Central Bank's intervention in debt markets. Considering the different types of interventions, we can distinguish other five sub-time periods:

- After the announcement of the Securities Markets Programme (SMP) which initially focused on Greek, Irish and Portuguese debt securities (10 May 2010). Italian and Spanish bonds were included in the programs starting from 8 August 2011 (Eser & Schwaab, 2016).
- SMP was replaced by the Outright Monetary Transactions (OMT) Program which contemplated the purchases of government bonds in the secondary markets (6 September 2012).
- Between 9 March 2015 and 19 December 2018, the Eurosystem conducted net purchases of public sector securities under the public sector purchase programme (PSPP) included in the asset purchase programme (APP). These purchases gave rise to what is technically defined as "Quantitative Easing". As of January 2019, the Eurosystem continued to reinvest the principal payments from maturing securities held in the PSPP portfolio.
- As of 1 November, 2019 the Eurosystem restarted net purchases under the PSPP.
- In March 2020 the ECB's pandemic emergency purchase programme (PEPP) initiated. The PEPP is a temporary asset purchase programme of private and public sector securities. On 4 June 2020 the Governing Council decided to increase the €750 billion envelopes for the PEPP by €600 billion to a total of €1350 billion. PEPP will not terminate before the end of June 2021.

We can notice several different ECB interventions whose effects are not easy to disentangle but surely affected country-specific Eurozone sovereign yields. In the literature, scholars have examined these different time periods and exogenous events with the following findings.

1. Before the introduction of the euro, identical financial claims issued in different euro-area currencies were imperfect substitutes and traded at different prices. EMU has eliminated this source of market segmentation (Pagano & Von Thadden, 2004). More specifically,

government bonds issued by some countries offered high yields determined by exchange rate risks and the fear of systematic devaluations which investors had to face (Aristei & Martelli, 2014). The yields decreased in the 1990s, arriving at the lowest levels around 1999, the year of the introduction of the single currency. It was so even if some countries registered deterioration in terms of levels of deficit and national debt. This was due certainly to the elimination of currency risk and probably to the process of financial integration that seemed to have cancelled also country's credit risk, regardless of the individual national fiscal policies (Bernoth et al., 2012; Antonakakis et al., 2017).

2. Since the introduction of the euro in 1999, with the removal of the intra-euro area exchange rate risk, there was a further decline of the spreads against German benchmark (Manganelli & Wolswijk, 2009). In fact, it has been demonstrated that soon after the introduction of the euro, the sovereign debt yields of the EMU countries were not very distant among them, because each country sovereign debt was perceived by the market as a part of the same group of countries (Schuknecht et al., 2009; Paniagua et al., 2017). Furthermore, a positive market sentiment led to the convergence of government risk premia which surely benefited high-debt countries (Giordano et al., 2012).

   In this regard also D'Agostino and Ehrmann (2014) find that in the first years of the EMU several macro fundamentals, general risk aversion and liquidity risks were not considered in the prices of sovereign bonds.

   Consequently, until the unfolding of the financial crisis, the international risk factor was an important determinant of bond yields and spreads in the Eurozone (Afonso et al., 2015).

   Several studies analyze the impact of the introduction of EMU on government bond yields (Jankowitsch et al., 2006; Pagano & Von Thadden, 2004). Among these papers we can particularly mention Gomez-Puig (2006) who decomposes European yield spreads into two main domestic risk components (liquidity and credit risk) that remain after EMU and she determines whether there has been a change in the price assigned to them by the markets since the introduction of the euro.

Also the paper of Maltritz (2012) provides answers to the question of what drives sovereign yield spreads (to German bond yields) of EMU countries' government bonds by analysing potential determinants of their sovereign yield spreads observed on secondary bond markets. These yield spreads result from several reasons; apart from default risk, the yield spreads are influenced by liquidity risk and market sentiments toward investments in risky bonds.

3. While at the start of the EMU, long-term government bond yields have been relatively stable at very low levels in Eurozone, they begun to rise specifically after the collapse of Lehman Brothers (Bernoth & Erdogan, 2012; De Santis, 2012).

In the time period after the onset of the financial crisis in the literature we find two widely shared findings (Afonso et al., 2015): (a) the widening of EMU sovereign yields driven by the increased international risk factor; (b) fiscal and other macro-imbalances penalize sovereign debt of some EMU countries much more heavily than before (Schuknecht et al., 2010).

In addition, Beirne and Fratzscher (2013) show that market pricing of sovereign risk has not been fully reflecting fundamentals prior to the crisis. Conversely, the rise in sovereign yield spreads during the crisis reflected the deterioration in countries' fundamentals, the fundamentals contagion and a sharp rise in the sensitivity of financial markets to fundamentals. In particular, a negative market sentiment on the resilience of the euro area favored a dispersion of the spreads, affecting more the high-debt countries and in this way advantaging countries perceived safer (Giordano et al., 2012; Poghosyan, 2012). Other authors demonstrate the so-called herding contagion, concentrated in time and among a few markets, in particular Greece and other bystander countries. In the literature the herding contagion has referred to as "wake-up call" contagion or fundamentals contagion (Bekaert et al., 2010). In fact, for some countries, such as the GIPSI countries (Greece, Italy, Portugal, Spain, Ireland), there is strong evidence in favour of this "wake-up call" contagion, though for other countries there is much less of such evidence.

The same phenomenon was described differently specifying that, the increase in sovereign risk premium in Eurozone countries after the financial crisis was uneven because of the "safe haven flows" which affected some bond markets after the Lehman Brothers collapse and again during some phases of the sovereign debt crisis (Ejsing et al., 2012). This effect is also known as "flight to quality" and deserves to distinguish the analysis between core and peripheral Eurozone countries: spreads on peripheral countries were on average significantly higher than what predicted by fundamentals due to a contagion effect (Giordano et al., 2012).

4. The sovereign crisis started from Greece in February 2009 and gradually spread to the whole EMU, particularly to the peripheral economies. According to Afonso et al. (2015) since March 2009 markets penalize fiscal imbalances more strongly than before, attaching an extra-premium on the stock of projected public debt. Furthermore, the number of macro and fiscal risks priced by markets has been significantly enriched including international financial risk and liquidity risk.

   In the literature there is wide understanding that most of the high-debt countries have experienced an under-pricing of sovereign debt in respect to their respective fundamentals in the period before the financial crisis and an overpricing after the inception of the sovereign crisis. Afonso and Jalles (2019) impute this to the fluctuation of the risk appetite and to country-specific concern related to economic fundamentals. Similarly, Beirne and Fratzscher (2013) find that most of the increase in the price of sovereign risk during the sovereign debt crisis among GIPSI and other euro area countries was due to a deterioration in countries' fundamentals and fundamentals contagion.
5. The analysis of the effects of the ECB quantitative easing programs on sovereign yield spreads in the Eurozone countries has not received much attention in the literature till now. Afonso and Jalles (2019) unveil that ECB's interventions contributed to contain sovereign yield spread, implying indirectly some sort of expansionary monetary developments, particularly when bonds are kept until maturity in the ECB balance sheet. De Santis (2020), in order to capture market sentiment and expectations, follows a new strand in the literature that employs indices based on social media, google and newswire reports. He finds that up to October 2015 the ECB policy reduced the GDP-weighted 10-year euro area yields by 72 basis points, with the vulnerable countries benefiting most.

All this considered, our empirical analysis focuses on different determinants of sovereign yields. We consider distinctively macroeconomic factors and exogenous events.

Macroeconomic determinants are considered very relevant as well in determining sovereign yields. There are many factors that can explain the macroeconomy and the macroeconomic situation and these factors surely impact the level of risk of the debt of that country. In this chapter we focus on addressing a series of relevant questions. The first and most straightforward one is:

I. What macroeconomic factors do influence sovereign bond yields the most?

Even if macroeconomic factors are very relevant, sometimes there can be exogenous events that might have an effect on sovereign bonds' yields, such as economic crises or extraordinary monetary policy measures enforced by European Central Bank (ECB). Because macroeconomic factors might react to such events themselves, parts of the effects of such events on sovereign yields should be incorporated in the effects of macroeconomic factors. However, the effects of the macroeconomic factors potentially do not contain the entire effects of such events, and therefore, they have to be investigated separately.

For example, as we have already said, it has been demonstrated an under-pricing of sovereign risk in the Eurozone before the 2008–2009 financial crisis and an overpricing of it during the subsequent sovereign debt crisis. Moreover, it is demonstrated that non-conventional monetary policy measures implemented by the ECB had an effect on country-specific sovereign yields. Furthermore, also non-specific sovereign bonds ECB programs such as the first Covered Bond Purchase Programme (CBPP1) contributed to reduced sovereign yield spreads (Afonso and Jalles, 2019).

These realizations lead us to consider some more questions. Namely:

II. What influence do exogenous events have on sovereign bonds yields?
III. What is the role of the issue currency?
IV. How North and South Euro countries differ in terms of sovereign bond yields?

8.3 Data and Variables

In this section, the dataset used for the empirical analysis is described. First we explain how we select our sample of sovereign bonds.

We select medium–long-term sovereign bonds issued in 12 (founding or almost founding) Eurozone countries (Austria, Belgium, Finland, France, Germany, Greece, Ireland, Italy, Luxembourg, Netherlands, Portugal and Spain) from 1999 to June 2020.

Our dependent variable is a time-variant variable and it represents the yields of the sovereign bonds. Our initial sample comprehends 2879 sovereign bonds. We eliminate 2091 bonds because they have missing values and most of them are strips or stripped bonds. Our final sample is composed of 788 medium–long-term sovereign bonds (T-Bills excluded) issued in more than 20 years.

Despite as pointed out by Maltritz (2012), there is no general consensus on which factors should be considered as key determinants of sovereign yields, based on the recent empirical literature in Table 8.1 we list even different variables as proxies of country-specific fiscal and macroeconomic fundamentals that have been found to affect sovereign default risk (Aristei & Martelli, 2014).

Data on the variables come from various sources. For Debt to GDP, Current account balance to GDP, Unemployment, Total (net) lending

Table 8.1 Overview of the variables

Variable	*Description*
• ***Bond-specificvariable***	
Dependent variable	
Sovereign bond yield	Sovereign yield in basis point
• ***Macroeconomicvariables***	
Independent variables	
Debt-to-GDP	Fiscal position
GDP growth	Economic activity
Real effective exchange rate	External competitiveness
Current account balance to GDP	External competitiveness
Unemployment rate	External competitiveness
S&P500 implied stock market volatility index (VIX)	Global risk aversion
Total lending to GDP ratio	Size of the financial sector

Source Created by the Authors

to GDP we use AMECO; for GDP growth we rely on IMF (International Monetary Fund); for the Real effective exchange rate our source is BIS (Bank of International Settlements); and for the S&P500 implied stock market volatility index (VIX), as well as the bond yields we employ Bloomberg.

We then propose a model that explains sovereign yields through a set of the most relevant macroeconomic determinants observed in the literature.

8.4 Methodology

In methodological terms, the full model planned to be estimated for each sample bond i at date t provides:

$$\begin{aligned} \text{sovereign}_{ti} = & \, b_0 + b_1\text{fiscal}_t + b_2\text{econact}_t + b_3\text{compet}_t \\ & + b_4\text{global}_t + b_5\text{size}_t + \alpha_i + \beta_t + \epsilon_{it} \end{aligned} \quad (8.1)$$

where *sovereign* denotes the sovereign European bond yields, *fiscal* is the fiscal position of the country alternatively proxied by the debt to GDP ratio, *econact* proxies the economic activity of the country measured as the GDP growth rate, *compet* is a proxy for the external competitiveness of the country, alternatively proxied by the effective exchange rate, or the current account balance relative to GDP, or the unemployment rate, *global* displays the global risk aversion of the country, measured as the implied stock market volatility index (VIX), and *size* measures the size of the financial sector proxied by the total lending to GDP ratio. α_i and β_t account for bond and time fixed effects, respectively. We expect that the dependent variable is associated with each independent one according to the signs provided in Table 8.2.

Concerning the fiscal position, we choose one of the most widely used indicators, the government debt to GDP because it is considered able to measure the country's fiscal fragility (Aßmann & Boysen-Hogrefe, 2012). It allows controlling for the fact that higher indebtedness increases ceteris paribus the default risk of a country and therefore sovereign yield spreads (Aristei & Martelli, 2014). In general, the higher the debt to GDP ratio, the more sensitive the investors are to a given increase in the ratio itself (Afonso & Jalles, 2019; Giordano et al., 2012; Gomez-Bengoechea & Arahuetes, 2019). We use this ratio also lagged by one period. In the literature, sometimes the expected debt to GDP ratio is used because

Table 8.2 Expected influence of variables in the model

Variables	*Expected influence*
Debt-to-GDP	+
GDP growth	−
Real effective exchange rate	+
Current account balance to GDP	− or +
Unemployment rate	+
S&P500 implied stock market volatility index (VIX)	+
Total lending to GDP	+

Source Created by the Authors

an expected fiscal position provides a proxy for credit quality, with an expected fiscal deterioration implying higher risk (Afonso et al., 2015).

The economic activity of a country is of paramount importance in assessing the ability to meet its payment obligation. In this regard we select one variable able to capture the overall state of the economy of a country such as the GDP growth rate. Empirically it has been demonstrated the negative impact of the economic growth on spreads (De Grauwe & Ji, 2013; Gomez-Bengoechea & Arahuetes, 2019), considering that sovereign debt becomes riskier during periods of economic slowdown (Afonso et al., 2015). In particular, Afonso and Jalles (2019) demonstrate that higher than expected GDP growth has negative impact on the yield spreads.

As far as the external competitiveness, we choose three variables: the real effective exchange rate, the current account balance to GDP and the unemployment rate. Sometimes in the literature they are included in the models as lagged values (Giordano et al., 2012) but we do not consider any time lag. The real effective exchange rate is relevant because if it increases, the external position of a country deteriorates since its residents pay relatively more for their imports and raise relatively less from their exports. Therefore, an appreciation of the real effective exchange rate is likely to lead to an increase in the sovereign risk premium demanded by the investors (Afonso and Jalles, 2019). On the other side, the current account balance to GDP ratio is calculated by exports minus imports and it permits to raise funds for debt servicing; therefore, as it improves the sovereign spreads should decline (De Grauwe & Ji, 2013; Gomez-Puig et al., 2014), even if Maltritz (2012) have justified also a positive sign for this ratio. Finally, considering the unemployment rate, the variable is useful in order to capture the country's growth potential, so if it increases it unveils a deterioration of growth potential and competitiveness, consequently sovereign yields should increase (Gomez-Bengoechea & Arahuetes, 2019; Gomez-Puig et al., 2014).

The global risk aversion, also called international risk factor is important as well because sovereign bond yields are driven not only by country-specific factors but also by time-varying international risk drivers which in turn affect international risk appetite. Following the literature, we capture such a factor with the VIX indicator, also lagged by one period (Giordano et al., 2012). This index tends to spike during market turmoil periods and represents a popular proxy for international risk. Usually the higher the VIX, the higher the sovereign yield spreads (Afonso & Jalles, 2019; Gomez-Bengoechea & Arahuetes, 2019).

Finally, we investigate the size of the financial sector with the Total credit to GDP ratio. In the literature Gomez-Bengoechea and Arahuetes (2019) use another variable with the same meaning and find that the size of the financial sector (Credit/GDP) is positively related to yield spreads.

8.5 Empirical Analysis: Baseline Results

First, the empirical analysis examines the unit root properties in the data through advanced panel unit root tests. Panel unit root tests of the first-generation can lead to spurious results if significant degrees of positive residual cross-section dependence exist and are ignored. Consequently, the implementation of second-generation panel unit root tests is desirable only when it has been established that the panel is subject to a significant degree of residual cross-section dependence. Therefore, before selecting the appropriate panel unit root test, it is crucial to provide some evidence on the degree of residual cross-sectional dependence.

The cross-sectional dependence (CD) statistic by Pesaran (2004) is based on a simple average of all pair-wise correlation coefficients of the OLS residuals obtained from standard augmented Dickey-Fuller regressions for each variable in the panel. Under the null hypothesis of cross-sectional independence, the CD test statistic follows asymptotically a two-tailed standard normal distribution. The results, reported in Table 8.3, uniformly reject the null hypothesis of cross-section independence for the sovereign European bonds variable, providing evidence of cross-sectional dependence in the panel-type of variables in Eq. (8.1), given the statistical significance of the CD statistics.

Next, a second-generation panel unit root test is employed to determine the degree of integration of the respective variables. In the case of the panel variables, the Pesaran (2007) panel unit root test does not require the estimation of factor loading to eliminate cross-sectional dependence. The null hypothesis is a unit root for the Pesaran (2007) test. The results of this test are reported in Table 8.4 and support the presence of a unit root for the only panel variable in our system, that is of sovereign European bonds. Moreover, Table 8.4 reports the results of the General Least Squared Dickey-Fuller test recommended by Elliott et al. (1996) for the remaining cases characterized as time series variables. The results illustrate the presence of a unit root in the levels across all variables, while in terms of their first differences, the testing procedure indicates the presence of stationarity across all of them.

To avoid the presence of potential endogeneity issues, we estimate the dynamic panel data model using the general method of moments (GMM) estimation recommended by Arellano and Bover (1995) and Blundell and Bond (1998). The presence of endogeneity potentially comes through reverse causality between yields and the number of the control variables involved. For instance, the literature has established the presence of mutual and bi-causal links between bond yields and economic growth (Ahrens, 2002; De Bondt, 2002).

The empirical results are reported in Table 8.5 with columns one and two indicating two alternative modelling specifications. In particular, column (1) displays the estimates when only the fiscal variable is included, while column (2) shows the estimates of the full model described in Eq. (8.1). The standard errors reported in both specifications have been

Table 8.3 Cross dependence tests

Variables	*p-values*
Sovereign European bonds	0
Debt-to-GDP	0
GDP growth	0
Real effective exchange rate	0
Current account balance to GDP	0
Unemployment rate	0
The S&P500 implied stock market volatility index (VIX)	0
Total lending to GDP	0

Source Authors' estimations

Table 8.4 Unit root tests

H₀: Contains a unit root		
	CIPS	
Variables	*Levels*	*1st Differences*
Sovereign European bonds	−1.196	−6.514***
GLS test		
Debt -to -GDP ratio	−1.216	−6.285***
GDP growth	−1.094	−6.752***
Real effective exchange rate	−1.236	−6.116***
Current account balance to GDP	−1.202	−5.994***
Unemployment rate	−1.316	−5.609***
The S&P500 implied stock market volatility index (VIX)	−1.116	−6.451***
Total lending to GDP	−1.322	−6.042***

A constant is included in the Pesaran (2007) tests. The results are reported under the null hypothesis of stationarity. Critical values for the Pesaran (2007) test: −2.40 at 1%, −2.22 at 5%, and −2.14 at 10%. The results are reported at lag = 3. ***: $p \leq 0.01$

Source Authors' estimations

clustered on the bond yields level through the methodological approach recommended by Petersen (2009). The results indicate that in both specifications, lagged yields account for yields persistence (Gerlach et al., 2010). In terms of the determinants of bond yields, the estimates are in accordance with theoretical expectations. More specifically, the drivers of the Debt to GDP ratio, the effective exchange rate, the implied VIX volatility, and the total lending to GDP ratio all exert a positive impact on bond yields. By contrast, the GDP growth rate has a negative effect on those yields. The relevant diagnostics are reported at the bottom of Table 8.5. In particular, the findings report the LM test for the appropriateness of the random effects modelling approach. The null hypothesis of no random effects is rejected, indicating that a random effects model is more suitable. Moreover, the AR(2) test fails to reject the respective null, providing solid support to the validity of the instruments used. The diagnostics also reports the Hansen test for overidentifying restrictions, leading to the validity of the employed instruments. In the estimation process, the number of instruments used has been by far lower than the number of observations; this did not create any identification problem, as reflected in the Hansen test.

Table 8.5 Sovereign European bond yield estimates (all bonds)

Variables	*−1*	*−2*
ΔSovereign European bonds(−1)	4.581***	4.127***
	[0.00]	[0.00]
ΔDebt-to-GDP	5.038***	4.782***
	[0.00]	[0.00]
ΔDebt -to -GDP(−1)	2.316**	2.194**
	[0.02]	[0.03]
GDP growth rate		−7.893***
		[0.00]
ΔEffective exchange rate		6.883***
		[0.00]
ΔVIX		7.372***
		[0.00]
ΔVIX(−1)		3.618**
		[0.02]
ΔTotal lending to GDP		9.547***
		[0.00]
ΔTotal lending to GDP(−1)		4.755***
		[0.00]
Diagnostics		
R^2-adjusted	0.44	0.71
LM test	[0.00]	[0.00]
AR(2)	[0.51]	[0.59]
Hansen test	[0.58]	[0.63]
No. of instruments	6	13

Figures in brackets denote p-values. LM stands for the Lagrange Multiplier test for random effects (Breusch & Pagan, 1980). AR(2) is the test for autocorrelation of order 2. Hansen is the test for the overidentification check for the validity of instruments. All estimations accounted for both time and bond fixed effects. Figures in parentheses denote p-values based on clustered standard errors (Petersen, 2009). The numbers of lags in the control variables was determined through the Akaike criterion. $^{**}p < 0.05$; $^{***}p < 0.01$
Source Authors' estimations

Table 8.6 repeats the above analysis, but this time the variable of the external competitiveness of the country is measured through alternative definitions. More specifically, column (1) measures it through the current account balance relative to GDP ratio, while column (2) measures it as the unemployment rate. The new findings offer robust support to those obtained in Table 8.5.

Table 8.6 Sovereign European bond yield estimates (all bonds)-Alternative definitions of the external competitiveness variable

Variables	*−1*	*−2*
ΔSovereign European bonds(−1)	4.836***	4.672***
	[0.00]	[0.00]
ΔDebt-to-GDP	5.277***	5.126***
	[0.00]	[0.00]
ΔDebt-to-GDP(−1)	2.409**	2.338**
	[0.02]	[0.02]
GDP growth rate	−7.569***	−7.391***
	[0.00]	[0.00]
ΔCurrent account balance relative to GDP	6.237***	
	[0.00]	
ΔUnemployment rate		5.483***
		[0.00]
ΔVIX	7.014***	6.884***
	[0.00]	[0.00]
ΔVIX(−1)	4.005***	3.985***
	[0.01]	[0.01]
ΔTotal lending to GDP	9.237***	9.052***
	[0.00]	[0.00]
ΔTotal lending to GDP(−1)	[0.00]	[0.01]
Diagnostics		
R^2-adjusted	0.68	0.74
LM test	[0.00]	[0.00]
AR(2)	[0.46]	[0.68]
Hansen test	[0.53]	[0.67]
No. of instruments	7	15

Similar to those reported in Table 8.4. $^{**}p < 0.05$; $^{***}p < 0.01$.
Source Authors' Estimations

8.5.1 *Robustness Check: The Role of Crisis Events*

This part of the empirical analysis explores the role of exogenous events for bonds yields; to this end, the analysis explicitly includes dummy variables across different periods. As crisis events the analysis considers first, the financial crisis following the collapse of Lehman Brothers, and second, the European sovereign debt crisis. Therefore, the analysis includes one dummy for each crisis event as follows: Dfin takes one between October 10, 2008 and October 8, 2009, and zero otherwise; Dsov takes one between October 9, 2009 and December 28, 2012, and zero otherwise.

The dates used for the dummy variables receive supportive evidence from Will and Kwon (2010).

The new results are reported in Table 8.7. Columns (1) through (3) correspond to the modelling specifications under the three alternative definitions of the external competitiveness of the country. The new findings provide robust evidence to those presented previously. Moreover, both the crisis dummies have a significant positive effect on bond yields.

8.5.2 *Robustness Check: The Role of the ECB Unconventional Monetary Policy Measures*

This part of the analysis investigates the role of the first unconventional monetary policy measures implemented by the European Central Bank (ECB) to attain its goals. Considering that the effects of ECB's asset purchases were not limited to the specific market of intervention (Szczerbowicz, 2015), we analyze the first two covered bond purchase programmes. Therefore, the analysis constructs two dummy variables for each program, i.e. ECBP1 and ECBP2. The two dummies are defined as follows: ECBP1, takes one from May 7, 2009 to June 30, 2010, and zero otherwise; ECBP2 takes one from October 6, 2011 to October 31, 2012, and zero otherwise. In the first purchase program, min requirements are not included since such requirements in relevance to the rating and the issue size were only set "as a rule" (ECB, 2010).

The new results are reported in Table 8.8 where the three columns again correspond to the three alternative definitions of the external competitiveness. They provide robust evidence to the baseline findings presented in Tables 8.5 and 8.6. In addition, when exploring the role of the two purchase programmes by the ECB, the estimates clearly document that both purchase programs exert a negative and statistically significant effect not only on covered bonds but also on sovereign bondyields (Afonso & Jalles, 2019). Finally, Wald F-tests indicate the rejection of the null that the ECB purchase programs have the same effect on premium yields.

8.5.3 *Robustness Check: The Role of the Issue Currency*

Provided that the currencies the bonds are issued can be an important determinant of bond yields, while influencing factors might differ between bonds denominated in different currencies, this part of the robustness

Table 8.7 Sovereign European bond yield estimates (all bonds)-Alternative definitions of the external competitiveness variable-The role of the financial and sovereign debt crises

Variables	*−1*	*−2*	*−3*
ΔSovereign European bonds(−1)	5.664***	5.329***	5.426***
	[0.00]	[0.00]	[0.00]
ΔDebt-to-GDP	5.895***	5.619***	5.706***
	[0.00]	[0.00]	[0.00]
ΔDebt-to-GDP(−1)	2.773**	2.581**	2.647**
	[0.02]	[0.03]	[0.02]
GDP growth rate	−7.683***	−7.417***	−7.542***
	[0.00]	[0.00]	[0.00]
ΔEffective exchange rate	6.328***		
	[0.00]		
ΔCurrent account balance relative to GDP		6.074***	
		[0.00]	
Δunemployment rate			6.195***
			[0.00]
ΔVIX	7.246***	7.038***	7.085***
	[0.00]	[0.00]	[0.00]
ΔVIX(−1)		3.673**	3.814**
		[0.02]	[0.02]
ΔTotal lending to GDP	8.652***	8.126***	8.275***
	[0.00]	[0.00]	[0.00]
ΔTotal lending to GDP(−1)	3.855**	3.549**	3.706**
	[0.02]	[0.03]	[0.02]
Dfin	217.552***	209.083***	216.932***
	[0.00]	[0.00]	[0.00]
Dsov	268.904***	247.423***	254.691***
	[0.00]	[0.00]	[0.00]
Diagnostics			
R^2-adjusted	0.7	0.66	0.73
LM test	[0.00]	[0.00]	[0.00]
AR(2)	[0.53]	[0.50]	[0.58]
Hansen test	[0.56]	[0.49]	[0.61]
No. of instruments	13	14	16

Similar to those reported in Table 8.4. $^{**}p < 0.05$; $^{***}p < 0.01$.
Source Authors' estimations

Table 8.8 Sovereign European bond yield estimates (all bonds)-Alternative definitions of the external competitiveness variable-The role of the QE programs

Variables	*−1*	*−2*	*−3*
ΔSovereign European bonds(−1)	5.349***	5.115***	5.266***
	[0.00]	[0.00]	[0.00]
ΔDebt-to-GDP	5.653***	5.484***	5.562***
	[0.00]	[0.00]	[0.00]
ΔDebt-to-GDP(−1)	2.509**	2.417**	2.478**
	[0.02]	[0.03]	[0.03]
GDP growth rate	−7.449***	−7.382***	−7.409***
	[0.00]	[0.00]	[0.00]
ΔEffective exchange rate	6.135***		
	[0.00]		
ΔCurrent account balance relative to GDP		6.942***	
		[0.00]	
ΔUnemployment rate			6.041***
			[0.00]
ΔVIX	7.065***	6.847***	6.954***
	[0.00]	[0.00]	[0.00]
ΔVIX(−1)		3.319**	3.452**
		[0.03]	[0.03]
ΔTotal lending to GDP	8.326***	8.285***	8.308***
	[0.00]	[0.00]	[0.00]
ΔTotal lending to GDP(−1)	3.542**	3.396**	3.462**
	[0.03]	[0.03]	[0.03]
ECBP1	−14.236***	−12.354***	−14.001***
	[0.00]	[0.00]	[0.00]
ECBP2	−19.453***	−16.218***	−18.107***
	[0.00]	[0.00]	[0.00]
Diagnostics			
R^2-adjusted	0.68	0.63	0.76
LM test	[0.00]	[0.00]	[0.00]
AR(2)	[0.55]	[0.53]	[0.67]
Hansen test	[0.58]	[0.51]	[0.66]
No. of instruments	14	14	17
Wald *F*-tests	[0.00]	[0.01]	[0.00]

analysis splits the sample in line with the currency of issue. The results, reported in Table 8.9, present two specifications when all variables are included, plus both a dummy crisis and the two dummies in relevance to

Table 8.9 Sovereign European bond yield estimates-The role of the issue currency

Variables	*−1*	*−2*
ΔSovereign European bonds(−1)	7.655***	5.219***
	[0.00]	[0.00]
ΔDebt-to-GDP	9.736***	2.675*
	[0.00]	[0.09]
ΔDebt-to-GDP(−1)	4.873**	0.853
	[0.01]	[0.17]
GDP growth rate	−9.916***	−4.125**
	[0.00]	[0.02]
ΔEffective exchange rate	10.744***	3.268*
	[0.00]	[0.07]
ΔVIX	11.452***	4.836**
	[0.00]	[0.03]
ΔVIX(−1)	7.538***	2.154*
	[0.00]	[0.09]
ΔTotal lending to GDP	13.709***	4.261**
	[0.00]	[0.04]
Δtotal lending to GDP(−1)	7.865***	1.853*
	[0.00]	[0.10]
Dfin	179.563***	138.004***
	[0.00]	[0.00]
Dsov	288.439***	109.236***
	[0.00]	[0.00]
Diagnostics		
R^2-adjusted	0.73	0.31
LM test	[0.00]	[0.00]
AR(2)	[0.68]	[0.35]
Hansen test	[0.62]	[0.38]
No. of instruments	14	12

Similar to those reported in Table 8.4. *$p \leq 0.10$; **$p < 0.05$; ***$p < 0.01$.
Source Authors' estimations

the QE programs by the ECB. Finally, the competitiveness of the country is measured through the effective exchange rate definition.

In column (1) the estimates are with reference to euro-denominated bonds, while in column (2) they are with reference to bonds issued in other currencies. The findings document that in terms of the main control variables, the estimates remain consistently similar as previously (Tables 8.5 and 8.8), but in the case of international currency issues they are lower and with a weaker significance in some cases that reaches only 10%. Moreover, in terms of both the financial crisis and the European sovereign crisis, the findings illustrate the presence of a positive effect associated with both dummies, and in both specifications, indicating that the European sovereign crisis exerted a risk increase associated with international yields as well. In other words, the European sovereign debt crisis has had a catalytic effect on bond yields issues in euro, vis-a-vis bonds yields issued in other currencies, potentially confirming the presence of a "flight to safety" case (Baele et al., 2013).

8.5.4 *Robustness Check: South vs. North Country Bond Issues*

The recent financial crisis brought the surface potential differences between the Northern and the Southern European countries. This part of the robustness analysis, therefore, is motivated to investigate whether such a split would be a differentiating factor. It splits the sample with respect to the country of issues within the Eurozone (North vs. South). The results, reported in Table 8.10, present two specifications when all variables are included, plus both dummy crises, and the two dummies in relevance to the purchase programs by the ECB. In column (1) the estimates are with reference to the Northern European countries' sovereign bonds, while in column (2) the estimates are with reference to the Southern European countries' sovereign bonds. In terms of the main control variables, the new findings highlight certain differences in terms of the role of their drivers. In terms of the dummy variables, the estimates also highlight differentiated findings. More specifically, the positive effect of the financial crisis remains positive and strong in both specifications. In contrast, in terms of the sovereign crisis event, the estimates display that the Southern yields react stronger than those in the North, confirming the literature that claim that the sovereign crisis yields stronger and more viciously to countries experiencing it, probably supporting higher market imperfections or a stronger herding behavior of investors (Beirne & Fratzscher, 2013). In other words, the spillovers are weaker, probably due to the different role of macroeconomic fundamentals across the two regions.

Table 8.10 Sovereign European bond yield estimates-North vs. South bond issues

Variables	*−1*	*−2*
ΔSovereign European bonds(−1)	6.472***	7.944***
	[0.00]	[0.00]
ΔDebt-to-GDP	6.128***	11.552***
	[0.00]	[0.00]
ΔDebt-to-GDP(−1)	2.347*	6.482***
	[0.08]	[0.00]
GDP growth rate	−12.585***	−9.547***
	[0.00]	[0.00]
ΔEffective exchange rate	5.493***	8.814***
	[0.01]	[0.00]
ΔVIX	7.219***	12.562***
	[0.00]	[0.00]
ΔVIX(−1)	2.845**	5.491***
	[0.04]	[0.00]
ΔTotal lending to GDP	7.883***	13.185***
	[0.00]	[0.00]
ΔTotal lending to GDP(-1)	3.407**	7.395***
	[0.03]	[0.00]
Dfin	168.355***	193.372***
	[0.00]	[0.00]
Dsov	214.773***	289.572***
	[0.00]	[0.00]
ECBP1	−10.657***	−17.238***
	[0.00]	[0.00]
ECBP2	−9.784***	−19.662***
	[0.00]	[0.00]
Diagnostics		
R^2-adjusted	0.65	0.76
LM test	[0.00]	[0.00]
AR(2)	[0.57]	[0.69]
Hansen test	[0.58]	[0.72]
No. of instruments	13	14

Similar to those reported in Table 8.4. *$p \leq 0.10$; **$p < 0.05$; ***$p < 0.01$.
Source Authors' estimations

8.6 Discussion

The outcomes produced by the models employed are fully in line with our expectations, as described in the Data and variables section. In all the approaches followed, i.e. baseline, with all different external competitiveness proxies, with the crisis occurrence variation, with the ECB QE programme differentiation as well as the North–South country separation, the Debt to GDP ratio, the VIX, and the Total lending to GDP ratio are positively correlated with the bond yield. The same holds true for the effective exchange rate, the current account balance relative to GDP and the unemployment, i.e. the three metrics of external competitiveness. In contrast, the GDP growth rate is negatively correlated with the bond yield. These correlations post different levels of significance; however, in their majority they are statistically significant at all levels. Our findings are in accordance with the applicable existing literature. In particular, as far as the current account balance relative to GDP is concerned, for which there were publications supporting both signs, our results are aligned with the evidence of Maltritz (2012) according to which its correlation with the sovereign bond yields is positive.

The regression results are comparable with all three external competitiveness proxies both in terms of significance as well as in terms of magnitude. The effective exchange rate seems to have the biggest coefficient, with the current account balance following and the unemployment rate succeeding both of them.

Both the financial and sovereign debt crises lead to an increase in yields with the impact of the latter being somehow higher. This is probably justified by the fact that investors require higher returns as a result of the increased risk they have to assume. In addition, they most likely fly to quality, seeking safe havens—which could be shorter term fixed income investments or cash or other alternatives (Bernoth et al., 2012). When the financial and sovereign debt crises dummies are inserted all variables seem to have a bigger impact except for the GDP growth and VIX in some of the models and the total lending to GDP ratio in all models. The financial and sovereign debt crises post a higher impact on the euro-denominated versus the non-euro denominated bond yields. As a matter of fact the trend is reversed in non-euro denominated bonds and the sovereign crisis has a smaller influence than the financial crisis. A potential reason for this is that non-euro denominated bonds had already higher yields than euro-denominated bonds. Furthermore, it could be that they were considered less risky in a period that the viability of the Euro was questioned as a result of the pressure that certain economies in the Eurozone had to overcome during the sovereign but also the financial crisis. Moreover, the financial and sovereign crises seemed to have a greater effect on the Southern countries compared to the Northern countries of the Eurozone. The latter clearly had the lead in both sets of countries. This is most likely the outcome of the difficulty they had in weathering both crises, especially the debt crisis; Greece, Portugal, Italy and Spain experienced a higher pressure compared to the remaining countries of the Eurozone and thus their yields grew more in relation to those of the Northern countries as investors requested a sufficient premium for the additional risk they (felt they) were exposed to.

The implementation of QE programmes by the ECB results in lower yields under all different definitions of the external competitiveness variables. This supports the success of the scope of the purchase programmes that have been (and are still) launched by the ECB; to provide liquidity and make borrowing more affordable. The effect was bigger in the Southern countries, as apparently their bonds benefited the most; the scope of the ECB was also to support the Euro, hence the relevant issues of these countries, whose economies were more distressed, took advantage of the programs. As a matter of fact it could be that their yields were already higher. Furthermore, the introduction of the QE programme dummies in the model makes the remaining coefficients smaller with the exception of GDP growth rate and VIX in some of the models. The latter holds true, also, for the external competitiveness proxies.

The issue currency, as has become apparent from the previous discussion, also has a role that cannot be ignored; we first observe that the coefficients are much higher for the euro-denominated bonds; we then realize that the significance for the euro-denominated bonds is always greater to or equal than the non-euro denominated bonds. This unveils the importance of the currency of issuance for the yield; the Eurozone countries that opted to issue bonds at a currency different from euro did so in order to achieve lower yields and most likely investors were willing to accept lower compensation for the risk they were being exposed to versus the euro. Furthermore, when a country opted to issue a bond in a different currency the impact of its macroeconomic as well as its financial market variables were smaller; there was potential dependence on the corresponding variables of the country of the issue currency.

Finally, the distinction between Northern and Southern countries reveals that all determinants seemed to have a bigger effect in the countries of the South—as measured by the respective coefficients, except for the GDP growth rate. This may come as no surprise, as the bond yields of these countries are higher than the yields of the Northern countries; investors are looking very closely at how well they perform—as reflected by their macroeconomic and financial market variables—and request the appropriate premium for it, realizing that are definitely behind the countries of the North. The lower magnitude of the coefficient of the GDP growth is probably justified by the fact that for a number of years these countries posted a negative GDP growth.

The evidence found through our research can be of use to all interested parties; these are mainly policymakers, central banks and market participants. The yields can become lower by appropriately steering the debt to GDP, the GDP growth rate, the external competitiveness as captured by the effective exchange rate, the current account balance relative to GDP and the unemployment rate as well the financial positioning of the country as reflected by the volatility and the total lending to GDP. Boosting GDP growth and containing the remaining variables can be beneficial for the level of sovereign bond yields. Going one step further they may select to launch part of their debt in a currency different from the Euro as it could result in a lower yield or lower incremental yield because of potential turbulence that is due to the Euro.

The aforementioned conditions most likely justify and/or secure increased creditworthiness of the issuing country and thus the bonds qualify for participating in the purchase programmes of the ECB. As a matter of fact the central bank will include such sovereign bonds with an increased level of confidence knowing that the examined parameters are in line with our findings. Furthermore it can forecast the route that the yields are anticipated to follow and decide on the extent of the inclusion of each and every bond in a potential (future) quantitative easing action.

The latter is of interest to the investors; they may value the safety net offered by the central bank when the bonds they (plan to) include in their portfolios qualify for participation in a purchase program. In addition, the higher risk that they are exposed to when going through a crisis period or when investing at a more distressed issuer (such as the countries of the South), seems to be compensated by higher yields, which potentially increases their comfort.

8.7 Conclusion

Bond yields attract the attention of a number of interested parties who need to know the factors that influence them. The study conducted in this chapter indicates that yields are positively correlated with the debt to GDP, the real effective exchange rate, the current account balance to GDP, the unemployment rate, the stock market volatility (VIX) and the total lending to GDP ratio. The yields are negatively correlated with the GDP growth rate. These variables depict the fiscal position, the external competiveness, the international risk factor (or global risk aversion), the size of the financial sector and the economic activity, respectively. As such they are key for decision-making for the issuing countries, the central bank(s) and the investors. The financial and sovereign crisis resulted in an increase of these yields. In contrast the ECB purchase programmes led to their decrease. The observed impact was bigger for the yields of the euro-denominated versus the non-euro denominated bonds. The same holds true for the yields of the bonds issued by the Southern compared to the Northern countries. The evidence documented by our research may be useful to issuing countries, central banks and investors as they can better understand the effect of quantitative easing policies as well as macroeconomic and financial conditions on yields. This allows them to appropriately select the level of yields they favor. These outcomes are particularly interesting in an environment that countries, markets and central banks are under the influence of and try to exit from a pandemic with unprecedented and to a great extend unknown consequences.

References

Aßmann, C., & Boysen-Hogrefe, J. (2012). Determinants of government bond spreads in the euro area: In good times as in bad. *Empirica, 39*(3), 341–356.

Afonso, A., & Jalles, J. T. (2019). Quantitative easing and sovereign yield spreads: Euro-area time-varying evidence. *Journal of International Financial Markets, Institutions and Money, 58,* 208–224.

Afonso, A., Arghyrou, M. G., & Kontonikas, A. (2015). The determinants of sovereign bond yield spreads in the EMU. *ECB Working Paper Series*, 1781.

Afonso, A., Furceri, D., & Gomes, P. (2012). Sovereign credit ratings and financial markets linkages: Application to European data. *Journal of International Money and Finance, 31*(3), 606–638.

Ahrens, R. (2002). Predicting recessions with interest rate spreads: A multi-country regime-switching analysis. *Journal of International Money and Finance, 21*(4), 519–537.

Antonakakis, N., Christou, C., Cunado, J., & Gupta, R. (2017). Convergence patterns in sovereign bond yield spreads: Evidence from the Euro area. *Journal of International Financial Markets, Institutions and Money, 49,* 129–139.

Arellano, M., & Bover, O. (1995). Another look at the instrumental variable estimation of error-components models. *Journal of Econometrics, 68*(1), 29–51.

Aristei, D., & Martelli, D. (2014). Sovereign bond yield spreads and market sentiment and expectations: Empirical evidence from Euro area countries. *Journal of Economics and Business, 76,* 55–84.

Baele, L., I Bekaert, G., Inghelbrecht, K., & Wei, M. (2013). Flights to safety. *NBER Working Paper Series*, *19095*, 1–51.

Beirne, J., & Fratzscher, M. (2013). The pricing of sovereign risk and contagion during the European sovereign debt crisis. *Journal of International Money and Finance, 34*, 60–82.

Bekaert, G., Ehrmann, M., Fratzscher, M., & Mehl, A. (2010). Global crises and equity market contagion. *NBER Working Paper, 17121.*

Bernoth, K., Von Hagen, J., & Schuknecht, L. (2012). Sovereign risk premiums in the European government bond market. *Journal of International Money and Finance, 31*(5), 975–995.

Bernoth, K., & Erdogan, B. (2012). Sovereign bond yield spreads: A time-varying coefficient approach. *Journal of International Money and Finance, 31*(3), 639–656.

Blundell, R., & Bond, S. (1998). Initial conditions and moment restrictions in dynamic panel data models. *Journal of Econometrics, 87*(1), 115–143.

Breusch, T. S., & Pagan, A. R. (1980). The Lagrange multiplier test and its applications to model specification in econometrics. *The Review of Economic Studies, 47*(1), 239–253.

D'Agostino, A., & Ehrmann, M. (2014). The pricing of G7 sovereign bond spreads–The times, they are a-changin. *Journal of Banking & Finance, 47,* 155–176.

De Bondt, G. (2002). Euro area corporate debt securities market: First empirical evidence. *European Central Bank Working Paper Series, Working Paper, 164.*

De Grauwe, P., & Ji, Y. (2013). Self-fulfilling crises in the Eurozone: An empirical test. *Journal of International Money and Finance, 34,* 15–36.

De Santis, R. A. (2020). Impact of the Asset Purchase Programme on euro area government bond yields using market news. *Economic Modelling, 86*, 192–209.

De Santis, R. A. (2012). The Euro area sovereign debt crisis: Safe haven, credit rating agencies and the spread of the fever from Greece, Ireland and Portugal. *ECB Working paper series, 1419.*

ECB. (2010). Covered bond purchase programme completed. Press releases June 30, 2010. https://www.ecb.europa.eu/press/pr/date/2010/html/pr100630.en.html. Accessed Nov 2020.

Ejsing, J., Grothe, M., & Grothe, O. (2012). Liquidity and credit risk premia in government bond yields. *European Central Bank Working paper series, 1440.*

Elliott, G., Rothenberg, T., & Stock, J. (1996). Efficient tests for an autoregressive unit root. *Econometrica, 64*(4), 813–836. https://doi.org/10.2307/2171846.

Eser, F., & Schwaab, B. (2016). Evaluating the impact of unconventional monetary policy measures: Empirical evidence from the ECB' s Securities Markets Programme. *Journal of Financial Economics, 119*(1), 147–167.

Favero, C., Pagano, M., & Von Thadden, E. L. (2010). How does liquidity affect government bond yields? *Journal of Financial and Quantitative Analysis*, 107–134.

Gerlach, S., Schulz, A., & Wolff, G. B. (2010). Banking and sovereign risk in the Euro area. *CEPR Discussion Paper, 7833.*

Giordano, L., Linciano, N., & Soccorso, P. (2012). The determinants of government yield spreads in the euro area. *CONSOB, Quaderni di Finanza, 71.*

Gomez-Bengoechea, G., & Arahuetes, A. (2019). The importance of being earnest: Macroeconomic determinants of sovereign bond yield spreads in the Eurozone. *Journal of Financial Economic Policy, 11*(1), 121–138. https://doi.org/10.1108/JFEP-02-2018-0026.

Gomez-Puig, M. (2006). Size matters for liquidity: Evidence from EMU sovereign yield spreads. *Economics Letters, 90*(2), 156–162.

Gómez-Puig, M., Sosvilla-Rivero, S., & del Carmen Ramos-Herrera, M. (2014). An update on EMU sovereign yield spread drivers in times of crisis: A panel data analysis. *The North American Journal of Economics and Finance, 30*, 133–153.

Jankowitsch, R., Mösenbacher, H., & Pichler, S. (2006). Measuring the liquidity impact on EMU government bond prices. *The European Journal of Finance, 12*(2), 153–169.

Maltritz, D. (2012). Determinants of sovereign yield spreads in the Eurozone: A Bayesian approach. *Journal of International Money and Finance, 31*(3), 657–672.

Manganelli, S., & Wolswijk, G. (2009). What drives spreads in the euro area government bond market? *Economic Policy, 24*(58), 191–240.

Pagano, M., & Von Thadden, E. L. (2004). The European bond markets under EMU. *Oxford Review of Economic Policy, 20*(4), 531–554.

Paniagua, J., Sapena, J., & Tamarit, C. (2017). Sovereign debt spreads in EMU: The time-varying role of fundamentals and market distrust. *Journal of Financial Stability, 33,* 187–206.

Pesaran, M. H. (2004). *General diagnostic tests for cross section dependence in panels*. Cambridge Working Papers in Economics, No. 435 and CESifo Working Paper, 1229.

Pesaran, M. H. (2007). A simple panel unit root test in the presence of cross-section dependence. *Journal of Applied Econometrics, 22*(2), 265–312.

Petersen, M. A. (2009). Estimating standard errors in finance panel data sets: Comparing approaches. *The Review of Financial Studies, 22*(1), 435–480.

Poghosyan, T. (2012) Long-run and short-run determinants of sovereign bond yields in advanced economies. *IMF Working Paper, WP/12/271.*

Schuknecht, L., Von Hagen, J., & Wolswijk, G. (2009). Government risk premiums in the bond market: EMU and Canada. *European Journal of Political Economy, 25*(3), 371–384.

Schuknecht, L., Hagen, J. V., & Wolswijk, G. (2010). Government bond risk premiums in the EU revisited: The Impact of the financial crisis. *ECB Working Paper, 1152.*

Silvapulle, P., Fenech, J. P., Thomas, A., & Brooks, R. (2016). Determinants of sovereign bond yield spreads and contagion in the peripheral EU countries. *Economic Modelling, 58*, 83–92.

Szczerbowicz, U. (2015). The ECB unconventional monetary policies: Have they lowered market borrowing costs for banks and governements? *International Journal of Central Banking*. December, 91–127.

Will, F., & Kwon, S. (2010). Was the ECB covered bond purchase programme a success? *European Covered Bond Council (2010), European Covered Bond Fact Book*, 27–34.

Index

T. Poufinas (ed.), *Debt in Times of Crisis*,
https://doi.org/10.1007/978-3-030-74162-4

D

E

The manufacturer's authorised representative in the EU is Springer Nature Customer Service Centre GmbH, Europaplatz 3, 69115 Heidelberg, Germany. If you have any concerns regarding our products, please contact ProductSafety@springernature.com

Printed and bound by CPI Group (UK) Ltd, Croydon, CR0 4YY

22/09/2026

02221063-0004